TF

144 13

Youthquake

YOUTHQUAKE
The growth of a counter-culture through two decades

KENNETH LEECH

SHELDON PRESS LONDON

First published
in Great Britain in 1973
by Sheldon Press
SPCK, Marylebone Road
London NW1 4DU

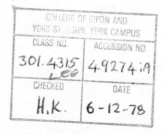

Printed in Great Britain by
The Camelot Press Ltd, London and Southampton

ISBN 0 85969 002 4

Acknowledgements

Thanks are due to the following for permission to quote from copyright sources:

Allen Lane The Penguin Press: *The Greening of America* by Charles Reich Copyright © Charles Reich, 1970. Reprinted by permission of Allen Lane The Penguin Press

George Allen & Unwin Ltd: *Sufi Essays* by Seyyed Hossein Nasr

Berkeley Barb: an extract from the 5–11 February 1971 issue

Jonathan Cape Ltd: *Playpower* by Richard Neville

Children of God: pamphlet published on 3 June 1972

Church Times: ' "Away with the Palaces" Say the Christian Radicals' (23 August 1968)

Dr Allan Y. Cohen: *LSD and the Search for God*

Andre Deutsch Ltd: *On the Road* by Jack Kerouac

Frendz: *Frendz 33*

Gandalf's Garden: *Gandalf's Garden 3*; *Gandalf's Garden 6*

Garnstone Press, London: *City of Revelation* by John Michell

Granada Publishing Ltd: *The Politics of Ecstasy* by Timothy Leary

Harper & Row Inc: 'The Journey Beyond Trips' from *Understanding Drug Use* by Peter Marin and Allan Y. Cohen

The Revd Leon P. Harris: *All Saints Episcopal Church Rector's Notebook*

Her Majesty's Stationery Office: *The Amphetamines and Lysergic Acid Diethylamide (LSD) Report* issued by the Advisory Council on Drug Dependence

Hodder and Stoughton Ltd: *The Street People: Selections from 'Right On'*

International Society for Krishna Consciousness Ltd: *Krishna Consciousness, What we Believe* (pamphlet)

IT, formerly International Times: an extract by Ian Dallas in *IT 64* (12–25 September 1969)

Lakeland Paperback No. 236: *Get Your Hands Off my Throat* by David Wilkerson

Life for the World Trust: The Revd Frank W. Wilson's 'Personal Word' insert in *Newscope* February 1973

Oliphants, London: *Purple Violet Squish* by David Wilkerson

Peace News, 5 Caledonian Road, London N1: *Resistance in Mass Society* by Ralph Shoenman; *Social Rebels or Juvenile Delinquents?* by David McReynolds; *The ELF Manifesto*

Roadrunner: 'Was Jesus a Freak?' by Alan Watts in *Roadrunner* 31 January 1972

Nicholas Saunders: *Alternative London* by Nicholas Saunders

SCM Press Ltd: *Theology of Hope* by Jurgen Moltmann

The Society of Saint Francis: 'The New Spiritual Quest' by Paulinus Milner OP in *The Franciscan* June 1970

The Spectator: 'Women and the Underground Press' in *The Spectator* 29 July 1969

Sweet and Maxwell Ltd: *Out of Apathy* ed E. P. Thompson

Student Assn. for the Study of Hallucinogens: 'Use of Amphetamines in the Haight-Ashbury Subculture' by Schick, Smith and Meyers in *Journal of Psycehdelic Drugs* 2.2, 1969

The International Headquarters of the Sufi Movement: extract by Pir Vilayat Inayat-Khan in *The Sufi Messenger Quarterly* January 1971

Transaction, Inc: 'Love Needs Care: Haight-Ashbury Dies' by Smith, Luce and Dernberg in transaction Vol. 7 (April 1970). Copyright © 1970 by Transaction, Inc.

Warner Brothers Music Ltd: 'The Times They Are A-Changing' by Bob Dylan © 1963 M. Witmark & Sons

The Revd R. L. York: *Viewpoints from California: Experimental Youth Ministries* by R. L. York; *The Covenant of Peace: A Liberation Prayer Book by the Free Church of Berkeley* by J. Pairman Brown and R. L. York

Contents

Preface

This is an attempt to describe one facet of the current youth scene: its search for spirituality. Some would claim that it is a marginal phenomenon, others would pin great hopes upon it. That there is such a search is obvious. I have tried to place the search in the context of youth culture as a whole, to relate it to the drug scene and to developments connected with it, and to discuss its implications for the church.

My own connection with the different trends and movements described here is varied. With some I have had close contacts over a number of years, with others my connection has been at second hand. Again it will be clear that I have more sympathy with some movements and viewpoints than with others. I hope that I have represented each one fairly and accurately.

I am very grateful to Sandra Bell and Maria James for help with the typing of the manuscript.

St Augustine's College, Canterbury.   KENNETH LEECH
April 1973

1
Youthquake

THE TEENAGE EXPLOSION

The 1950s was supremely the decade of the teenager. His coming to consciousness was aided and exploited by commercial interests in both the textile and record industries. The teenager is an international phenomenon: from San Francisco to London, from Leningrad to South Africa, the youth revolution is continuous. In recent years much of the energy which had formerly been directed towards social reform and political protest by the young has been diverted towards a search for spirituality, for the expansion of consciousness, for inner wholeness. So one has seen what some observers have described as a new spiritual quest. Out of a disillusionment with a violent society, and out of the ruins of the drug culture, has come a concern for the inner life of man. The language of revolution is used, often uncritically and loosely, about many facets of contemporary culture: Youth Revolution, Drug Revolution, Sexual Revolution, Political Revolution, Jesus Revolution—commonly used slogans which may hide, or even smother more complex developments, and become a substitute for serious thinking. But clearly something has happened. Richard Neville has referred to it as a 'youthquake'.[1] Others point to the widespread rejection of 'established' authority in most developed industrial countries. T. R. Fyvel in 1961 referred to the 'Teddy boy international' with *stilyagi* in the Soviet Union, *skinnknuttar* in Sweden, *blousons noirs* in France, and *taiyozoku* in Japan.[2]

The 1950s certainly saw the growth both of teenage group violence and of political protest movements against international violence, though how far 1945 inaugurated an era of total crisis in the sphere of youth culture is debatable. Statistics from a variety of sources suggest a high degree of consistency and conservatism in patterns of behaviour among the young between the 1930s and the present. It is very likely, for instance, that the 'sexual revolution' has been overstated. So, almost certainly, has the phenomenon of the 'teenage rebel'. Much youthful activity and behaviour is highly traditional and unrebellious. It is dubious too whether young people are, on an overall basis, more 'delinquent' than their parents were. But, while qualifications may be made, there is no doubt that there has been a major social upheaval and that the youth revolution is one aspect of a more broadly based pattern of social change. In the early period after the 1939–45 war, social change was indicated in an apparent contentment at the availability of welfare and the benefits of affluence. The Young Conservatives became the biggest youth movement in Britain, while in an opinion survey in 1959, 77 per cent of the young people interviewed regarded themselves as happy.[3] But by the middle years of the '50s a new mood was becoming apparent. Teenage riots began to assume significant dimensions around the world. *West Side Story* gave widespread, if romanticized, publicity to the gang warfare in New York City. In West Germany and Austria, the *halbstarken* initiated large-scale riots. In Britain it was the era of the Teds.

In 1955 *Rock Around the Clock*, featuring Bill Haley and the Comets, was shown at the Trocadero Cinema in the Elephant and Castle in South London. It provoked rioting, vandalism and assaults, seats were torn out, and in the general mood of chaos, the performance was brought to an end. The riots spread from the Elephant to other parts of Britain. The previous year there had been a murder in Clapham Common in South London when a seventeen-year-old youth was stabbed to death by a group of what had become known as Teddy Boys. Incidents like these brought the increasing teenage violence to the notice of the British public. However, it has been suggested that there were three quite separate waves of adolescent gang activity in London in the post-war years: first, the period of cloth-cap gangs of 'razor boys' in the years immediately after the war. Then followed the Teddy Boys, 'washed and spruced up, strangely and expensively dressed, moving about in large gangs, lawless and dangerous in their way, yet driven on by recognizable social urges and ambitions'.[4] Finally, in 1955–6 came the more sophisticated groups of adolescents in Italian clothes. The big Ted gangs were breaking up as the fashion spread and as it became impossible to distinguish a 'true Ted'. It was at this point that the

Notting Hill race riots of 1958 occurred, with gangs of youths armed with knives, chains and other weapons, converging in that area of North Kensington.

It is important to notice that, unlike the razor gangs of the Glasgow slums, or gangs such as the Mooney Boys in Sheffield, which flourished in pre-war days, the Teddy Boy movement was not directly the product of economic poverty, but rather of developing affluence combined with boredom. In the 1950s, particularly in London, a marked drift of many young people from the pub to the juke-box café occurred, though such groups of adolescents were not structured gangs in the American sense, but rather fluid, street-corner groups. Certainly there was talk of 'gang warfare' in the Teddy Boy period,[5] but there is little evidence that organized gangs of the type described by Yablonsky in the United States[6] played any significant role in British delinquency. David Downes, who studied delinquent patterns in the East End of London in the late 1950s and early '60s, concluded that ' "gangs proper", i.e. "with a leader, definite membership, persistence in time, a den, initiation procedure and criminal objectives" are extremely unusual'.[7] Downes's work suggested that American subcultural theories, inseparable as they were from the concept of the delinquent gang, were inapplicable to Britain. What was occurring in Britain was not the planned activities of a syndicated gang of juvenile criminals, but sporadic outbursts of irrational teenage rebellion. In the early 1960s this rebellion erupted again in the form of the Mod–Rocker conflict.

Mods began in London around 1960 and quickly grew into the largest young teenage group in Britain. Out of the Mod culture came the Carnaby Street revolution, the male fashion industry, 'Ready, Steady, Go', and, to some extent, the amphetamine traffic in the discotheques of Soho. To the Mods, clothes were the central feature of the world. Two contrasts with earlier teenage movements are important: unlike the Teddy Boys of the 1950s, the Mod was not simply concerned with aggressive rebellion or with achieving adult standards; moreover, the Mod image was in sharp conflict with the conventional picture of masculinity. It was an implicitly homosexual, or, more accurately, a bisexual phenomenon; girls were not popular in the Mod world, and it was in this period that homosexuality became more culturally acceptable to British youth. The Mods of 1960 rejected women, and built up their own male fashion scene. They were teenagers, and their world revolved around the teens:

some of the original Mods were only little boys of eleven or twelve. Later came music, dancing, scooters, and 'purple hearts'. But in the beginning was clothes. These post-war kids, the first generation for whom the Second World War was not even a memory, could be extravagant without guilt. To some extent the Mod extravagance could be seen as a defence against the earlier explosion of female clothes-buying. By 1961 the Mod scene had become commercialized: record companies, Carnaby Street, the Rolling Stones, all combined to create a highly lucrative teenage industry, and from this period the familiar accusation, 'phoney Mods' began to be made. The Mod scene spread in areas of West London, eastwards to Barking and Dagenham, south to Richmond, and in Soho, clothes, clubs and pills were easily available in adjoining streets. So Mod violence, helped along by amphetamines and alcohol, became national news though it was in the seaside resorts, not in the West End, that the Mods-versus-Rockers violence erupted.

There were riots at Brighton at Whitsun 1964 and at Margate in August of that year, and sporadic outbursts continued. The stereotypes which were built up around Mods and Rockers obscured the fact that both groups were deeply committed to conventional values and to the accumulation of wealth. But the Rockers were the more conventional, and tended to regard the Mods as effeminate. The Rocker prided himself in being straightforward, and in his social and political outlook was very much the little Englander, suspicious of foreigners and fairly reactionary. Both Mods and Rockers tended to live at home, and few seemed to come from broken homes. Rockers were more likely to be in unskilled manual jobs.[8] The treatment of the Mod–Rocker clashes in the popular press helped to reinforce the image of the Rocker as an inarticulate, working-class moron, while the Mod was extolled as gentle, inoffensive and pleasant. It would be an exaggeration to say that the press was running an anti-Rocker campaign, but there was certainly an intensive support for the Mod style, and this was supported too by commercial interests. Radio Luxembourg ran a special programme for Mods, while one of the daily papers ran a quiz, 'Are you a Mod or a Rocker?' In addition, not surprisingly, the clashes at the seaside resorts were used by some sections of the press to call for the restoration of National Service. Thus: 'The cure for the ills which manifest themselves in mods and rockers is intensive discipline. And the way to instil it? Reluctantly, one is forced to use a word which has become almost dirty—conscription. Two years of toeing the line made men of previous generations of aimless, spotty-faced youths.'[9]

This was not untypical comment. The chairman of the Margate magistrates on the following day sent a young man to detention centre with a reference to 'the dregs of those vermin which infested this town'.[10] 'These long-haired, mentally unstable, petty little Sawdust Caesars', commented the same magistrate,[11] 'seem to find courage, like rats, by hunting only in packs'. The tendency to lump Mods and Rockers together, and the belief that they differed only in their dress was common at the time. In fact, there were very marked differences between the two groups, and large numbers of adolescents identified themselves with one or other of them. This division of adolescent society over a very wide area was in startling contrast to the Teds who, at their peak, represented only a fringe group. By 1964 the identification as a Mod or a Rocker affected large sections of young people. A technical school teacher, writing in May of that year, suggested that over half of the boys aged 13–18 in his school identified themselves in some way with the Mod–Rocker groupings, and claimed that in nearby secondary modern schools the involvement was even more evident.[12]

The key differences between the groups might be summarized under four headings. First, clothing. Mods took over a variety of traditionally feminine fashions, such as long hair, make-up, hair lacquer, brightly coloured and flimsy clothes, and high heels; Rockers, on the other hand, wore hard-wearing jackets suitable for motor-cycling. Secondly, masculinity. Mods would be criticized as 'effeminate', but they would themselves criticize Rocker girls for 'trying to look like men'. Rockers dominated their women, who would ride on pillion and who were expected to be faithful to one boy, for male solidarity and cooperation were emphasized in the Rocker culture, and the motor bike symbolized the stress on physical skill. Thirdly, literary expression. Between January and April 1964, at least five Mod-oriented magazines appeared, of which *Ready Steady Go* (named after the TV programme) was the best-known. Rockers, on the other hand, read very little, and attached no importance to reading. Fourthly, social attitudes. While both groups were at heart conventional, Mods saw themselves as individualists and innovators, while Rockers were very conservative and even reactionary.

It was probably in 1967 that the Skinhead style first appeared in London. The Skinheads' use of boots and braces, even more than the

Rockers' cycle gear, represented a 'formalization of work clothes'.[13]
The first major appearance of Skinheads in large numbers was at
the sit-in at 144 Piccadilly in the summer of 1969 and in anti-Pakistani
episodes in Leeds and later in the East End of London, and only in
that year did the term become widely used. Previously these youngsters had been treated as ordinary working-class youth, very conventional in their behaviour and outlook.[14] They represented a
return to the old working-class culture of alcohol, and a rejection of
the new hippy culture. Like Rockers, they stressed working-class
values, were very conservative, and held the same belief in manliness
and physical prowess.

In their different ways, the Teds, Mods and Rockers, and Skinheads represented the conventional patterns of juvenile rebellion, of
protest within the accepted framework of materialism. They certainly aroused hostility and fear by their violence, but they offered no
real threat to the nature of society as such. They accepted the underlying materialism of the social order, and their rebellion took place,
for the most part, within the assumptions of that social order; only
with the emergence of the beat generation and of the hippy scene
were these assumptions questioned. But during the 1950s and 1960s
a good deal of adolescent frustration and boredom was channelled
into aggression: for noticeably the non-academic working-class adolescent found the leisure demands of a forty-hour week difficult to cope
with, which his parents who grew up in a totally different situation
found difficult to comprehend. Even so, large sections of youth
remained only marginally affected by the labelled minority groups.
London was affected most of all by these movements. A study in
Lancashire, however, suggested that the image of swinging youth as
delivered by the mass media was, and is, incorrect: 'These young
people are mostly not angry and active, but apathetic and unasser-
tive, especially in the face of "them". Even where few minorities
threaten them directly, a deep-seated bigotry often bitterly obtrudes,
as they seek to defend the little they do possess. Far from challenging
the world around them with an insistent individuality, they seem
personally and socially incarcerated.'[15]

These youngsters, typical of so many in the country, are not
affluent, nor noticeably 'deviant': their sexual behaviour and their
job expectations are extremely conventional, and they lack idealism
and personal ambition. Their political views on such issues as
capital punishment or immigration are reactionary. A National

Opinion Poll of teenagers in 1971 showed that the most popular personalities among them included their own mothers, the Queen, Harold Wilson, President Johnson, Prince Philip, Elvis Presley, and Bobby Charlton.[16] Hardly the most radical set! So one must set against the 'youth revolution' this pervasive conservatism.

Until the mid-1960s the trend in juvenile delinquency was also extremely conservative. The concept of a 'subculture' had been introduced into criminological theory by Albert Cohen in the United States in 1955.[17] This was applied to the delinquency neighbourhoods of American cities, where 'cultures within cultures' were inextricably bound up with delinquent gangs. It is interesting that 'counter-culture', a term which has now become highly fashionable, was also originally used in a criminal context.[18] American writing on delinquency invariably stressed 'delinquent gangs, or subcultures, as they are typically found among adolescent males in lower-class areas of large urban centres'.[19] The studies of Cloward and Ohlin referred to criminal, conflict and retreatist types of subculture: the criminal pattern was concerned primarily with material gain and power; the conflict pattern was clearly seen in the fighting gang; the retreatist pattern was largely viewed in terms of drug use. The contrast with the British youth scene of the late '50s and early '60s was most clearly distinguished by Downes who claimed that 'the English evidence lends no support for the existence of delinquent subcultures, on the Cloward–Ohlin basis. . . . Gangs of the distinctive "criminal"/"conflict"/"retreatist" subcultural varieties clearly do not exist.' Of the retreatist subculture, he argued:

> There is probably more chance of the middle-class adolescent jazz enthusiast coming into contact with the genuine retreatist culture, and indulging in marginal addictive practices such as ether or gasoline sniffing—or smoking an experimental 'reefer'—than there is of the working-class adolescent 'double failure' taking to drug use. The current retreatist pattern in this country is sophisticated, 'hip' and upper-class or middle-class or 'student'-class, rather than connected with working-class subcultural delinquency, though this is not to deny the probability of the drug cult spreading down the socio-economic scale.[20]

Yet the notion that 'gang delinquency' was a central element in British life has remained popular and is frequently revived by the national press. In fact, delinquent gangs were probably more common before and immediately after the Second World War than they are today. Colin Fletcher's study of Merseyside[21] suggests that gangs were prevalent in Liverpool until the 1950s when they virtually disintegrated with the growth of teenage culture and affluence, and later of the beat scene. Gangs gave birth to beat groups. So in June 1958 the Park Gang evolved into The Tremeloes, one of the earliest exponents of the Mersey Sound, and between 1960 and 1964 around three hundred groups had sprung up on Merseyside. But if beat killed the gangs, it did not kill delinquency. Since the mid-1960s, the radical and retreatist or bohemian traditions of youth revolt have increased, but not at the expense of the delinquent tradition.[22]

THE POP SCENE

In attempting to trace the growth of a counter-culture—a way of life and a philosophy which at central points is in conflict with the mainstream society—pop music is of crucial importance. In one sense, of course, pop music is essentially part of the mainstream society, for capitalist ethics control the record industry as much as any other. But the ideas expressed through pop songs may still be potentially and actually subversive of the established order, and there can be little doubt that it is in pop music, rather than in political or religious literature, that the values of the emerging youth culture are expressed. In order to make sense of spirituality among young people, it is necessary to look at the pop scene, and examine the underlying life-styles and ideas.

Since the war years, when Vera Lynn sang 'There'll be bluebirds over the white cliffs of Dover', there has been a tremendous change in popular songs. We have seen a progression from rock 'n' roll to skiffle, from beat to contemporary folk, from protest to psychedelic music. Overseas influences, from India, Africa and the Caribbean, have helped to create new western styles in music and dancing, such as blue beat, calypso, high-life, reggae, and soul. The psychedelic drug culture, the Vietnam war and other conflicts, the disillusionment with institutional religion, have all in some way affected popular songs.

During the 1950s rock and roll hit the West. Historians of pop distinguish between *rock 'n' roll*, the type of music which became popular in the early '50s and petered out around 1958, *rock and roll*, the name given to the wider musical tradition, and *rock*, the post-

1964 derivations of rock 'n' roll.[23] The origins of rock 'n' roll lie in the 1940s, but it was not until Bill Haley and the Comets in 1953 that it became popular among the teenage public in Britain. When the term 'rock 'n' roll' was first used, probably by Alan Freed, an American disc-jockey, it was as a synonym for what had previously been known as rhythm and blues. The difference was that now this music was being directed at white audiences, and in its new setting its character changed. In 1956 the *New York Times* reported attempts by white southern church groups to have rock 'n' roll suppressed: they saw it as a leftist operation aimed at corrupting the youth of the south. Many adults viewed the new music with suspicion. It was seen as inciting primitive sexual urges, as encouraging violence, and (particularly in the United States) as being of Negro origin. Bill Haley's film *Rock Around the Clock*, released in 1955, shook the teenage public and there were riots throughout cinemas all over Britain. All the forms of rock 'n' roll which developed were based on Negro dance rhythms, and it was out of the fusion of rhythm and blues with country and western music that there emerged the phenomenon of 'country rock', or 'rockabilly', exemplified most clearly by Elvis Presley.

During 1956–7 there developed a species of song which focused almost exclusively on adolescence. Elvis Presley's 'Teddy Bear', Tab Hunter's 'Young Love', Tommy Sands' 'Teenage Crush', and Paul Anka's 'Diana' were fairly typical. It was the age of the teenage dream boy, and out of this period came Cliff Richard. Rock 'n' roll became transformed into pop music. Out of the early rock 'n' roll era too came skiffle, represented by Lonnie Donegan, by Johnny Duncan and the Blue Grass Boys, and by the large number of skiffle groups who appeared on the BBC Light Programme's Saturday Skiffle Club. Young working-class teenagers throughout Britain began to feel themselves actively involved in the new muscial culture, and cheap guitars and banjos became a profitable business. Elvis was the major inspiration of such singers as Sonny James, Tab Hunter, and Tommy Sands, and with them, and the early successors of Haley, such as Pat Boone, the lyrics became as important as the big beat itself. In the skiffle movement, as developed by Lonnie Donegan, the folk traditions of the United States, the songs of such men as Leadbelly and Woody Guthrie were used as source material. The songs of skiffle ranged from direct adaptations of American events—'I gambled down in Washington'—to specifically British creations—'My old man's a dustman' and 'Cumberland Gap'. But the dominant influence on all popular music was American until about 1962, when Britain began to make its own unique contribution to the pop scene, and the arrival of The Beatles was the most significant event of this period. Although they were influenced by Chuck Berry, The Miracles, and Buddy Holly and the Crickets, The Beatles appeared to represent a new and authentic British beat style. With working-class backgrounds in Merseyside, they set the precedent for the appearance of vast numbers of small beat groups and clubs throughout the north-west and Britain as a whole.

The influences on popular song and dance were not only American —the Caribbean was a major factor for the ska dance pattern, popular among the Jamaican working-class, was the basis of blue beat. The rhythm of blue beat goes back many centuries in the culture of Africa, although medieval Europe had its counterparts. The precise dance was created in Jamaica in 1961 and it was accompanied by a continuous, monotonous, pulsating rhythm. From Jamaica, blue beat spread to London, originally to Soho and the black areas of Brixton; the success of Millie's 'My Boy Lollipop' in 1964 was the first big turning-point in the spread of blue beat throughout the country. The Negro rhythm was 'essentially the recreational pattern of an alienated people, developed to express the rage, the anger, the violence and the vitalism of a subculture which, for various historical reasons, is basically hedonistic in orientation'.[24]

After The Beatles had introduced a decade of groups, rock music became allied increasingly in some circles with social comment. The Who, originally the Mod group *par excellence*, produced 'My Generation'. The Beatles themselves provided, on their LP 'Revolver', both tragic songs of protest like 'Eleanor Rigby' and cynical ones like 'Dr Robert', and also inward-looking psychedelic hymns such as 'Yellow Submarine' and 'Turn off your mind, relax and float downstream' (the words taken directly from Timothy Leary's version of *The Tibetan Book of the Dead*). The Rolling Stones produced such songs as 'Satisfaction', 'Get Off Of My Cloud' and 'Nineteenth Nervous Breakdown'. At the same time, Bob Dylan and Paul Simon became the first important representatives of a style of contemporary folk sound which was very preoccupied with social and moral protest. The Byrds, an American west coast group, became famous through their version of Dylan's 'Mr Tambourine Man', and they later recorded 'The Times, They Are

A-Changing'. Paul Simon wrote such songs as 'I am a Rock', 'A Church is Burning', 'The Sound of Silence', 'He Was My Brother' and 'A Most peculiar Man'. Their themes were loneliness, freedom, communication, martyrdom for justice, and the suicide of the lonely. It was at this point that the folk scene began to assume the identity of a quasi-religious movement, combining elements of prophecy (as in Dylan's 'A Hard Rain's a Gonna Fall'), hymns of dereliction (as in Simon's 'Blessed'), songs of faith and doubt (as in Simon's 'Kathy's Song'). The old order, Dylan warned, was crumbling.

> Come, mothers and fathers, throughout the land,
> And don't criticise what you can't understand.
> Your sons and daughters are beyond your command.
> Your old world is rapidly ageing.
> Please get out of the new one if you can't lend your hand,
> For the times, they are a-changing.

Dylan, however, also changed. His early songs were old-fashioned folk protest, attacks on social injustices, on war, exploitation, and so on. But later Dylan became surrealist and psychedelic. His individual progress in many ways symbolizes the much larger phenomenon of rock music's transformation. As Charles Reich has written:[25]

> What the new music has become is a medium that expresses the whole range of the new generation's experiences and feelings. The complex, frantic, disjointed, machine-like experiences of modern urban existence were presented, with piercing notes of pain, and dark notes of anger, by The Cream. The mystical transcendence of ordinary experience achieved by the hippies, the drug world and the spiritual realm, soaring fantasy and brilliant patterns of rhythm and sound, are the domain of the San Francisco acid rock of Jefferson Airplane, and the psychedelic meditations of the early music of Country Joe and The Fish. Irony, satire, mockery of the Establishment and of rational thought were the speciality of Mothers of Invention. A uniquely personal but universal view of the world has been achieved by The Beatles, gentle, unearthly, the world transformed. Another highly personal view of the world, but one close to the experience of young listeners, is that of Bob Dylan. Dylan has gone through a whole cycle of experiences, from folk music to social protest and

commentary, next to folk rock, then to the extraordinarily personal
world of the ballad 'Sad-Eyed Lady of the Lowlands', and
finally to the serene, but achieved, innocence of the country
music of the album *Nashville Skyline*. Perhaps more than any
other individual on the field of music, Dylan has been, from the
very beginning, a true prophet of the new consciousness.

Eastern Europe has not been left untouched by the international
pop scene. In Prague, the Socialist Youth Organisation chose to
take pop into its system, and the term 'popsocialism' has been used
to describe the fusion of western pop culture and Eastern European
socialism. The impact of pop has met with considerable resistance
from those who, like the East German paper *Volksarmee*, see pop
tunes as ammunition in the psychological warfare of imperialism.
Radio Prague has described the pop scene as escapist, a diversion
from the 'real problems of society', a 'senseless imitation of petty
bourgeois models'. Others have seen rock music as potentially
revolutionary, maybe too revolutionary, while a widespread official
communist line has been to view pop as innocuous and inevitable.
So in 1971 there were some four thousand rock ensembles in Hungary,
while in Poland there were some four hundred 'big beat' groups,
and five thousand smaller, amateur groups.

> The unanswered question in Eastern Europe is still whether
> young people can enjoy mass culture, and even dabble with its
> outward trappings, without being influenced politically or
> morally. The 1960s produced no 'sexual revolution' in Eastern
> Europe—but they did produce student protest movements and
> 'alienation'. Whether the mass culture that the youth of the East
> finds so appealing represents an ideological challenge is still
> being debated.[26]

In the West too, the political significance of rock music is still a con-
tentious question.

On the one hand, rock music is felt to be subversive, not simply
in terms of the views and attitudes expressed by musicians, but in
the area of behaviour.[27] On the other hand, it is the capitalist world
which controls the rock industry. To many young revolutionaries,
the 'inner revolution' of which John Lennon spoke seemed only a
modern psychedelic version of the old Christian 'change of heart'
view, and Richard Neville quotes a clash which occurred on this

argument between Lennon and John Hoyland, a British leftist, in the pages of *Black Dwarf*. Lennon argued that what was wrong with the world was people, to which Hoyland retorted, 'What makes you so sure that a lot of us haven't changed our heads in something like the way you recommend—and then found out it wasn't enough, because you simply cannot be turned on and happy when you know that kids are being roasted to death in Vietnam, when all around you, you see people's individuality being stunted by the system.'[28] Some rock groups, such as The Fugs, which grew out of the bohemian literary scene in New York City, saw themselves as politically and culturally subversive. Others have remained cynical, and have pointed to Dylan as the prime example of how social protest fades into psychedelic fantasy, and revolution is marketed as a commodity by Columbia Records Ltd.

THE ALDERMASTON GENERATION

The years that saw the emergence of Presley and the creation of the scene that welcomed The Beatles also saw the growth of the anti-bomb movement. The Campaign for Nuclear Disarmament, which grew out of the Direct Action Committee Against Nuclear War, came into existence in 1958. Soon it became the largest political mass movement outside the political parties, and it was predominantly a youth movement. Associated with the protest against nuclear madness was the creation of a new folk culture: indeed the importance of the marches to and from Aldermaston lay less in their direct, or even symbolic, effect on the public, than in their creation of a sense of solidarity among the marchers. The success of the anti-bomb movement too was inseparable from the growing sense of disillusionment with the major parties, the sense of moral disgust at the policy of deterrence, the feeling of betrayal by the men in power.

The theoretical basis of the Campaign, in so far as it had one, lay in the thinking of the New Left. Of course, there were—and particularly after 1960—large numbers of unconnected or mutually hostile groups associated with the movement, and many individuals who were 'non-political', religious or old-style pacifists. But the New Left was the only group which offered a clearly argued socialist alternative to the nuclear power structure. It saw the alternative in moral terms, and described it in the context of pop culture. One of its leaders referred to the 'Great Apathy' and pointed to the increase in crime, drug addiction, gang conflicts and race riots, and he went on, 'Sometimes the protest is just *against*: against nothing, as in the rock 'n' roll riots.' On the other hand:

> The young marchers of Aldermaston, despite all immaturities and individualistic attitudes, are at root more mature than their critics on the Old Left. They have understood that 'politics' have become too serious to be left to the routines of politicians. As for 'moral and spiritual values', what can Old Left or New Right offer, after all?
>
>> The fourth day there'll be darkness
>> The last time the sun has shone,
>> The fifth day you'll wake up and say
>> The world's real gone . . .
>
> (Tommy Steele, *Doomsday Rock*)[29]

The New Left combined critical analysis of the social and economic structure, diagnosis of the way of life of 'welfare capitalism', rejection of the deterrent approach to nuclear weapons, and a commitment to the recovery of a truly socialist humanism. During the late '50s and early '60s, the *New Left Review* group constituted the most important body of dissent in British youth politics. It represented a moral repudiation of nuclear weapons: for the New Left, 'unilateralism is founded upon a moral judgement rather than upon political calculation'.[30] It represented also an emphasis on culture. Writings such as Richard Hoggart's *The Uses of Literacy* and Raymond Williams's *Culture and Society 1780–1950* and *The Long Revolution* helped to shape the form of its protest.

The *New Left Review* group was the result of a merger between two distinct socialist bodies. The first was the opposition group ('revisionists') within the British Communist Party which published a journal *The Reasoner*. Its editors, who were from the North of England, where they were active in working-class movements, had by 1957 left the Communist Party, and begun a new journal, *The New Reasoner*. John Saville, E. P. Thompson and Peter Worsley were the key figures in this group. The second group was the *Universities and Left Review* which began in Oxford and later centred on the Partisan Coffee House in Carlisle Street, Soho. The central figure in this movement was Stuart Hall. In 1960 a symposium *Out of Apathy* appeared, in which the New Left's concept of the current struggle emerges.

Two essays in *Out of Apathy* by E. P. Thompson[31] best convey the atmosphere of the New Left—most strongly apparent is its *moral* emphasis. Thompson rejoices in 'the long and tenacious revolutionary tradition of the British commoner'. 'From the Chartist camp meeting to the dockers' picket line it has expressed itself most naturally in the language of moral revolt.'[32] He hopes that this age will be 'the age in which the rebellion of socialist humanism began'.[33] He argues that the New Left was born when the disillusionment with the old Left met the threat of nuclear destruction.

> Just as the rituals and resounding absolutes of orthodox Stalinism have induced a nausea in the younger Soviet generation, giving rise to the critique of the 'revisionists', the positive rebellion of '56, the negative resistance of the *stilyagi*; so Napolitan ideology has engendered within itself its own negation—a new critical temper, the positives of Aldermaston, the negatives of 'hip' and 'beats'.
>
>   Out of the truth of quietism there stems a new rebellious humanism: the politics of anti-politics. The post-war generation grew to consciousness amidst the stench of the dead, the stench of the politics of power. . . . The old Left, because it refused to look evil in the face, because it fudged the truth about Communism or suggested that human nature could be set right by some stroke of administration, appeared mechanical, 'bullying', de-humanised: it could only speak in the language of power, not of socialised humanity.

But out of quietism came a new socialist protest.

> It was the threat of nuclear annihilation which made the quietists rebel. At Aldermaston the clouds began at last to release their store of compassion . . . And so this rebellious humanism stems outwards from the offence which power gives to the personal—the offence of power against people with different pigment in their skins, the offence of power against people of different social class, the offence of the bomb against human personality itself. The anti-political find themselves once again in the arena of political choice. Because, in retreating to the personal, they found themselves in the atomised, impersonal jungle of *Room at the Top*, they find that they must reach out once again towards the values of community. Because 'love' must be thrust into the context of power, the moralist finds that he must become a revolutionary.[34]

The New Left grew out of the threat of nuclear destruction, and was primarily a recovery of the moral basis of socialism. The movement that showed the largest post-war political organisation of youth however was the Campaign for Nuclear Disarmament, formed in 1958. The marches to and from Aldermaston and the emergence of the New Left were inseparable; what began as a simple protest against the bomb soon became a wider social protest movement on a major scale. But in its origins the anti-bomb movement was a moral protest in the name of humanity and with a strong Christian basis, although it received slight support from the Churches, and clergy were sufficiently rare in marches that those who did march became well known. The anti-bomb movement was international. In the United States, the National Committee for a Sane Nuclear Policy was founded a few months before CND, and soon anti-bomb movements, using the CND slogan, were established in every major West European country and elsewhere. CND officially began at a public meeting on 17 February 1958 at the Central Hall, Westminster. On that occasion Dr Alex Comfort said:[35]

> Within the coming weeks we intend to raise throughout the country a solid body of opposition to the whole strategy of moral bankruptcy and ceremonial suicide which the hydrogen bomb epitomises, to all the mentally under-privileged double-talk by which it has been justified. . . . We can make Britain offer the world something which is virtually forgotten—moral leadership. Let us make this country stand on the side of human decency and human sanity.

Between 1958–60, the campaign grew: the 1958 Easter march only collected about two thousand people, but by 1960 there were twenty thousand. Many of those who took part were young people for whom neither the Labour Party nor the Communist Party had much appeal. Both parties realized that CND threatened to become the biggest movement of socialist youth in the country, and it was in 1960 that the Young Socialists came into being, and the Communist Party threw its support behind the anti-bomb movement.

The Young Socialists, the official Labour Party youth section, came into existence in 1960 as the result of a Working Party set up by the National Executive. The Labour Party, conscious of the fact that it was failing to attract large numbers of radical youth, decided the Young Socialist movement was 'an integral part of the Party'.[36] Regional Youth Officers were appointed and sent out to every branch. By October 1960, there were 608 branches, and they had grown to 726 by April 1961. The Party had been spurred into action by its defeat in the election of October 1959 and by the threat from the growing anti-bomb movement. In fact, the Young Socialists at their first conference in Easter 1961 passed a resolution calling on the Party to campaign for the cessation of the manufacture of nuclear weapons by Britain, removal of all nuclear bases, withdrawal from NATO, and for the discontinuing of H-bomber patrol flights over British soil. The second conference of the Young Socialists in Easter 1962 maintained this unilateralism, although the Labour Party had retreated from such a stance at its Blackpool Conference. There were very strained relations between the Young Socialists and Transport House, and soon the energy of the young Left became centred on two unofficial journals, *Keep Left* (which was soon proscribed) and *Young Guard*. The official Young Socialist paper *New Advance* began to warn of dangers from the *Keep Left* section: 'They believe in a world-wide revolution of the proletariat and dictatorial communist world government. They have turned their attention to the YS movement because they are dismayed to see such a brilliant organ of democratic socialism. They want to smash it in its early stages and take away many of its members.'[37] The spectre of Trotskyism was haunting the Labour establishment as they viewed the increasing alienation of the young radicals from the Labour Party.

The Communist Party position on the bomb was ambivalent. In May 1960 the Executive Committee of the Communist Party called on all party members to support the Campaign for Nuclear Disarmament. But the Communist record on nuclear weapons was not good. The *Daily Worker* had been the only British newspaper to have called, after the bombing of Hiroshima, for use of the atomic bomb on a large scale.[38] By 1947, however, in face of the nuclear superiority of the United States they changed their line, and the Stockholm Peace appeal called for the banning of nuclear weapons, though not for unilateral action. The Communist Party were never unilateralist, and they supported the Soviet doctrine of the pre-emptive nuclear strike (American development of nuclear weapons was aggressive militarism, Soviet development of them was a contribution to world peace). Palme Dutt, the vice-chairman of the British Communist

Party, explained in 1955 that it was the Soviet hydrogen bomb which constituted the 'Great Deterrent'.[39] Consequently the attitude of the Communist Party towards CND was not friendly at the start, and Communists at trades union conferences opposed unilateralism. The *Daily Worker* saw unilateralism as a divisive force which split the peace movement, and would place the Soviet Union in an embarrassing position. The 26th Congress of the Communist Party in 1959 reiterated this view: 'unilateralism only divides the movement and diverts attention from the real issue, namely international agreement to ban nuclear weapons'.[40] In May 1960 they apparently changed their position, but this was because they saw that it would be expedient, even necessary, to jump on the bandwaggon of what promised to be the biggest mass socialist movement since the war. Yet even in October 1960, Communist spokesmen continued to describe unilateralism as 'unrealistic and in the short run simply opportunistic'.[41] The Communists may have marched with CND, but they did not support its basic belief, a moral commitment to unilateralism. To many young people, the Party was thus discredited.

But moral disillusionment with the Communist Party went deeper than the single issue of unilateralism. For years the literature of disenchantment with Communism had been increasing on the Left. To many of those who took part in the protest movements of the '50s and '60s, the Communist Party appeared as a conservative force. The bureaucratic control of the Party, the apparent conflict between intellectual honesty and party loyalty, the exposure of the atrocities and distortions of the Stalinist period: all this contributed to the irrelevance of this Party to the new revolutionary thinking among the young.[42] The rejection of the authoritarian and anti-intellectual elements in Marxism, associated particularly with the Stalin period, was an international phenomenon. Interest in 'the young Marx', in 'Marxist humanism' and ethics was revived, and in the concept of freedom. There was a rejection of dogmatism and determinism, and after the Hungarian rising of 1956 'a world-wide and continuing movement of Communist dissidence' developed,[43] particularly among young people. But many older intellectuals felt, with A. H. Hanson, 'I could remain no longer in the Party without forfeiting my moral and intellectual self respect: so I got out'.[44]

Meanwhile the course of the anti-bomb movement was changing. After the peak year of 1960, support for CND among the young waned, for two reasons: first, the vagueness of the Campaign's position. Its propaganda was aimed too much at the heart and at human fears, and, apart from the New Left intellectuals, paid little attention to serious thought about alternatives to nuclear deterrence. Second, the method which the Campaign had espoused, constitutional change aided by polite, law-abiding marches, was proving to be fruitless. Many young people were impatient with constitutional methods and they found a leader in a man who was probably the oldest member of CND, Bertrand Russell. Russell believed that civil disobedience was necessary if governments were to be brought to their senses, and his speeches were far more militant and outspoken than the more restrained words of the official CND spokesmen. In the summer of 1960 the clash between the supporters of constitutional methods, led by Canon Collins, and the direct action group, led by Russell, came to a head. As a result the Committee of 100 was set up in October 1960, supported by over a hundred prominent names. The Committee organized its first mass sit-down in front of the Ministry of Defence in February 1961, with further demonstrations in April and September.

Between 1958 and 1961 the anti-bomb movement became increasingly a youth protest. The *Daily Mail* on 8 April 1958 had described the supporters of the first march as 'mainly middle class and professional people' and 'quiet suburbanites'. The tone of the press in 1963 was quite different. *The Times* claimed that a large group within CND were 'very young or very immature' and were 'carefully dishevelled exhibitionists', simply protesting against authority.[45] In between these dates, a survey in 1959 of a 10 per cent random sample of marchers estimated that 41 per cent were under 21 years of age, and nine out of ten of the young people said that they supported the Campaign for moral reasons. (The proportion was even higher among the over 25s.) Significantly, some 34 per cent of the young people professed a religious faith.[46]

The announcement of the first Committee of 100 demonstration was made by Bertrand Russell on 14 December 1960. It would be on 18 February 1961 outside the Ministry of Defence, would last for four hours, and would coincide with the arrival of the submarine tender *Proteus* in the Clyde. Estimates of the numbers who did sit down on that day varied from one thousand to six thousand. A declaration which was stuck to the door of the Ministry by Russell and Michael Scott demanded 'the immediate scrapping of the agreement to base Polaris carrying submarines in Britain' and 'the complete rejection by our country of nuclear weapons and all policies and alliances that depend upon them'. The declaration ended, 'We call upon the scientists to refuse to work on nuclear weapons. We call upon workers to black all work connected with them and to use their industrial strength in the struggle for life. . . . We hereby serve notice on our Government that we can no longer stand aside while they prepare to destroy mankind.'[47]

Among the thinkers who influenced supporters of non-violent direct action was a young American, Ralph Schoenman, who for a time became personal secretary to Russell. Schoenman's theoretical position was that the values derived from the liberal, democratic and socialist traditions were no longer operative; instead we had entered an age in which 'power is concentrated, and in western societies it is private'. He pointed out that the oil corporations possessed over a quarter of the United States on lease, and that directorates were in control of production, television, newspapers and cinemas:

> I believe that in fundamental ways the Cold War has served as a Metternich programme on the part of the West, designed to create the climate and the ideological myths necessary to prevent serious challange to the power of the vast corporations whose control over planetary resources is maintained at the expense of the agony and starvation of its population at large.

 The United States was geared to an economy based on war and violence. Mass society, Schoenman claimed, was now totalitarian.

> It is as true of Britain as it is of the United States or the Soviet Union. In these countries individuals find vast impersonal institutions in which they are absorbed like ciphers. More depressingly these institutions feed and breed men for quiescence. The efficient operation of a highly ordered institution, whether private or publicly, rests on a man who does not question ends, make demands, or display the characteristics of one not disposed to guide his manner to the dictates of the organisation he inhabits or of its bureaucracy.[48]

In April 1961 Bertrand Russell addressed the first Annual Conference of the Midlands Region Youth Campaign for Nuclear Disarmament in Birmingham.[49] Here he put the case for civil disobedience by non-violent action. The forces which control public opinion,

Russell argued, were heavily weighted on the side of the rich and powerful: although we lived officially in a democracy, the great newspapers belonged to powerful people, and, like television and radio, had strong reasons for not offending the Government. 'Most experts would lose their position and their income if they spoke the truth. . . . There is in every modern state a vast mechanism intended to prevent the truth from being known, not only to the public, but also to the Governments. Every Government is advised by experts and inevitably prefers the experts who flatter its prejudices.' So Russell saw the Committee of 100 as the central element in a campaign against 'massive artificial ignorance' about nuclear warfare. Non-violent civil disobedience was 'a method of causing people to know the perils to which the world is exposed and in persuading them to join us in opposing the insanity which affects, at present, many of the most powerful Governments in the world'. Russell and his followers accepted the argument that civil disobedience as a means of propaganda was hard to justify except in extreme cases: but he argued that the prevention of nuclear war was extreme, and demanded radical action of this kind.

The Committee of 100 for a time became the focal point of civil disobedience in Britain, and after the two major demonstrations in April and September 1961, began to emphasize the need for large-scale social change. Michael Scott, one of its leaders, urged the establishment of 'people's assemblies' which would relate military preparations to social deprivation and injustice. Since direct action was not now seen only as a means of propaganda, in their demonstrations of 9 December 1961 the Committee planned to occupy eight nuclear air bases. Subsequently, six of the leaders were tried in February 1962 under the Official Secrets Act of 1911, five were sent to prison for eighteen months and one woman, for twelve months. From this period the Committee and the anti-bomb movement generally went into decline. Few would deny that it performed a major educational role in creating an informed body of people with an awareness of the facts about nuclear weapons, and that it had consolidated a large body of radical youth, among whom it helped to create a political consciousness. But its policies were too vague, and its language too unreal for people who needed to be shown how a violent society could be changed. Out of the disintegration of the non-violent movement grew a concern for alternative life-styles, for demonstrating non-violence in local situations. This tendency to

*A way
to
escape
+ change
society*

move into small-scale community action was seen by some as escapist, a retreat to the ghetto, while others saw it as the only practical way of changing society.

After its peak period of influence in the days of big Aldermastons and of the Partisan Coffee House, the New Left also entered a period of what appeared to be decline, or at least a sabbatical reflection period. What was to emerge some years later was a very different protest style, very unlike traditional Marxism in its ideology, and deriving its impetus from the American and European student revolts and from the Underground. But the *New Left Review* tradition did not wholly disappear. In 1968 *The May Day Manifesto* attempted to produce an analysis of contemporary capitalism,[50] but those responsible for this were the older, non-student leftists of the previous decade. From 1968 onwards the influences on the left-wing youth scene were different: Yippies, Marcuse, *Black Dwarf*, Students for a Democratic Society (SDS) in the United States, Che Guevara, Cohn-Bendit. Tariq Ali has observed about the New Left clubs of the CND era: 'The notion was seriously entertained that these clubs constituted the embryo of a new socialist movement, but they disappeared without a trace in a couple of years.' But he concedes that the New Left was 'an important component of the radicalization of youth in the late 'fifties and early 'sixties'.[51] Since a new team took over *New Left Review* in 1962 it has made a significant contribution to the popularizing in Britain of the works of European socialist thinkers such as Marcuse, Sartre, Mandel and Lukacs.

Today the term 'New Left' is used in a vague way to describe a whole range of distinct and unrelated groups and movements. At the present time, one can identify at least five strands within the political consciousness of the young. First, a Communist group consisting of the Communist Party itself and such groups as the Communist Party of Britain (Marxist-Leninist), a Maoist splinter movement which broke away from the Communist Party. Secondly, a Trotskyist group represented by a large number of bodies, the three largest being the Socialist Labour League, International Socialism and the International Marxist Group. Thirdly, community action movements such as the Claimants' Unions and squatters' groups. Fourthly, a large number of movements concerned with the liberation of various minority groups—Black Liberation Front, Women's Lib, Gay Liberation Front, and so on. Finally, anarchist groups (although anarchist *ideas* have had a much wider influence than the traditional anarchist organizations).

SEX REVOLUTION

An important element in the changed youth scene is the so-called sex revolution. There are three distinct areas which concern us here: the changes in research into sexuality, the changes in attitude and behaviour, and the changes in Christian thinking. In the first area, there has been a tremendous amount of research into, and writing about, human sexual behaviour. The early studies by psychoanalysts tended to approach sex by way of the study of neuroses, and emphasized the central role of sexual repression. Such studies as Freud's *Three Essays in the Theory of Sexuality* (1905), Krafft-Ebing's *Psychopathia Sexualis* and Havelock Ellis's *Psychology of Sex* (1933) were pioneers in this field. A major landmark in sexology was the appearance of Wilhelm Reich's *The Function of the Orgasm* in 1942, and this was followed by *The Sexual Revolution* (1945). It was Reich who, above all others in his day, related sexual repression with the political order, and introduced the study of sex into the world of revolutionary politics. Reich's works have recently recaptured considerable popularity. Another better known set of studies has concentrated on sexual behaviour. Kinsey's *Sexual Behaviour in the Human Male* (1948) was followed by his *Sexual Behaviour in the Human Female* (1953). In 1956 Chesser published *The Sexual, Marital and Family Relationships of the English Woman*, and more recently the famous studies by Masters and Johnson *Human Sexual Response* and *Human Sexual Inadequacy* have appeared. In Britain, there have been two important studies, Michael Schofield's *The Sexual Behaviour of Young People* and Geoffrey Gorer's *Sex and Marriage in England Today*. Sexuality is a popular area of study and writing.

But has there been a 'sexual revolution'? Maybe the term is too strong as a description of what is rather a gradual shift in attitude and, to a lesser extent, in behaviour. In one sense, of course, there has been a revolution—in technology—which has left its mark indelibly on the sexual sphere. For a major area of sexual behaviour is concerned with the refinements in technique, and with the chemical revolution which has produced both oral contraceptives and penicillin (against sexually transmitted diseases). Those who naively associate 'sex and drugs' as part of a massive campaign of 'moral

B

pollution' have at least grasped the point that both sexual activity and drug use have been radically changed by chemistry. The spread of contraception in fact represents the first major change in sexual attitudes and practice: the use of contraceptives has enabled sex to be viewed in terms of relationship and not merely of reproduction. The separation of sex for pleasure from sex for procreation is fundamental. One result of the change (which Christians ought to welcome) is the clarification of the nature of moral decisions, which are no longer confused and smothered beneath worries about unwanted babies. The spread of contraception has not only affected the non-Roman Catholic world. A Roman Catholic writer, Dominian, in his *Marital Breakdown* (1968) has argued that birth control is necessary for a concept of marriage-as-relationship. In fact, the number of children born to Roman Catholics differs by only 0·5 per cent from that of others. Between 1966–7, sales of the contraceptive pill increased in Roman Catholic countries—by 87 per cent in Austria and Portugal, 98 per cent in Spain, and 122 per cent in Italy.

Secondly, there has been a change in the pattern of pre-marital sexual relationships. In Kinsey's studies, 85 per cent of the males had had pre-marital intercourse, including 70·5 per cent by their late teens. Schofield's figures for Britain however are only half of this, but Schofield estimates that around 350,000 young people under the age of 20 have had some pre-marital sexual intercourse.[52] Schofield studied 1,873 young people aged 15–19. Of these only 12 per cent of the girls had had sexual intercourse, but of the engaged ones, 37 per cent were sleeping with their boyfriends. Again, illegitimacy has increased, but the number of pregnant brides has decreased. What emerges from the studies is not a pattern of promiscuity (although Schofield and Martin Cole believe that some promiscuity at some stage is valuable and necessary), but rather a gradual relaxation and change in behaviour. Behaviour changes less rapidly than does attitude. Thus a study of third-year students at Durham University in 1970[53] showed that 70 per cent did not think that wives should be virgins, and 66 per cent did not think that premarital sexual intercourse was immoral, although 46 per cent thought that the couple should be in love. But 27 per cent (38 per cent of females, 21 per cent of males) had had sexual experience first at university, and 93 per cent of the girls were virgins when they came to university. By the third year, only 49 per cent were still virgins, but even so this means that 46 per cent had still no sexual experience.

The degree of change can therefore be overstated, but there is certainly a more widespread acceptance of casual sex among young people. Richard Neville expresses this attitude well:[54]

> Thousands of young people all over the world are quietly accomplishing an authentic sexual revolution without even knowing they are part of it. . . . No more tedious 'will she or won't she by Saturday?' but a total tactile information exchange, and an unambiguous foundation upon which to build a temporary or permanent relationship. The pot of gold at the end of the rainbow comes first: later one decides whether the rainbow is worth having for its own sake. If the attraction is only biological, nothing is lost except a few million spermatozoa and both parties continue their separate ways. If there is a deeper involvement, the relationship becomes richer, and so does the sexual experience. One way to a girl's mind is through her cunt.

Thirdly, there has been a good deal of questioning of the ideas of marriage and the family structure by many young people, and this has led to a search for alternative forms of living, communes, extended families, and so on. The family is seen as an instrument for maintaining the present social order, and rejection of that order and its values demand rejection of the family.

Fourthly, the attitude to homosexuality has changed. The use of terms such as 'pervert' or 'perversion' is now less common, though the view that homosexuality is a form of sickness, a sexual neurosis, still persists. But today more people will hold the view that there is some homosexual orientation in everyone and that the sickness theory is untenable. However, at the level of behaviour, persecution and blackmail of male homosexuals still continues. There have been changes not only in the attitudes towards homosexuals but also in the attitudes within the homosexual communities: today women are more readily accepted in the male homosexual society; there has been an increase also, particularly since the emergence of the Gay Liberation Front, of homosexual militancy. The growth of Carnaby Street was, as was shown earlier, a phenomenon with important consequences for male sexual mores. Trends such as the male fashion explosion, the movement towards a bisexual concept, the popularity of 'camp' humour in theatre and TV, and the growth of a homosexual press, with newspapers such as *Gay News* and journals such as *Jeremy* (now defunct), *Quorum* and *Lunch*, are all significant elements in the changed view of homosexuality.

Fifthly, there is certainly an increased openness and frankness of discussion about sex. This is shown not only in the use of so-called 'four letter words' but also in the removal of many of the inhibitions, anxieties and fears about sexuality which were common in the older generation. The influence of the cinema and theatre—with such performances as *Hair* or Ken Russell's film *The Devils*—has helped to bring about a greater degree of honesty, and has reduced the level of fear and repression.

Sixthly, there is a changed view of women. No longer is it possible to see women as tools. The exploding of the myth of the vaginal orgasm has called into question the view that women are, sexually and socially, the passive partners. Early gynaecology was entirely in the hands of men, and, while Samuel Collins in his *Systema Anatomicum* (1685) described the vagina in active terms, for the most part the female organs have been seen as merely passive. Today the 'Freudian vaginal ethic' is rejected by the movement for women's liberation. 'The definition of feminine sexuality as normally vaginal', wrote Susan Lydon in *Ramparts*, 'was part of keeping them down, of making them sexually as well as economically, socially and politically subservient.'[55] So today the movement for female emancipation has been carried into the field of sexuality.[56]

Finally, there has been a rediscovery of the body and a search for physical ecstasy, a phenomenon to which I shall return.

In spite of these changes, however, there remains a marked conservatism in the field of sex. Whole areas of ignorance remain—about sexual intercourse, menstruation, venereal diseases, contraception, and so on. Myths about 'flying sperms' are still held and propagated. Again, Gorer's study showed that premarital sex was by no means universal, and that conventional social mores had changed very little. Most couples still did not use contraceptives of any kind. Eighty-eight per cent of women and 46 per cent of men married the person with whom they first had intercourse. Only 2 per cent of men and 3 per cent of women admitted any homosexual attraction, and nearly a quarter said that they were revolted by homosexuals. As one reviewer observed:[57]

All in all, this is a picture of an extremely conventional society: chaste, limited, prejudiced, serious and dull. Lord Longford, Malcolm Muggeridge and Mrs Whitehouse can pack up and go home. We swing not, neither are we lechers. The majority of English people lead sexual lives of extreme respectability, in spite of Soho, television and the erotic bletherings of the press.

The Christian approach to sexuality has been severely hampered by the inheritance from the past for according to much Christian thinking over the centuries, sex is a necessary evil. The Book of Common Prayer explained that one of the purposes of marriage was that 'those who have not the gift of continency' might control their urges in this way. The priest, on this view, must assume that couples who stand before him are incontinent, or they would not be there. But if everybody *did* have the gift of continency, then presumably none of us would be here at all! St Augustine saw sex as tolerable for the purpose of procreation, which was the sacramental means of forgiveness for the sin of pleasure in coition. St Thomas Aquinas believed that marriage without intercourse was preferable, and quoted Xystus: 'He who loves his own wife too ardently is an adulterer.' Considerable influence has been exerted by the Gnostic and Manichee tradition wherein the flesh was seen as evil, and sexuality was seen as the source of most, if not all, of the sin in the world. Some groups, such as the Abelites, who opposed procreation on the ground that it was the perpetuation of sin, became, on their own principles, extinct. But the Christian anti-sex tradition is by no means extinct. Since the Reformation, the Calvinist influence has added to the burden. Thus Sherwin Bailey has written:[58]

> The general impression left by the Church's teaching upon simple and unlearned people can only have been that the physical relationship of the sexes was regarded by religion as unworthy, if not shameless and obscene. The effect of such teaching must necessarily have been grave. It caused a distortion of principles and values which has left an indelible mark upon Christian sexual thought, and we can only guess at the psychological disturbance and conflicts which it has produced in the lives of individuals.

Today there is a recovery of the relational approach to sex. Studies such as the reports *Towards a Quaker View of Sex* (1963) and *Sex and Morality* (British Council of Churches, 1966) have been

significant, as have been Hugh Warner's *Theological Issues of
Contraception* (1954), John Robinson's *Christian Morals Today*
(1964) and the writings of Sherwin Bailey. But a good deal of moral
theology is in straight conflict with contemporary scientific evidence.
The conflict is most marked over masturbation. While well-
known Roman Catholic textbooks such as G. Kelly's *Medico-Moral
Problems* (1960) can still insist that masturbation is never permitted,
the scientific and psychological study of man shows conclusively
that it is not merely an inevitable but also an important element in
sexual development.

Inevitably, there has been renewed attention to the question of
non-marital sexuality. It is significant that Canon Demant, in a
series of lectures given at Oxford in the early 1960s on sex ethics had
very little to say on the matter.[59] Others have defended the traditional
position by the use of illogical and intellectually disreputable
arguments, on the principle, presumably, that ten bad arguments
together might make one good one.[60] Writers such as H. A. Williams,
however, have refused to isolate the physical act from its context.
'I believe,' says Williams,[61] 'that goodness consists in generous self-
giving, and evil in refusal or incapacity to give. Where sex outside
marriage is the medium of self-giving of this kind, then I would
unhesitatingly say that it is not sinful.' The Quaker Report takes
the same line.

A good deal has been written too on the theology of homosexuality, although the Church as a whole has probably not been
affected to any significant extent. The Church of England Moral
Welfare Council's Report *The Problem of Homosexuality* anteceded
the Wolfenden Report of 1957, and the thought of Sherwin Bailey,
its secretary, was firmly imprinted upon it. More recent discussion,
in the Quaker Report and in the writings of Norman Pittenger,[62]
has focused on the physical expression of homosexual love. Related
to this writing has been a growing pastoral contact with homosexuals
by many clergy, both in this country and in the United States, and
this has brought a deeper understanding of the need for experienced
counselling and an awareness of the danger of ignorant advice.

Against all the positive indications of Christian response to the
'sexual revolution', there are two ominous negative signs. The first
is the emergence in recent years of a Christian backlash, evident in
such movements as the Festival of Light, which could well undo
much of the good which has been accomplished over several decades.

The second is the continued survival of the Manichean heresy, evident in a false spirituality and attitude to both the material world and sexuality. The future will show whether the Church will continue to regress, and so reinforce the false stereotype which so many young people hold about the Christian view of sex.

'ON THE ROAD'

In considering the 'youthquake' which has hit the West since the Second World War, I have needed to assess several factors. First, the phenomenon of mass teenage violence, against the background of a youth culture which is predominantly very conventional. Secondly, the growth of pop music, embodying and shaping new forms of youth expression. Thirdly, the political protest movements, particularly those against the bomb, and the formation of a left-wing youth scene. Fourthly, the changing approach to sex. There is a fifth phenomenon which had become evident by the 1950s but whose roots go back many centuries: the phenomenon of the beatnik. The beat generation as it emerged in the United States was a form of protest by disengagement—that is, it did not fight the mainstream social order, but ignored it. It was the early manifestation of the process of 'dropping out', although that term was not widely used until the hippy years of the late 1960s.

The term 'beat generation' was first coined by Jack Kerouac, and was made popular by John Clellon Holmes, the American novelist, in the *New York Times Magazine*. 'The origins of the word "beat"', wrote Holmes, 'are obscure, but the meaning is all too clear to most Americans. More than mere weariness, it implies the sort of feeling of having been used, of being raw. It involves a sort of nakedness of mind, and, ultimately, of soul; a feeling of being reduced to the bedrock of consciousness. In short it means being undramatically pushed up against the wall of oneself. A man is beat whenever he goes for broke and wagers the sum of his resources on a single number.'[63] To be beat demanded a considerable self-consciousness and a sense of isolation, and this led to the cultivation of a religious faith, predominantly Zen-based. But it was in poetry that the beat voice was most powerfully expressed. Beat poetry is spontaneous, uncontrolled and, to many people, incomprehensible, since there is no respect for convention or syntax. The poem expresses the beat quest for self-authenticity, for salvation. Thus in the poetry of Allen Ginsberg, man, God and the Void wrestle.

I am a Seraph and I know not whether I go into the Void
I am a man and I know not whither I go into death—
Christ Christ poor hopeless
lifted on the Cross between Dimension—
to see the Ever-Unknowable.[64]

The roots of the beat generation lie precisely in its lack of roots, its sense of alienation from past, present and future, its lack of interest in industrial and technological progress, its lack of confidence in reason, the Church or political parties. The beats strictly did not reject society: they claimed that there was no society left to reject. Philosophically, the major influence on the beats came from existentialism though unlike the French existentialist, the beatnik was not concerned with the problem of choice—he simply opted out, and chose voluntary poverty. Uninhibited and free sex was central to the beat philosophy, but it was certainly not 'mere promiscuity'. There was a mystique of sexuality which was reminiscent of D. H. Lawrence, or in Kenneth Rexroth's words, 'Against the ruin of the world, there is only one defence—the creative act.' The beat, in his exile from square society, was concerned primarily with the search for identity, for salvation, for the revolution which begins within each man.

So the beats of the 1950s took the way of disaffiliation, 'a voluntary self-alienation from the family cult, from Moneytheism and all its works and ways'.[65] They chose voluntary poverty, jazz was their staple musical diet, and marijuana their drug of awareness. It was in fact in the beat generation that marijuana as a social drug became popular among sections of American youth. Lawrence Lipton wrote of it:[66]

The joint is passed around the pad and shared, not for reasons of economy but as a *social ritual*. Once the group is high, the magic circle is complete. Confidences are exchanged, personal problems are discussed—with a frankness that is difficult to achieve under normal circumstances—music is listened to with rapt concentration, poetry is read aloud and its images, visual and acoustical, communicated with maximum effect. The Eros is felt in the magic circle of marijuana with far greater force, as a unifying principle in human relationships, than at any other time except, perhaps, in the mutual metaphysical orgasm. The magic circle is, in fact, a symbol of and preparation for the metaphysical orgasm.

Without doubt the most famous novel of the beatnik era was Jack Kerouac's *On the Road*, and its influence was considerable. Kerouac wrote of 'the sordid hipsters of America, a new beat generation that I was slowly joining', and saw himself as being like 'the Prophet who has walked across the land to bring the dark Word, and the only Word I had was "Wow" '.[67] Kerouac's books were noted for their vivid descriptions of beatnik areas—such as the account of South Main Street, Los Angeles.

> You could smell tea, weed, I mean marijuana, floating in the air, together with the chili beans and beer. That grand wild sound of bop floated from beer parlours; it mixed medleys with every kind of cowboy and boogie-woogie in the American night. Everybody looked like Hassel. Wild Negroes with bop caps and goatees came laughing by; then long-haired broken-down hipsters straight off Route 66 from New York; then old desert rats, carrying packs and heading for a park bench at the Plaza; then Methodist ministers with raveled sleeves, and an occasional Nature Boy saint in beard and sandals.[68]

Kerouac's characters have a crazy prophetic wildness about them— 'holy flowers floating in the air were all these tired faces in the dawn of Jazz America',[69] and in *The Subterraneans*, he characterized the San Francisco beats:[70] 'They are hip without being slick, they are intelligent without being corny, they are intellectual as hell and know all about Pound without being pretentious or talking too much about it, they are very quiet, they are very Christlike.'

How important were these early American beatniks in the emergence of social protest and of the youth counter-culture? The public image of the beats was that of long-haired, dirty delinquents, permanently high on pot, influenced by Zen, spending most of their time writing obscene poetry and driving recklessly round the United States. Greenwich Village in New York City has been cited as the original source of the beat philosophy, but this is clearly not the case. In origin, beat was not a literary movement, indeed Kerouac was one of the few writers it produced. Nor were the beats delinquents, but rather middle-class young Americans who turned their backs on violence and wealth. In 1960 a well-known American pacifist commented:[71]

If society fears the Beat it is because he cannot be understood in the present materialistic frame of values. He alone—not the church, long since compromised to the system—has said a clear No. No, he will not fight the wars of the United States. No, he will not hate the Negro. No, he will not sell his talent to Madison Avenue. No, he will not dress respectably because he does not seek the respect of society. . . . And so it is, oddly enough, that the juvenile delinquent with his criminal record of violence and theft is really the conformist, while the Beat who murders no one and rarely robs is the real rebel, the ill-clothed and confused potential revolutionist sprung from the fatted loins of the great American middle class.

As another observer put it, 'the juvenile delinquent or hood is simply a square in a hurry'.[72] The beat rejects square values alto-gether. 'The beat and the juvenile delinquent are only kissin' cousins. They have the same enemies, which is the slender thread that some-times unites them in temporary alliance. Both are outlaws, speak a private language and put down the squares, but in beat circles the J.D. is regarded as a square, a hip square in some things, but still a square.'[73]

At heart the beats were a religious movement, a quest for spirit-uality outside the institutional American religious framework. Lipton was emphatic about this:[74]

It is all part of what Carl Jung has called modern man in search of a soul. This spiritual search is not confined to the beat genera-tion: it is in such waters that Monsignor Sheen has been fishing for years. But it is not peace of mind or positive thinking or re-conciliation with tradition or the Church that the beats are seeking. It is something deeper in the human psyche and farther back in the history of the numinous experience, farther back and farther out, than any church of our time has to offer. . . . The aim, of course, is wholeness, personal salvation, in a word, holiness. . . .

There was thus a spiritual search among some sections of the alienated young prior to the development of the drug culture. But the spread of drug use was a central phenomenon in the growth of this search, and remains important for understanding its direction and progress.

2
The Drug Culture

One of the most widely held beliefs, and most frequently repeated statements, about the drug scene in the West is that most of those involved are young people. In fact, drug abuse occurs most frequently among middle-aged and elderly persons. Not only are there more drug addicts in the older age groups, but adults consume far more psycho-active chemicals. Drug abuse in fact is a well-established conventional western phenomenon. It is therefore quite wrong to claim that 'most drug misuse is predominently among the younger generation' or to imagine that the thesis 'that drug misuse is at present largely a phenomenon of youth is clearly well documented'.[1] The abuse of alchohol, barbiturates, minor tranquillisers and the newer sedative agents is principally among the middle-aged. In 1966 G. B. Adams who studied an urban general practice in London reported that 407 patients out of a practice of ten thousand were regularly receiving barbiturates. They were mainly women aged 49–54. If Adams's figures are in any sense representative of the country as a whole 'approximately two million people in Great Britain are receiving barbiturates at any one time and 80 per cent of the total are female'.[2]

More recently, Parish has shown that in 1970, 47·2 million prescriptions for psychotropic drugs—sleeping pills, appetite suppressants, tranquillisers and anti-depressants—were issued in England and Wales. From 1965 to 1970 prescriptions for these drugs increased by 19 per cent, from 39·7 million to 47·2 million. During these six years 120 million prescriptions for hypnotic drugs were dispensed in England and Wales, and there was a remarkable shift from the barbiturates to non-barbiturate hypnotics. These increased by 145 per cent, 'a figure entirely accounted for by the prescribing of two drugs (Mandrax and Mogadon) both introduced in 1965'.

Parish has described this widespread use of these agents as 'a pharmacological leucotomy on a large section of contemporary society'.[3] The majority of those to whom these drugs go are not young people. Indeed, during the period, there was a 220 per cent increase in the prescribing of the minor tranquillisers, particularly Librium and Valium, drugs used to combat anxiety. Parish noted:[4]

> . . . twice as many women as men received them and the number of patients of both sexes receiving these drugs increased rapidly from the age of eighteen to twenty-five. For women the increase continued up to the age of fifty and then levelled off until sixty-five when it rose again. By contrast there was a continued and progressive increase in the number of men receiving treatment from twenty-five to seventy-five years of age.

The use of centrally acting drugs is a well established feature of life in Britain.

Moreover, in the 1950s most addiction to narcotics—including morphine and heroin—occurred among the middle-aged and was of therapeutic origin. As late as 1967, 36 per cent of women addicts were aged over fifty.[5] Barbiturate addiction fatalities have long been features of the middle-aged and elderly drug scene, and amphetamines were abused by middle-aged women as slimming agents before they spread to the young. Alcoholism too is not principally a young person's disease. The evidence is very clear that our society is saturated with centrally acting drugs, and it would be odd if such a high level of use did not carry with it an incidence of abuse, however small. To see the growth of drug abuse among the young as an alien phenomenon is to distort its significance. It would have been surprising if the young had not turned to drugs when they were born into a society which had accepted, and depended upon, their use. Drug abuse therefore is well within the conformities of western culture. What is new is the precise types of drug used. Objectively, it is hard to say whether there has been any overall increase in drug abuse and addiction, but there has certainly been an alteration in the pattern. Among young people, there have been four major areas in which drug consumption has risen: first, amphetamines and other centrally acting pills and capsules; secondly, heroin and other 'needle drugs'; thirdly, cannabis. Fourthly, LSD and other psychedelics, consideration of which I shall leave to Chapter Three.

PURPLE HEARTS AND BEYOND

In 1951 Smith, Kline and French manufactured Drinamyl, a small blue pill containing dexamphetamine (a stimulant) with amylobarbitone (a hypnotic). It quickly became known as 'purple heart' (although it was not strictly either purple or heart-shaped but blue and triangular!) and its appearance can be seen as the beginning of the pep pill era in Britain. Amphetamine had been in use for some time. It had been introduced in the form of the Benzedrine inhaler in 1932, and in tablet form amphetamines had been widely used as stimulants and anti-fatigue drugs. Misuse of amphetamines had been noted in the 1930s, and amphetamine psychoses had been described in the medical literature.[6] Though there had been epidemics of amphetamine misuse in Japan and Scandinavia, there was no major incidence of abuse among adolescents in Britain until about 1960. In 1963–4 there was a good deal of publicity about the use of 'purple hearts' in Soho, and largely as a result of this publicity, the Drugs (Prevention of Misuse) Act was passed in 1964, which made possession of these drugs without prescription an offence. Since then there have been efforts to curb illicit distribution as well as irresponsible prescribing by general practitioners, but the illicit market in these drugs has remained. After 1965 the traffic in pep pills became decentralized, and London ceased to be the one focal point of distribution.

In the United States, amphetamine abuse has reached epidemic proportions in certain areas, although as recently as 1963 the American Medical Association's Council on Drugs could claim that 'at this time, compulsive abuse of the amphetamines (is) a small problem'.[7] By 1966 concern was greater, and a report commented that sufficient amphetamines were available in the United States to supply 25 to 50 doses to every man, woman and child in the country.[8] Much of the concern in the United States has focused around intravenous use of illicitly manufactured methamphetamine crystal. Colonies of intravenous amphetamine users ('speed freaks') have grown up in San Francisco, Los Angeles, New York and other cities, and abuse of amphetamine constitutes one of the most serious health problems in most drug-using communities.[9] In Britain, abuse of amphetamine by young people was principally by mouth, but after 1967 intravenous use of methylamphetamine increased particularly in the Central London area. The spread of methylamphetamine (Methedrine) in injectible form was one factor which helped to create links between the oral and intravenous drug cultures, for prior to 1967, the pill-taking youth of the Soho discotheques had not been associated with the intravenous drug scene represented by heroin and cocaine addicts. The Methedrine epidemic brought them closer together.

There are crucial differences between the ways in which British and American drug scenes have developed.[10] Nevertheless in many respects the history of the last few years provides striking parallels. In Soho, as in San Francisco, it was amphetamine which transformed the character of the drug culture, and in each country serious psychological problems have been reported with amphetamine abuse. The most serious of these, amphetamine psychosis, was described at length in Britain by P. H. Connell in 1958: 'the psychotic picture is identical with paranoid schizophrenia but, without a lengthy follow-up with biochemical control, only speculation is possible'.[11] The condition is characterized by paranoid delusions and vivid hallucinations, and there may be confusion and violence. Towards the end of 1965 the Second Brain Report noted:[12] 'Witnesses have told us that there are numerous clubs, many in the West End of London, enjoying a vogue among young people who can find in them such diversions as modern music and all-night dancing. In such places it is known that some young people have indulged in stimulant drugs of the amphetamine type.' In fact, however, the peak period of amphetamine abuse in the Soho clubs had been earlier, in 1963-4. By 1965 the traffic was beginning to disperse, although Soho has remained an important centre of the pill scene to the present day.

In contrast to the American situation where many of the original hippy community in San Francisco moved on to the 'speed freak' scene, in Britain amphetamines never really caught on in the Underground. LSD and cannabis were far preferable. The pill takers tended to be working-class youths, predominantly conventional in outlook and life-style, conforming more to the stereotype of the old-fashioned juvenile delinquent. The growth of the popularity and use of amphetamines coincided with the 'Mod' period in Britain, and to this extent, amphetamines must be seen as an important element in youth culture. Again, as the intravenous use of Methedrine grew—although the numbers of young people affected were very much smaller—a highly disturbed needle-using group became evident in Central London. Methedrine introduced a high degree of paranoia and violence into the needle culture.

In spite of these factors, the Underground and hippy groups were not affected to any significant extent by amphetamine. The 'Speed Kills' notices issued by Release, an Underground welfare agency, were effective, and Methedrine was never a popular drug. The organs of Underground opinion tended to frown on the needle and disapproved of the use of needle drugs. The pill scene remained fairly conservative, consisting mainly of delinquent adolescents with conventional backgrounds and of low intelligence.

NEEDLE CULTURE

Similarly, the rise of intravenous drug addiction cannot be said to have played any role in the formation of the current youth culture. William Burroughs pointed out that 'junk is not, like alcohol or weed, a means to increased enjoyment. Junk is not a kick. It is a way of life.'[13] Richard Neville, one of the leading blue-eyed boys of the British Underground, has no time for junk either. 'Being a junkie is a full-time occupation and has little to do with being alive. It is one of many ways to destroy yourself, if that's what you want.'[14] Nevertheless, the symbolic role which heroin has played in poetry and music should not be underestimated. The themes of despair and destruction, as represented by the heroin addict's ritualized self-murder, frequently occur in current writing. Pop groups have utilized the heroin experience musically, one of the best examples being The Velvet Underground's track 'Heroin'. But heroin itself has been little used in the Underground; among heroin addicts, there have been some who identified more than others with the Underground culture, but they have been viewed as fringe figures. Heroin is not part of the scene in which the alternative society is set.

This is not, of course, to deny that abuse of and addiction to heroin has increased among young people in recent years, but those involved are a very small section of the total drug-taking population. They are a severely damaged group with a high incidence of family pathology and psycho-social disturbance. A study of female heroin addicts in a London prison in 1968 concluded:[15] 'The women in this study were a highly disturbed group. Viewed in the context of their personality damage as shown by their disturbed, delinquent and grossly unstable conduct, their often profound lack of self

esteem and their obvious emotional deprivation, their heroin dependence appeared almost a minor symptom, and could be regarded as
but the most recent development in their long history of maladjust-
ment.' A similar study of male addicts in another London prison
also concluded that intravenous heroin addiction in Britain 'occurs
predominantly in individuals of markedly sociopathic character
structure which predated the addiction'.[16] The majority of drug-
takers, on the other hand, show no such pathological characteristics,
nor do they tend towards heroin use.

CANNABIS—THE NEW SOCIAL DRUG

Cannabis is by far the most important drug of the new youth culture.
It is more widely used as a purely recreational agent than any drug
except alcohol, and its use is increasing among all sections of young
people except the ultra-conservative. No study of patterns of change
can ignore cannabis. At the same time the drug has provoked more
heat, more hysteria, more irrational argument than any other drug.
Enormous volumes continue to be published about it. Its use is
more extensive than most lay observers realize, although accurate
assessments are extremely difficult. In 1956 the United Nations
Commission on Narcotic Drugs observed that consumers of cannabis numbered millions in the world, and that it was the most
widespread drug of dependence.[17] National figures are dependent
to a large extent on convictions, and since the fluctuations in numbers
are related to variations in law enforcement, such figures are not in
any sense a reliable indication of the overall size of the cannabis-
using community. The witnesses to the Wootton Committee, which
reported in Britain in 1968, emphasized that there had been a gradual
growth in cannabis use in the United Kingdom since the Second
World War. Estimates of the numbers of users were largely guesswork and ranged between thirty thousand and three hundred
thousand,[18] but Bewley's estimate in 1966 was twenty-four
thousand,[19] Aitken's in 1970 was a million,[20] and others have
claimed two million users.[21]

Although it is generally believed that cannabis use is associated
with late adolescence, it is probable that it is 'quite widespread
throughout the age spectrum and not exclusively restricted to the
student and adolescent populations'.[22] An advertisement sponsored
by SOMA Research Association in *The Times* on 24 July 1967
claimed: 'The use of cannabis is increasing and the rate of increase

is accelerating. Cannabis smoking is widespread in the universities, and the custom has been taken up by writers, teachers, doctors, businessmen, musicians, artists and priests. . . .' In a study in 1971, Michael Schofield, a well-respected social psychologist, suggested that 'there are very few men and women over the age of forty who use cannabis, and most people who smoke pot are nearer twenty than thirty'.[23] But estimates of the number of smokers in Britain, and attempts to analyse their age, class and social structure, are very largely informed guesswork. It is certain that there exists a sizeable 'invisible' cannabis-using population, and that the stereotypes of the 'delinquent' or 'freak' users are quite inaccurate. There is no one 'cannabis subculture'.

This is not to deny that historically cannabis use has been statistically associated with recognizable subcultures or minorities of different kinds in different periods. In the 1940s there were a number of dockland cannabis-using districts in England and Wales where the drug was used mainly by immigrant and other merchant seamen. There were groups of smokers among jazz musicians, among beatnik poets, among the followers of Aldermaston marches. The Wootton Report agreed that cannabis smoking in this country was a social rather than a solitary activity, and that the cannabis 'society' was predominantly young and without class barriers. 'It was not politically inclined and our witnesses saw no special significance in the popularity of cannabis among members of radical movements.'[24] However, an American study in 1970 commented:[25] '. . . in analyzing the various youth protest movements—whether political activists and the Peace and Freedom Party, centred in Berkeley, or the Bohemians in Haight-Ashbury—one finds a number of common slogans: "end the war in Vietnam, eliminate racism, and legalise marijuana". A very definite drug culture involving young people in various stages of rebellion has developed in the United States.' On this view, the use of cannabis is one facet of a battle against the establishment.

Though there are very major differences between the drug cultures of Britain and the United States, it is helpful to consider the role of cannabis in the youth movements of American society in the last decade or so. In the late 1930s the Federal Bureau of Narcotics in the United States was responsible for an all-out attack on marijuana, and the most ludicrous claims were made about the drug. It was alleged that it led to insanity, crime, violence and moral

degradation. The Mayor of New York's Committee which reported
in 1944 rejected most of the false claims[26] and subsequent reports
have continued to repudiate them, but many of the myths survive.
The Mayor's Report noted that the use of marijuana was largely
restricted to working-class Negroes and other minorities. The anti-
marijuana campaign was led by Commissioner Harry Anslinger
whose views, whilst invariably inaccurate, at least varied from time
to time. At the House Ways and Means Committee hearings in 1937,
Anslinger held that marijuana led to rape, homicide and insanity,
but denied that it led to heroin. 'No, Sir,' he told a questioner, 'I
have not heard of a case of that kind. I think it is an entirely different
class. The marijuana addict does not go in that direction.' However,
by 1955 he has changed his views, and held that 'if used over a long
period, it does lead to heroin addiction'.[27] Subsequent studies have
demolished the Anslinger view, and, while his position is still popular among the ignorant and very prejudiced, it would be virtually
impossible to find intellectual defence for it.

Today the extent to which cannabis is used in the United States
is incalculable. A Gallup poll in the spring of 1969 indicated that
around one-quarter of the American college population had tried
marijuana at least once,[28] while the largest Federal survey of
marijuana smoking in American universities in 1971 showed that
almost one-third of students had tried marijuana and one-seventh
used it regularly.[29] This study claimed that use had increased and
was continuing to increase in the United States but that the increase
had slowed down in the last few years and that in some areas, such
as the West Coast, use seemed to have 'crested'. In addition, between
1965–7, arrests for marijuana offences among soldiers in Vietnam
increased by 2,553 per cent. Smith commented drily:[30] 'It is
interesting that the politicians who are most vigorously supporting
the war effort are also the most vocal in their attacks on marijuana and
"its associated evils such as the hippies". It is ironic that the war of
these politicians is serving as one of the major forces in strengthening
marijuana's acceptance by American society.'

In such areas as Berkeley, California, marijuana is used almost
universally by college students. Some of these users are part of
what has been called 'a new bohemianism'. Among them, the lyrics
of folk rock music constitute the central body of oral folk lore, and
there is a strong religious sense. Within this new bohemian culture,
cannabis plays a crucial role. The use of cannabis by many radical

and militant students has led some writers mistakenly to assume that it is a revolutionary drug, used principally by left-wing persons. An FBI official was quoted in 1966 as referring to 'the evil of the Communist, beatnik, peacenik conspiracy . . . those dirty non-conformists who smoke marijuana and revel in free sex'.[31] In fact, in both the United States and Britain, the use of cannabis cuts across many social and cultural divisions. Statistically it is probably true to say that cannabis use tends to be associated with a left-wing or apolitical viewpoint. But many leftist writers view the drug culture with suspicion, as a diversion and an escape route from the revolutionary struggle and some of the black power groups have waged war on the drug as another facet of white enslavement of the black population. To see cannabis as allied to the new left is therefore inaccurate. Cannabis users have nothing in common except their use of cannabis, for within their number is a very wide range of social and political viewpoints. Again, not all the Underground groups are entirely favourable to the drug. A Digger magazine in 1968 complained that 'its narcotic effects tend to be cumulative' and that chronic users show 'a lack of interest in communicating about anything except the drug'.[32] One should not make too grandiose claims for cannabis, either on the negative or positive front. As Richard Neville wrote, 'the contribution of marijuana to the evolvement of the New Man is marginal'.[33]

What is cannabis? *Cannabis Sativa* is the name of the hemp plant which grows throughout the world. From the plant is derived not only hemp rope but also substances with drug effects, chiefly marijuana (the flowering leaves and tops) and hashish (the sticky resinous substance). In tropical climates the resin is plentiful, and it is resin which finds its way to Britain, while the American market consists largely of marijuana. Marijuana is commonly referred to as 'pot', hashish as 'hash', though 'pot' tends to be used as a general term. But it is the resin which contains most of the active principles and therefore is most potent. It has been estimated that marijuana as smoked in the United States is between one-fifth and one-eighth the strength of the hashish used in India.[34]

The use of cannabis can be traced back thousands of years in history. It is often claimed that the first reference to it occurs in the pharmacopoeia of the Chinese Emperor Shen Nung in 2737 B.C., although Shen Nung was a mythical figure and his pharmacopoeia cannot be traced beyond the ninth century. But there are Indian references from around 500 B.C. and English references in *Culpepper's Herbal* of 1652. Culpepper regarded it as 'so well-known to every good housewife in the country that I shall not need to write any description of it'. There is no evidence of *smoking* cannabis before the sixteenth century, that is, before the practice of smoking with its American origins came into contact with cannabis, an old-world drug. During the nineteenth century, cannabis was very widely used in Britain by physicians, one of the more prominent being Russell Reynolds, the physician in ordinary to Queen Victoria![35]

Today the use of cannabis is virtually obsolete medically although some would still claim that it is a valuable drug. The medical use of cannabis, usually in tincture of alcohol solution, occurred before the manufacture of the minor tranquillisers and newer hypo-sedative drugs, and before the discovery of the active chemical principles of the cannabis drugs themselves. It was in the years between 1930 and 1942 that three kinds of related compounds were identified in analysis of hashish: cannabidiol, cannabinol and tetrahydrocannabinol (THC). It is now believed that the main active component of cannabis is $\triangle^9$-tetrahydrocannabinol. In 1967 Isbell and his colleagues in the United States published 'the first demonstration of hashish-like activity of a tetrahydrocannabinol of known chemical structure in men'.[36] There is no doubt that THC is a powerful chemical, but its occurrence in individual samples of raw cannabis is variable. 'Samples of resin vary greatly in the amounts and proportions of these cannabinoids according to their country of origin, and as the sample ages, its THC content declines. As a result the THC content of samples can vary from almost zero to eight per cent.'[37] Unfortunately, for cultural, sociological and legal reasons we know more about the effects of THC on rats in laboratories than we do about those of smoked cannabis on non-psychotic humans in their environment.

However, there have been a number of important studies of the effects of cannabis in humans, the most famous of which is that by Zinberg and Weil.[38] This study concluded that in a neutral setting persons who were naive to marijuana did not have strong subjective experiences after smoking low or high doses of the drug, but did show impaired performance in simple tests. Regular users, on the other hand, did get high in a neutral setting but did not show the same degree of impairment of performance as did the naive subjects, and on occasions actually improved slightly in their performance.

No change in respiratory rate, pupil size or blood sugar levels were observed, but there was a moderate increase in heart rate. The authors described the drug when smoked as 'a relatively mild intoxicant'. Earlier studies had for the most part concluded that cannabis was a drug of intoxication whose moderate use did not lead to seriously harmful consequences, although reports from the Middle and Far East had suggested that very heavy consumption might lead to 'a syndrome of increasing mental and physical deterioration'.[39] The study of marijuana toxicity by Smith and his colleagues in San Francisco noted a tendency to over-emphasize the role of the drug, but accepted that cannabis 'can however, produce toxic reactions, both acute and chronic'.[40] Those who are critical of cannabis use tend to focus on two kinds of danger: that of psychosis, and that of progression to more dangerous substances.

Is there a 'cannabis psychosis'? Can the drug induce severe psychological breakdown? Many writers in the Near and Middle East have argued for such a syndrome, and it is described in various studies from Morocco, India and Nigeria.[41] Benabud speaks of 'mass addiction' and 'cannabis psychosis', and the Chopras of 'cannabis insanity'. In Britain, Dr Elizabeth Tylden has argued the case for a cannabis psychosis, and in 1967 she warned of 'the beginning of a crop of cannabis psychotics':[42] 'There are innumerable articles about the cannabis psychosis. Some of them are of considerable antiquity, but the state observed is clearly recognizable from them. In this century there are reliable accounts of cannabis psychosis from India, America, Brazil, Morocco, U.S.S.R. and more recently in the U.K.'[43] In the United States, Isbell's research with THC has led to the view that psychosis is directly related to dosage, and that the low incidence of psychotic relations in the United States 'may reflect nothing more than the low tetrahydrocannabinol content of most of the marihuana available in the United States'. Isbell points out:[44]

It has long been known that marihuana and hashish can cause psychotic reactions, but usually such reactions were ascribed to individual idiosyncrasies rather than being usual or common reactions to the drug. The data in these experiments, however, definitely indicate that the psychotomimetic effects of Δ^1-THC are dependent on dosage and that sufficiently high doses can cause psychotic reactions in almost any individual.

However, there is considerable doubt among researchers whether cannabis is the direct cause of a psychosis or merely triggers off the condition in certain predisposed individuals. Sir Aubrey Lewis in an extensive survey of the world literature observed that '"cannabis psychoses" have been frequently described and the accounts include practically every known variety of mental disorder'. He went on: 'The term "cannabis psychosis" begs the question of the existence of such a syndrome.'[45] The main conditions described as 'cannabis psychoses' in the literature have been schizophrenia, paranoid states, manic excitement, depression and anxiety, and dementia. The Indian Hemp Drugs Commission of 1894 expressed serious doubts about the diagnosis, concluding that 'the usual mode of differentiating between hemp drug insanity and ordinary mania was in the highest degree uncertain and therefore fallacious'.[46] Moreover, today the view that psychosis is a mental disorder with a single cause is no longer tenable. 'Psychosis' is not something which is *in* an individual, but a label which one individual pins on another. 'The *fact* is that the subjects experienced perceptual changes, it is not a fact but merely an *opinion* whether one wants to call these changes "consciousness expansion" and "transcendence of the ego" (with Timothy Leary) or "hallucinations" and "psychotic reactions" (with Dr Isbell).'[47] Nor is it certain that 'psychoses' resulting from drug use are not largely affected by social and cultural factors.

The view that psychosis is a function of the stage of development of drug-using cultures has been put by the American sociologist Howard Becker who points out that 'verified reports of drug-induced psychosis are scarcer than one might think',[48] and that in many cases the 'psychosis' is a panic reaction to the drug experience. He points out that psychotic episodes occur less frequently within a culture as the drug spreads and the range of possible effects becomes understood. The Interim Report of the Canadian Government's Commission of Inquiry, published in 1970, commented that 'earlier notions of a specific "cannabis psychosis" have generally been abandoned since there is little evidence of such a distinct psychiatric entity'.[49] Ungerleider's study in Los Angeles in 1968 reported 1,887 'adverse reactions' to cannabis, but no definition of 'adverse reaction' was given, and in any case the survey was restricted to the observations of psychiatrists and other professionals.[50] Unwin in Montreal, on the other hand, reported only three 'adverse reactions' to cannabis in two years, all involving large quantities of hashish and all in individuals with previous psychiatric histories.[51] Smith in San Francisco reported that he had never observed 'cannabis psychosis' in over thirty-five thousand marijuana users seen at the Haight-Ashbury Free Clinic.[52]

Another view, frequently expressed, is that use of cannabis leads to involvement with more dangerous drugs such as heroin. This is entirely mistaken and now is virtually discredited. It is partly based on the undoubted fact that most heroin users have at some point used cannabis; it would have been surprising if they had not, in view of their involvement in the drug culture where cannabis is the most popular drug. But the number of cannabis users who become heroin addicts is very small indeed, and it is doubtful if most cannabis users have ever encountered heroin addiction. Indeed, contrary to the popular 'escalation thesis', there has over the last few years been a 'de-escalation' process, for as cannabis use has spread geographically and socially, it has more and more become disconnected with the narcotic and amphetamine cycles. The sources and the clientele are quite different. If cannabis users progress to any other drug, it is more likely to be LSD, the progression from a mild to a potent psychedelic. Whether this progression occurs depends to some extent on the personality and motivation of the individual and to some extent on the local scene. Many cannabis users have not only failed to progress to other drugs, but have actually reduced their use of cannabis itself and in some cases ceased to use the drug. On the other hand, the American evidence shows that movement from cannabis to the opiates is swift in the inner-city ghettoes. Here the liberal cries for legalization have a hollow ring, and are revealed as middle-class demands made by those who will never suffer any adverse consequences. In the deprived areas, concern about cannabis can only deflect attention away from the crucial issues of class and poverty.

There is no doubt that the dangers of cannabis use have been grossly distorted and exaggerated not only by the popular press but also by many well-meaning professionals. Tragically, this ill-informed propaganda has often had the disastrous effect of discrediting all information about drug abuse which emanates from adult sources, and has sometimes led young people to more dangerous drugs under the belief that all adult warnings were incorrect. On the other hand, one should not be misled by the equally inaccurate view that cannabis is totally harmless, a concept rejected by all researchers including those who are most friendly to the drug. Smith has drawn attention to an 'amotivational syndrome' which may be developed by the chronic heavy user.

> He loses his desire to work, to compete, and to face any challenges. His interests and major concerns may centre around marijuana to the point that his drug use becomes compulsive. He may drop out of school or leave work, ignore personal hygiene, experience a loss of sex drive, and avoid most social interaction. The picture in terms of social consequences is then similar to that of a chronic alcoholic, but *without* the physical deterioration.[53]

There are a number of reports of personal deterioration, of psychological dependence, and of toxic effects such as 'accumulation in body fat, brain damage, interference with the repair processes of the body, teratogenicity, tachycardia, interference with certain liver enzymes'[54] and so on.

What is the significance of the spread of cannabis use for the growth in spirituality? First, cannabis is an Eastern drug, and its spread in Western Christian societies has naturally led to a revival of interest in Eastern culture and religions. In India cannabis has been used for centuries as an aid to concentration and prayer. 'The mere sight of bhang (an Indian name for cannabis) cleanses from us as much sin as a thousand horse sacrifices' according to a Bengali sect. Secondly, cannabis is a drug of relaxation, and tends to encourage a tranquil, reflective and dreamily meditative attitude. The revival of such a passive approach to religion has provoked hostile reactions in an alcohol-oriented activist 'Christian'(!) culture which is alien to the meditative spirit. Thirdly, the use of cannabis is identified with a questioning of, or rejection of, the values of 'straight' society with its conventional lip-service to Christianity. The break with that society inevitably involves a break with its Christian superstructure. The spread of cannabis use among young people must be seen as having profound effects on their spiritual orientation. Timothy Leary has written:[55] 'If it seems surprising to you that marijuana can be considered as a key to the spiritual experience, don't forget that there are 200 million people in the world today who use marijuana regularly in their spiritual life or in their pursuit of serenity.'

Today this pursuit has spread to the West.

3
The Psychedelic Experience and Beyond

WHAT IS LSD?

Lysergic acid diethylamide is a synthetic drug which was discovered in 1938 by the Swiss scientist Hofmann during the course of work on ergot derivatives. Hofmann had prepared lysergic acid diethyla- mide (LSD) and in 1943 accidentally ingested some of it. He described his experiences:[1]

> In the afternoon of 16th April 1943 when I was working on this problem, I was seized by a peculiar sensation of vertigo and rest- lessness. Objects, as well as the shape of my associates in the laboratory, appeared to undergo optical changes. I was unable to concentrate on my work. In a dream-like state I left for home, where an irresistible urge to lie down overcame me. I drew the curtains and immediately fell into a peculiar state similar to drunkenness, characterized by an exaggerated imagination. With my eyes closed, fantastic pictures of extraordinary plasticity and intensive colour seemed to surge towards me. After two hours this stage gradually wore off.

Subsequent experiments convinced Hofmann that LSD had pro- duced these effects which were not unlike those of mescaline, a drug which had been synthesized about 1918. The use of similar naturally occurring substances for hallucinogenic effects is, of course, very ancient and well documented.

LSD is derived from ergot, a substance produced by fermenting rye. Ergometrine maliate, which is used in obstetrics, is very similar in chemical structure to LSD, as is ergometrine tartrate, the standard cure for migraine. The therapeutic use of LSD was introduced to Britain at Powick Hospital in about 1954 by Dr R. A. Sandison, a

psychiatrist with a Jungian background. Sandison believed that
through LSD the patient could relive his experiences in the first
year of life. The drug produced 'a sort of detached ego' where the
conscious self was separated from the body and there was a symbolic
disintegration of the real world.[2] The drug, Sandison claimed,
'produces an upsurge of unconscious material into consciousness',
and 'repressed memories are relived with remarkable clarity—with
therapeutically beneficial consequences'.[3] After this early work, LSD
was used by a number of psychiatrists within the framework of
psychotherapy. The drug was administered in order to facilitate
abreaction and the reliving of experiences and associational, dream-
like material was produced which was utilized in subsequent
analysis. In 1957 Humphrey Osmond began to use a single high
dose of LSD in the treatment of alcoholism, and from this work
developed the concept of 'psychedelic therapy', a form of treatment
which was to produce a peak overwhelming experience. It was
Osmond who first used the word 'psychedelic' about the LSD
experience in 1957: 'A psychedelic compound is one like LSD or
mescaline which enriches the mind and enlarges the vision. It is this
kind of experience which provides the greatest possibility for
examining those areas most interesting to psychiatry, and which has
provided men down the ages with experiences they have considered
valuable above all others.'[4]

The earlier work with mescaline, however, had led to two lines of
study: first, that concerned with the enriching of consciousness,
which Aldous Huxley described as 'the chemical conditions of
transcendental experience'.[5] This 'artificial paradise' of mescaline
had been described as early as 1897 by Havelock Ellis from his
study of the naturally occurring substance.[6] But the second line of
study saw mescaline and related drugs as important aids to the
understanding of schizophrenia. A study in 1940 argued that mescaline brought about a psychosis, and suggested that non-organic
psychoses were in fact variants of the same disease and might well be
caused by an amine resembling mescaline.[7] If this were true, the
correct approach to psychotic illness might lie in the fields of bio-
chemistry and pharmacology.

The discovery of LSD led to further interest in a chemical
approach to psychosis.[8] The terms 'psychotomimetic' (psychosis-
mimicking) and 'psychotogenic' (psychosis-producing) were used
about LSD. The later discovery that the LSD experience is generally

different from the natural psychoses has lessened interest in this aspect.[9] However, during the 1950s there was a good deal of clinical work in the United States and some in Europe. Malleson[10] has shown that about eighty doctors in the United Kingdom had used the drug clinically or experimentally, but by the early 1960s its use had become more confined. 'It seemed increasingly unlikely that it had any effective place in the treatment of psychoses. In recent years its use has been largely confined to two groups of cases: chronic alcoholics and persons suffering from character disorders or psycho-sexual difficulties.'[11] A number of doctors believe that the drug has a real, if limited, therapeutic value, though its efficacy is not proved, and there are clearly a number of risks attending it. However, Malleson's study of all psychiatrists who had used the drug in Britain suggested that, out of five thousand cases (fifty thousand doses of LSD) there were three suicides, and thirty-seven acute psychotic reactions most of which cleared up quite quickly.

However, by the mid-1960s the widespread, illicit use of LSD raised more serious problems. Very small amounts of LSD can affect the mind profoundly. One millionth of a gram taken by mouth can have considerable effect and only about one per cent penetrates the brain. The effects of a single dose may start some 15–30 minutes after oral use of the drug, and will reach a peak between 2–6 hours later, and last for 12–24 hours or longer. There are three elements in the LSD experience. First, that of an intensifying of experience of light and colour and of all sensual experience. There are not necessarily hallucinations but rather perceptual changes, and perhaps 'synesthesia', the translation of one sense into another. Secondly, depersonalization or 'ego-loss'. It is this transcendence of the ego which is seen as the central characteristic of psychedelic experience. Thirdly, the illumination of reality and of the universe. There are two effects of the drug which are important here: the reduction in the critical faculties, and the change in method of processing in-coming data. Because of these changes, trivial experiences and phenomena may become tremendously important. The structure of reality will look very different. This experience of illumination of the universe is described by Pahnke and Richards as the 'psychedelic peak, transcendental or mystical' experience.[12] In this state the user feels a sense of unity, transcendence of space and time, positive moods of joy, peace and love, awe and reverence, philosophical insight, and ineffability.

Not all LSD experiences are of this type, and there are serious dangers. The most obvious danger is that of accident whilst under the influence of the drug. A person under LSD is intensely distracted and his judgement of reality seriously distorted. He may believe that he can fly out of a window, or walk on water, or that he is being threatened or prosecuted. There are, however, psychiatric dangers associated with the drug itself, the most common of which is the 'bad trip'. In fact, most 'bad trips' only involve a few hours of terror and alarm which can be extremely unpleasant but will wear off. The bad trip is actually an anxiety reaction to the drug effect, and is most likely to occur in a disturbing or threatening environment with inexperienced user or users with ambivalent attitudes to the drug. Therapy consists of reassurance, explanation and support. Medication may be necessary, but the administration of an antidote in a hospital setting may only lead to long periods of depression: bad trips often get worse when the parient is admitted to hospital, and the patient may find it harder to recover from the effects of the 'coming down' medication (usually chlorpromazine) than from the bad trip itself. The best treatment for bad trips is the 'talk down' approach in a calm, non-threatening atmosphere. However, a more serious form of bad trip occurs when a toxic psychosis is produced. A Canadian study of 225 adverse reactions to LSD prior to June 1967 showed that 142 were cases of prolonged psychotic conditions with paranoid delusions, schizophrenic-like hallucinations and overwhelming fear.[13]

LSD can be extremely dangerous and the literature, as well as personal experience, is full of cases of users whose trips have ended in disaster or permanent hospitalization. Yet young people continue to take the risks. For what an increasing number of them are seeking through psychedelic chemicals is an experience of transcendence. It is such experiences which to a large extent our society has lost, and this has resulted in the contemporary spiritual impoverishment. But if LSD is capable of inducing the vision of God, or even of helping people to reach it, then, many will argue, the dangers are beside the point. It is worth the risk. The view that chemicals can aid religious experience is an old one, and in the last century Benjamin Blood[14] made similar claims about nitrous oxide. In 1902 William James, pursuing Blood's work, devoted a good deal of space in *The Varieties of Religious Experience* to an examination of experiences under this drug by which 'the opposites of the world, whose contradictoriness and conflict make all our difficulties and troubles, were melted into unity'; ascribing 'some metaphysical significance' to these experiences.[15] It has been claimed that all the issues raised by psychedelic experience were covered by Blood and James.[16] But in this century it was Timothy Leary who picked up the results of the work with LSD and drew out the implications for spirituality. It is Leary who 'stands out as that of promoter, apologist and high priest of psychedelia'.[17]

LEARY—THE HIGH PRIEST OF PSYCHEDELIA

Leary's significance is that it is he 'who has managed to embed the younger generation's psychedelic fascination solidly in a religious context' and made 'turning on' into 'the sacred rite of a new age'.[18] Leary took a Ph.D. in clinical psychology at the University of California, Berkeley, in 1950 and worked in the field of psychological research until he joined the Centre for Research in Personality at Harvard. It was here that he became involved in experiments with the psilocybin mushroom, and in 1961 he began turning on the students. According to one of his graduate students, Allan Y. Cohen, it was in 1962 that Leary came to see the spiritual dimension of the drug experience.

> For me, watching him, it was in the summer '62 when we were in Mexico and it was one of those classic nights when everyone had turned on. We'd taken over a hotel completely . . . all heads . . . it must have been 2 o'clock in the morning and everyone was coming down. Leary walked upstairs on a cliff to the ocean, we were quietly discussing and hallucinating, he looked out with a kind of glazed look in his eyes and said, 'We're going to have to write a bible about this.'[19]

It is possible that this represented a turning-point. Certainly about this time both Leary and some of his students were strongly influenced by Eastern spiritual texts.

But Leary's religious interests began earlier than this. After his vacation in Mexico in the summer of 1960, when he obtained the fungi containing psilocybin, Leary had gone to Massachusetts where he encountered Aldous Huxley. Huxley had already published accounts of his experiences with mescaline and in an article in the *Saturday Evening Post* in 1958 he had claimed that drugs would 'make it possible for large numbers of men and women to achieve a

radical self-transcendence and a deeper understanding of the nature
of things. And this revival of religion will be at the same time a
revolution.'[20] Leary was clearly impressed by Huxley, and his
subsequent writing shows the strong influence of Huxley's ideas. In
1963 Leary was dismissed from Harvard, and in June of that year
The Psychedelic Review was inaugurated as a forum for the psychedelic movement. The following year *The Psychedelic Experience*, an
adaptation of the *Tibetan Book of the Dead*, was published, and soon
became the bible of the movement. It began:[21]

> A psychedelic experience is a journey to new realms of conscious-
> ness. The scope and content of the experience is limitless, but its
> characteristic features are the transcendence of verbal concepts,
> of space time dimensions, and of the ego or identity. Such experi-
> ences of enlarged consciousness can occur in a variety of ways:
> sensory deprivation, yoga exercises, disciplined meditation,
> religious or aesthetic ecstasies, or spontaneously. Most recently
> they have become available to anyone through the ingestion of
> psychedelic drugs such as LSD, psilocybin, mescaline, DMT, etc.

In 1966 Leary published his *Psychedelic Prayers after the Tao Te
Ching*, and that year the League for Spiritual Discovery was set up
as 'a non-profit religious association'.

Leary's writing continued to become more and more religious in
tone: in 1963 he told a meeting of Lutheran psychologists that he
had repeated his original psychedelic experiment some fifty times
and on each occasion had been 'awed by religious revelations as
shattering as the first experience'.[22] He added that at least 75 per cent
of his subjects also reported intense mystico-religious responses, and
over half claimed to have received the deepest spiritual experience of
their life. He prophesied that the day would come when 'sacramental
biochemicals like LSD will be as routinely and tamely used as organ
music and incense to assist in the attainment of religious experience',
and added, significantly, that then 'it may well be that the ego-
shattering effect of the drug will be diminished'.[23] How did Leary
understand religious experience? He defined it in this way in 1963:
'The religious experience is the ecstatic, incontrovertibly certain,
subjective discovery of answers to four basic spiritual questions', the
four questions being about the ultimate power which moves the
universe, the nature, origin and destiny of Man, and the nature of
the self.[24]

But Leary did not, and does not, believe that LSD is an automatic ticket to religious illumination. Professor Zaehner has written that 'Dr Leary and his friends claim that drugs can produce an authentic religious ecstasy by a short cut'.[25] This description is misleading for two reasons: first, what Leary suggests is that the drug does not actually produce the religious experience but opens the door and makes the experience possible. Secondly, Leary insists that the psychedelic path is not a short-cut but is hard and demanding. 'The psychedelic yoga is the toughest, most demanding yoga of all. . . . The discipline of LSD is without doubt the most complex and demanding task that man on this planet has yet confronted.'[26] He points out that LSD sessions 'puzzle, enrapture awe and confuse' but 'mainly they confuse'.[27] Because of this, there was a need of guides, maps, models. So Leary turned to the East for help. In his *Psychedelic Prayers* he provided hymns, poems or prayers which could be used at various stages of the experience: as preparation, or invoking energy flow, or cellular consciousness and sensory experiences, and as aiding re-entry. Leary defines prayer as 'ecstatic poetry' or 'psychedelic communication', which may be used of 'those transition moments of terror, of isolation, or reverence, of gratitude . . . when there comes that need to communicate'.[28]

The establishment of the League for Spiritual Discovery had three purposes: individual worship, communal worship and glorification and public illumination of the human race. Each member was to be encouraged to use the sacraments and so discover 'the divinity within' and to practise the motto 'Turn on, tune in, drop out'. Ashrams (monastic centres) were to be set up for renunciants (drop outs), and education towards illuminating and liberating humanity was to be carried on. 'The LSD is an orthodox, psychedelic religion. Like the founding group of every great world religion, the LSD aims to expand consciousness, to pursue internal union and revelation, and to express these revelations in actions of glorification.' The sacraments of the League were 'psychedelic chemicals which at every turning point in human history have been provided by God for man's illumination and liberation'. But Leary's scheme certainly was not solely concerned with ingesting chemicals. There was an emphasis too on meditation, solitude, silence, mantras, and the use of ascetic techniques.[29] Nevertheless, the drugs were central. 'We believe that dope is the hope of the human race, it is a way to make people free and happy. . . . Our lives have been saved from the plastic

nightmare because of dope.' So Leary quoted approvingly some
young dealers,[30] and he himself wrote:[31] 'There are three groups
who are bringing about the great evolution of the new age that we
are going through now. They are the *dope dealers*, the *rock musicians*
and the Underground *artists and writers*.'

Leary's most widely read book is *The Politics of Ecstasy*, much of
which consists of reprints from elsewhere. Here esoteric religious
language occurs on virtually every page. 'The instruments of syste-
matic religion are chemicals. Drugs. Dope. If you are serious about
your religion, if you really wish to commit yourself to the spiritual
quest, you must learn how to use psychochemicals. Drugs are the
religion of the twenty-first century.'[32] 'In the current hassle over
psychedelic plants and drugs, you are witnessing a good, old-
fashioned, traditional religious controversy.'[33] 'LSD turns you on to
God'.[34] 'I consider my work basically religious. . . . The aim of all
Eastern religions, like the aim of LSD, is basically to get high: that
is, to expand your consciousness and find ecstasy and revelation
within.'[35] 'To turn on you need a sacrament. . . . Today the sacrament is LSD.'[36] 'The panoramas and the levels that you get into with
LSD are exactly those areas which men have called the confrontation
of God. The LSD trip is the classic visionary-mystic voyage.'[37] 'The
real trip is the God trip. . . . I can teach you how to find God.'[38] 'The
sacramental process in our religion is the use of marijuana and LSD,
and nothing can substitute for that.'[39] There is much more to the
same effect, and it is perfectly clear that for Leary the use of LSD is
a religious activity.

The impact of Leary on the counter-culture has been a major one.
Throughout all his writing and speaking, he emphasized four major
points. First, our society fears and suspects ecstasy, and the experience of the transcendent. Secondly, psychedelic drugs are the most
efficient and speedy way of achieving the religious ecstasy which
men have sought for centuries by non-chemical as well as chemical
means. Thirdly, religious ecstasy is inseparable from sexual ecstasy,
and the search for fulfilment in sexual relations is a major element in
the LSD trip. Fourthly, the use of psychedelic drugs will bring
about a major change both in consciousness and in social and
political life in the West. For a while Leary's psychedelic cult had
only a restricted following, but in 1966 a series of events in the West
Coast brought about a crisis which brought LSD into the centre of
the youth culture.

HAIGHT–ASHBURY AND THE HIPPY CULTURE

The decay of the Haight-Ashbury district of San Francisco began over forty years ago, and was accelerated by overcrowding and by the division of large houses into small apartments during the Second World War. Soon after the war adjacent areas of the City began to be redeveloped. The Haight-Ashbury district remained a middle-class area, and the neighbourhood was relatively prosperous, but a population of transients began to develop soon after the war. At the same time the commercial complex of Haight Street was declining, and the growth of huge supermarkets elsewhere helped to kill the small shopping area. In 1965 Haight-Ashbury appeared to be on the brink of a new phase with the development of fine art studios and boutiques. Soon all the vacant stores were occupied in Haight Street, and there was a movement from North Beach, the old beatnik area—now heavily commercialized—of poets, writers and artists into Haight-Ashbury. Some had moved there earlier, and there was a significant, but unpublicized, bohemian colony in Haight-Ashbury by 1962. The colony managed to remain unnoticed for several years, but in 1964 the spread of Timothy Leary's psychedelic cult, and the popularizing of an LSD-based life-style brought Haight-Ashbury towards the limelight. The beats were very vulnerable to psychedelic drugs which might aid their aesthetic powers. It was the coming of Ken Kesey which initiated the hippy explosion that was to make LSD known throughout the world.

Kesey and his group the Merry Pranksters probably first took LSD in August 1965. From then they moved around the cities of the West Coast introducing people to 'the Acid Test', and out of the combination of LSD and electronic equipment came the San Francisco sound which was to shake and transform American pop music. Kesey's contribution to the acid scene was to make it a spectacular, wild, playful happening in contrast to the 'high church' intensity of Leary. In the evolving San Francisco drug culture, experiments with LSD, light-shows and new sounds and rhythms were all part of one great event. Among the earliest converts to LSD were the Thelin brothers who opened the world's first Psychedelic Shop in Haight Street on 1 January 1966, at a time when 'you might see maybe fifteen people with long hair and strange dress walking down the street on a good day'.[40] Two weeks later Ken Kesey was the host to a Trips Festival at Longshoreman's Hall. Fifteen thousand

c

people attended, and it was out of this period that the word 'hippie'[41] was born. A year later, at the beginning of 1967 came the world's First Human Be-In. Haight-Ashbury became the centre of the new phenomenon. *Newsweek* predicted that around one hundred thousand would move into the district for the summer of 1967. 'Haight is Love' and similar slogans ushered in the 'Summer of Love'.

In Britain too in the summer of 1967 Scott McKenzie's record 'San Francisco' topped the charts. 'If you go to San Francisco', it said, 'be sure to wear some flowers in your hair'. These were the 'gentle people' representing 'a new generation with a new explanation'. San Francisco was portrayed as a paradisal state of flower children, LSD and universal love. In the formative period of the movement, drugs, rock music and mystical groups were all present. The Hare Krishna chanters were in at the beginning. Groups like the Grateful Dead and Jefferson Airplane were there. LSD was a powerful binding force for the new culture. An observer of the scene in San Francisco in 1967 has suggested that the civil rights movement's idea of building 'parallel structures' and a loving community —as developed by the Student Non-Violent Co-ordinating Committee (SNICK) in 1963–4—became the foundation rhetoric for the hippy culture. People like Rock Scully, one of the managers of the Grateful Dead, had worked with SNICK and was involved in the early days of Haight-Ashbury. Other musicians, painters, writers and actors were deeply imbued with the sense of creating social alternatives, 'Dope was associated with ideas which have no necessary connection with the dope business: the sharing, the search for community, the looking for an alternative way of life, the love and flower-power themes. . . . Love and acid fused in muzzy associations through these non-political youngsters.'[42] As the community of youngsters in Haight-Ashbury grew, much of the original vision became obscured. The hippy scene became commercialized.

Father Leon Harris, the elderly parish priest of All Saints in Waller Street, described the events of 1967–8 in a parish newsletter.[43]

The news of interesting developments in the Haight-Ashbury was heard by hordes of unhappy, alienated, confused and rebellious young people who lived all over the nation and beyond, in numbers without precedent in the world's history. These, believing that developments in 'the Hashbury' had provided a locus for founding of a new society, based on peace and love and rejecting materialism, immigrated to the Haight-Ashbury in a great mass movement, thousands and thousands strong. Soon our streets were impassable, a solid mass of young humanity jammed the thoroughfares, housing and sanitation problems became acute, and all difficulties were compound by the hordes of tourists and bemused San Franciscans who came from other neighbourhoods to view this strange phenomenon.

After this came a third phase: a massive influx of delinquents and chronic drug users, and the final death of the original hippy community. Today nothing is left of the old Haight-Ashbury. 'We're all frightened,' one 60-year-old resident commented, 'the Haight has become a drug ghetto, a teenage slum. The streets aren't safe, rats romp in the Panhandle; the neighbourhood gets more rundown every day. The only thing that'll save this place now is a massive dose of federal aid.'[44]

The transformation of the Haight-Ashbury district from a colony of peaceful hippies, Diggers and flower children into a district of crime and violence was paralleled by a change from LSD and marijuana to amphetamine and heroin.

The Haight-Ashbury in early 1967 was an area composed primarily of persons using marijuana and LSD. Prior to the summer of 1967 intravenous amphetamine misuse was practically unknown in the Haight. During the summer and fall of 1967 we began to see an increasing number of adverse reactions to intravenous amphetamine at the Haight-Ashbury Clinic which heralded the beginning of a new pattern of drug abuse in this area. . . . As the community of 'speed-freaks' emerged, the persons who were the 'acid heads', that is the more moderate users of marijuana and LSD, began to dwindle in number as they left the Haight when the two diverse groups began to conflict. Although the shift from the periodic and repeated use of LSD to the compulsive use of intravenous amphetamine appeared on the surface to involve merely a change of intoxicating agent, in retrospect it represented a dramatic transformation of the community and was to have far-reaching consequences for drug using subcultures all over the nation.[45]

So between 1967 and 1969 the high-dose 'speed scene' dominated the district.

By 1970 the storefronts on Haight Street were covered with steel gates and sheets of plywood, and the sidewalks littered with rubbish and broken glass. It was claimed in that year that over fifty grocers, florists, druggists, haberdashers and other merchants had moved off the street since the summer of love three years earlier. Today there are few 'flower children' in the district, and the Psychedelic Shop is empty. Leary, Ginsberg and Kesey no longer visit the district, and all that seems to be left of the old community is a group of Diggers who still operate a free bakery and housing office based on All Saints Church. Most of the long-haired radical youth whom the press describe as 'hippies' have moved back to North Beach, over the bay to Telegraph Avenue in Berkeley, or out to the communes.

> A new population has moved into the district and taken over Haight Street like an occupying army. Transient and diverse, its members now number several thousand persons. Included are a few tourists, weekend vistors and young runaways who still regard the Haight-Ashbury as a refuge for the alienated. There are also older white, Negro and Indian alcoholics from the city's Skid Row; black delinquents who live in the Flatlands or the Fillmore ghetto; Hell's Angels and other 'bikers' who roar through the area on their Harley Davidsons. Finally there are the overtly psychotic young people who abuse any and all kinds of drugs, and psychopathic white adolescents, with criminal records in San Francisco and other cities, who come from lower class homes or no homes at all.[46]

The new population is involved in no search for mystical illumination and is in no way comparable to the original hippies.

What was the early hippy community like? Its public symbol in the 'straight' press was a flower, and flowers did in fact accurately symbolize its concern for gentleness, non-violence and love of nature and the body. But, beyond the official image, one can identify a series of philosophical strands in the hippy culture. First, the rejection of anger, and the commitment to love and gentleness. Brickman has argued that, by the stress on the death and rebirth experiences of LSD, the hippy has accepted death, and so removed the necessity for the externalizing of destructiveness which Freud saw as the basis of aggression.[47] However, the subsequent history of the Underground has seen the abandonment of the early concern for gentleness. Secondly, there was an emphasis on 'doing your own thing', on the expression of individuality. Thirdly, intimacy—in personal and sexual relationships—was central, and involved a rejection of the sexual repressiveness and conventional mores of the larger society. Fourthly, there was a commitment to the group and its welfare, a concern for community, and finally, a rejection of the mainstream society, including its religious and eductional system. But unlike the political radicals, the hippy did not oppose 'the system' by a head-on conflict: he turned his back on it, rejecting its values totally. Because of this, the hippy culture was seen by Marcuse as providing a more threatening attack on the establishment because 'their opposition hits the system from without and is therefore not deflected by the system'.[48]

The use of LSD was central to the hippy culture of 1967, and the dependence on the drug was probably the major factor in the failure of the movement. For if the acid trip presented the experience of universal love and self-loss without the corresponding ability to practise love and to live in a self-transcending way, then the alternatives seemed to be permanent frustration or continual 'turning on'. Moreover, once one had accepted the chemical basis of the counter-culture, it seemed inconsistent to reject other more powerful drugs which might aid different aspects of life. The switch from LSD to methedrine and later to heroin was an inevitable consequence of the commitment to chemicals as the foundation elements of a social movement. Of course, for many, this was not so. LSD was used within the framework of a social philosophy, and its benefits or hazards evaluated in relation to that philosophy. Those whose lifestyle was not chemically-centred often survived best in the psychedelic culture. But for large numbers, the 'universal love' inspired by LSD could not be translated into actual love of one other person.

The pop music which came out of the post-1967 period was heavily influenced by the drug culture. Songs by The Beatles ('Lucy in the Sky with Diamonds', 'Tomorrow Never Comes'), and the Rolling Stones ('Connection', 'Need Somebody to Love') as well as American groups such as the Fugs ('I couldn't Get High'), the Doors ('Crystal Ship'), The Mothers of Invention ('Hungry Freaks', 'Help I'm a Rock'), Jefferson Airplane ('White Rabbit'), Procul Harum ('Whiter Shade of Pale') and the Byrds ('Eight Miles High', 'Mind Gardens'), were among many which reflected or propagated the drug experience. All this cultural ferment came out of the Haight-Ashbury experiment of 1966–7.

DISILLUSIONMENT SETS IN

By the end of 1967 the Haight-Ashbury experiment seemed to have gone sour. The incidence of physical and psychological disease was high. Measles, influenza, hepatitis, urinary and genital tract infections, venereal diseases were prevalent. Uncontrolled drug use was at epidemic level and there was a very high number of 'bad trips' in 1967. By 1968, however, it was amphetamine psychosis and overdose which were more common, and in 1969 heroin addiction increased ten-fold. The Haight had been transformed from a paradise to a jungle. Not surprisingly, disillusionment with the psychedelic gurus was increasing, though some of their early disciples had questioned the validity of the chemical approach to consciousness before the hippy scene had run its course. One, Allan Y. Cohen, a former graduate student of Leary at Harvard, disputed the claims of LSD to bring about ego-loss, religious experience and changed lives, rejecting the first and third claims, but accepting the second with some reservations.

First, is the LSD experience an authentic meta-ego experience? Cohen did not accept that it was:

> The main point is that psychedelic chemicals stimulate one's imagination. But the point that the mystics have made is that it is an illusory experience. Clearly it is a *real* experience, because everybody can remember it, but is it an experience of *reality*? The problem is *not* to intensify your experience of duality, separatedness and limitation, but to get rid of it. If there is a sense of knowing God, it is a sense of getting rid of the ego. In the old days we were certain that you would have an ego-dissolution experience, a disintegration of the ego, under LSD. But who remembered the ego-loss experience? It was the ego, still there. I may have floated out of my body, but I was still there. God was not there completely, because there was still duality. The emphasis in mystical aspects of spirituality, however, is on the oneness and infinite love, God everywhere and in everything, and this can be experienced.[49]

According to this view, drug-induced experience of ego-loss is an illusion, a dream within a dream.

Secondly, Cohen accepted that 'religious experiences' could be the result of psychedelic drug use.

It was very clear that the psychedelic movement was taking a spiritual direction by 1963. It was inevitable, because people were encountering levels and alterations of consciousness which they couldn't explain by any psychological conception. The word 'consciousness' was suddenly discovered and was responsible for the link between chemical experience and religious experience. People discovered that spiritual figures, particularly in the east, talked about consciousness in the same was as western men talked about the search for God. The experience under these materials was sufficiently dramatic that, with the proper set and setting you could be 100 per cent sure that you had experienced God. But the question which had to be faced was: *did* you experience God? There is no question that chemicals, and other forms of external manipulation (for example, fasting, flagellation) can produce alterations of consciousness and religious experiences. If I stick you in a church and give you 500 microgrammes of LSD I will guarantee you a religious experience. (It might be of hell—but that's religious!)[50]

Thirdly, Cohen rejected the authenticity of the chemical approach, primarily because it does not show positive fruits in terms of spiritual change.

> . . . one of the phantasies we used to have is now demonstrably false. This is the belief that if you take enough psychedelic drugs, you will become holy, spiritually sophisticated, wise, expanded consciousness, love will flow from you. It doesn't happen to work. Haight-Ashbury in San Francisco in the last six years has turned from a reserve of flower children to a jungle where even the police aren't safe. The use of psychedelic chemicals in that culture did not lead to a social utopia. Our attempts too failed not because of the quality of the people but because these results do not accrue from chemical-induced experiences. You can't carry over even the profound experiences you have. You can feel very loving under LSD but can you exert that love to someone whom previously you didn't like? The long-range answer is No. It is almost beyond controversy. The controversy has now shifted into: Maybe it can get you started, but something else has to end it—one's own effort. But when you see the psychedelic leaders of the world, after a gorgeously mystical brotherhood love session, as they are coming down, having a bitter argument about who should wash

the dishes, a sense passes through one that somehow sainthood has been missed![51]

Cohen's loss of faith in LSD was similar to that of many others. Not many people today would deny the ability of drugs to induce 'religious experiences'. It is not necessary to claim, as a leader in *The Times* did in 1967, that drug-induced mysticism is only to be compared with the mysticism of the psychotic.[52] Some writers would see LSD as a desperate remedy which one should be neither too proud to accept, nor too eager to try if one can manage without.[53] The studies by Pahnke[54] and by Masters and Houston[55] have suggested that virtually all the known kinds of mystical experience have been reported on LSD. Pahnke in particular has listed nine characteristics of spontaneous mystical experiences which are also reported in the drug-induced states: unity, transcendence of time and space; a deeply felt positive mood; a sense of sacredness; a feeling of insight on an intuitive level; paradoxicality; alleged ineffability; transiency; and persisting positive changes in attitudes and behaviour.[56]

However, the ability to achieve such experiences through drugs was known to William James in 1902. On his experiences with nitrous oxide James wrote:[57] 'Looking back on my own experiences they all converge towards a kind of insight to which I cannot help ascribing some metaphysical significance. The keynote of it is invariably a reconciliation. It is as if the opposites of the world, whose contradictoriness and conflict make all our difficulties and troubles, were melted into unity.' One could indeed go many centuries beyond James to consider the role played by drugs in aiding religious reflection and meditation. But the mere multiplication of examples of reported mystical states does not help to solve the problem: are the mystical experience and the drug experience comparable? Certainly there are close similarities, but it has been suggested that these are superficial, and that closer examination shows that the two kinds of experience differ fundamentally.[58] The states reported under psychedelic drugs are due, it has been argued, to perceptual changes brought about by the action of the drug on the mind. LSD 'seems to trigger a depth charge into the unconscious process. The direction that the explosion will take is the result of factors other than the drug.'[59] Within the context of a developing religious life, then, it is possible that LSD could aid the life of prayer, and equally possible that it could provide a glimpse of another dimension to experience which might lead some towards religious life.

However, it was only the *context* of mystical experiences which, for the Christian mystics, made them meaningful. Only against the background of a continuing life of prayer and sacrament could the believer make sense of his experiences, and only this background helped him to integrate them into conscious working life. But for the psychedelic disciple, as Leary saw only too plainly, there was little guidance, and the experience brought confusion more often than peace. In addition, the problem of how to integrate the unconscious material which had been revealed by LSD became a very difficult one for the immature and the undisciplined. Many found the transition phase impossible. Yet for the traditional mystics, it was the ability to produce fruits in daily life which was the test of true experience of the Divine. The disintegration of Haight-Ashbury and the failure of the psychedelic gurus to provide 'spiritual direction'[60] —Alan Watts had suggested retreat houses for the LSD trip—led to a growing doubt about the possibilities of the drug route to consciousness expansion. It was at this point that Eastern teachers began to hit the drug scene, and initiated a new phase of the movement.

4

Stars in the East

DRUGS AND EASTERN RELIGIONS

There had been a revival of Eastern spiritual methods in the early years of the century when such movements as Vedanta (supported by Aldous Huxley, Gerald Heard and Christopher Isherwood), theosophy, anthroposophy and the systems of Gurdjieff and Ouspensky became popular. Rudolf Steiner was writing about the mystical quest for self-transcendence.[1] The Theosophical Society had been set up in 1875, and H. P. Blavatsky's *The Secret Doctrine* published in 1888. In 1924 the Buddhist Lodge of London had been established, and there was a good deal of interest in Eastern teachers such as Krishnamurti. The quest for Eastern spirituality is not, therefore, merely a by-product of the drug scene. Nor is it correct to see the recent revival of interest as evidence solely of disillusionment with psychedelic drugs. Indeed, as we have seen, the initial revival of interest in Eastern religious disciplines grew out of the early psychedelic drug culture and its need to find guidebooks, maps of the spiritual journey. It was thought that drugs and the spiritual path could go well together, and Eastern religious traditions had more to offer, it seemed, than did Christianity.

Apart from Leary, probably the major intellectual influence which helped to direct the psychedelic religious search towards the East was that of Alan Watts. Watts was a former Anglican priest who had resigned his orders, became America's leading exponent of Zen, and in recent years a popular writer on psychedelics. Watts saw psychedelic drugs as a Western means of helping the human organism to attain the sensation of being integrated, but he believed that this experience needed support by other procedures such as psychotherapy, spiritual disciplines and basic changes in one's pattern of life. The crucial task was the attainment of the unity of man, the

body-mind

elimination of the mind-body separation. Taoism and Zen Buddhism
did not presuppose the division between mind and body, spirit and
matter, which had become so basic an element in Western thought,
and, with the help of LSD and proper direction, the Westerner
could help to escape from this false position. Christianity, on the
other hand, treats God as a monarch, the 'high and mighty, King of
Kings, Lord of Lords, the only Ruler of princes'. The Westerner
who claims consciousness of union with God clashes with conventional notions of religion, whereas in most Eastern cultures he will
be congratulated for penetrating the true secret of life. Watts sees
mystical experience as a threat to Christianity, and points out that
attempts to describe the drug experience in religious terms have to
borrow vocabulary from the East—*Samadhi* or *Moksha* from the
Hindu tradition, or *Satori* or *Kensho* from the Japanese.[2] Watts was
not the first person to make this kind of claim: Gerald Heard had
argued that the concepts which gave to Western religion itself its
deepest insights were imported from India, and he suggested that
Eastern influence was necessary today in providing a frame of
reference for contemporary Christians.[3]

Ironically, the very Eastern teachers to whom the acid-religionists
turned for guidance were most critical of the psychedelic claims. In
addition, the study of Eastern religions which was inspired by the
drug experience, became for many people a confirmation of the fact
that the two experiences had as many differences as similarities. It
was found, for example, that even the alteration of body chemistry
by means other than drugs—fasting and meditation—was looked
upon with suspicion by spiritual masters. The Buddha condemned
asceticism. The *Bhagavad-Gita* similarly warned against ascetical
excess.[4] 'Yoga is not for him who eats too much nor yet for him who
does not eat at all, nor him who is all too prone to sleep, nor yet for
him who always stays awake. Rather Yoga is for him who is moderate
in food and recreation, controlled in his deeds and gestures, moderate
in sleeping as in waking.'

Nor is mind-expansion viewed by Eastern spiritual teachers as a
necessary contribution to enlightenment. One Zen master observed:[5]
'An ancient Zen saying has it that to become attached to one's own
enlightenment is as much a sickness as to exhibit a maddeningly
active ego. Indeed, the profounder the enlightenment, the worse the
illness.' The Sufis too warn, 'Be chary of expansion and beware of
it.'[6] Also, as Zaehner has shown, the Buddhist notion of Nirvana is

the reverse of cosmic consciousness, and has nothing to do with sense perceptions.[7]

Again, there is a profound concern among the spiritual teachers of the East that enlightenment should not be confused with inflation of the ego. Leary's claim that 'the aim of all Eastern religion, like the aim of LSD, is basically to get high: that is, to expand your consciousness and find ecstasy and revelation within'[8] was seen to be false. For not only is there a wide diversity within Eastern religions, but also there are constant warnings against the search for ecstasy. Humility is valued more highly, and there is a stress throughout on darkness and silence which is in sharp contrast to the sensuality and egocentricity which often characterizes the drug experience. Rather does psychedelic mind expansion seem to resemble Jung's description of 'inflation' where 'the personality becomes so vastly enlarged that the normal ego-personality is almost extinguished. In other words, if the individual identifies himself with the contents awaiting integration, a positive or negative inflation results. Positive inflation comes very near to a more or less conscious megalomania; negative inflation is felt as an annihilation of the ego.'[9] This is so far from the mystical goals of East or West that it is not surprising that many moved away from drugs towards the Eastern paths themselves.

THE ZEN REVIVAL

The revival of interest in Zen among young people in the West goes back beyond the psychedelic drug culture to the beats of the 1950s. In his earliest poems, Allen Ginsberg was expressing the need for God: 'The cry is not for revolution, but for an apocalypse: a descent of divine fire'.[10] In 1956 Kerouac's *The Dharma Bums* contained assorted Zen slogans which he had picked up from the San Francisco poet Gary Snyder, who was responsible for introducing both Kerouac and Ginsberg to Zen in the early 1950s. Later he went to Japan to study Zen at a deeper level. But the major intellectual influence was Alan Watts, who had begun to teach in the School of Asian Studies in San Francisco. At the age of 19 Watts had been editor of *The Middle Way*, the English Buddhist journal, and more than Suzuki, he popularized Zen in the West. Watts has been unkindly called 'the Norman Vincent Peale of Zen', but he was by no means uncritical of the n 'beat Zen' as his essay 'Beat Zen, Square Zen, and Zen' of 1958 shows. Here he attacked 'beat Zen' as 'a pretext for license', and referred to 'the cool fake-intellectual hipster searching for kicks, name-dropping bits of Zen and jazz jargon'.[11]

Part of the attraction of Zen was the apparent absence of doctrine. Buddha himself saw his doctrine (dharma) as the way to enlightenment. Bodidharma brought Zen to China in the sixth century and by the time of Hui Neng, it had become a Chinese movement. After Hui Neng came the so-called Golden Age of Chinese culture and of Zen. The essence of Zen has been summed up as:

> A special transmission of Enlightenment outside the Scriptures;
> No dependence upon words and letters;
> Direct pointing to the soul man;
> Seeing into one's own nature.[12]

Two crucial ideas in Zen are *Satori*, a sudden realization of truth bringing a sense of release, and the *Koan*, a baffling problem which appears to be nonsensical but through which one achieves *Satori*.[13] In Zen communities the meditation hall is crucial, and there are regular interviews with a Master on the Koans. The consumption of tea is of major importance in the quest for contemplation. 'In the tea ceremony we find Zen in its most peaceful aspect.'[14] There is a stress throughout Zen on direct knowledge (Buddhi) and intuition; there is a need to turn inward, mistrusting the senses and the deceptions of the world, and seeking the impersonal, the Eternal Man. There is a rejection of metaphysics and intellectual speculation. 'Zen shuns abstractions, representations and figures of speech. No real value is attached to such words as God, Buddha, the soul, the infinite, the One and such like words.'[15] The fundamental idea is to pass beyond the world of opposites, of intellectual distinction, and attain a spiritual world of non-distinction.

The rejection of a 'system', and the absence of a view of God as 'out there', a supreme being, are among the main reasons why Zen has attracted so many young people. For Zen rejects even the authority of Buddhism, in so far as it represents a system of thought. 'To the extent that "Buddhism" limits Zen, Zen is not Buddhism.'[16] There is no view of any outside God. On the contrary, 'the Zen view, borrowed from Buddhist philosophy, is that behind or beyond the manifest is the absolute Void of Emptiness wherein no "thing" essentially exists'.[17] It would be wrong to describe Buddhism as atheistic; it simply rejects the point of view where such terms as theist, pantheist or atheist are meaningful. 'The Zen insight cannot be communicated in any kind of doctrinal formula or even *in any precise phenomenological description*. This is probably what Suzuki means when he says it is "not mystical": that it does not present clear and definitely recognisable characteristics capable of being set down in words.'[18] Zen seeks to get beyond subject and object to pure being. The absence of thought is true freedom according to Suzuki: one achieves a level of seeing that is without subject or object and is 'pure seeing', when the mind has become empty and void. The void is not a mere negation, but a true emptiness and a true light. It was this light and darkness, this emptiness that was also the fulness of being which some felt they had glimpsed on drugs. Zen seemed to offer a way of making further progress.

Some critics look cynically at the popularity of Zen among the young. It is unusually vulnerable, claims Theodore Roszak,[19] to 'adolescentization'. Zen in a vulgarized form, he argues, dovetails with various adolescent traits: moody inarticulateness, intellectual confusion and immaturity, the search for freedom. But there is a more serious aspect of the quest. Through Zen the young seeker hopes to cut through the verbosity and the intellectual camouflage of Western society, to escape from its rationalized and restricted religious understanding. Ninian Smart has pointed out that the powerful impact of Zen in the West has been largely due to the fact that it 'accords with some intellectual and artistic tendencies in the modern West'.[20] Thus the anti-intellectualism of Zen appeals to those who have intellectual difficulties, for it seems to remove religion and enlightenment from the areas of intellectual thought. In addition, there is an aesthetic approach in Zen which draws many from the field of the creative arts. The spread of existentialist ethics too has merged easily with a Zen approach. So, at the very moment that Zen is rapidly declining in Japan, it is becoming more popular in the West. 'The Japanese . . . are more eager to master the scientific techniques of the West than they are to attain enlightenment. On the other hand, the West is showing some desire for the enlightenment of the East.'[21]

The vulgarized Zen which Watts described as 'beat Zen' was an easy development from the 'nature mysticism' side of Zen, 'a caricature to which Zen all too easily lends itself'.[22] Zaehner has compared it to the way in which the fourteenth-century Brethren of the Free Spirit vulgarized and distorted Eckhart's mystical theology: there is the same antinomianism and amoralism. Freedom from

Karma is freedom from both actions and the responsibility for them. In Hui Neng's words, 'So long as there is . . . neither right nor wrong . . . and so long as you are quiet and tranquil, that is the Great Way.'[23] The true Zen enlightenment requires arduous discipline and guidance. Enlightenment needs to ripen, and during those years there will be the experience of false enlightenment and self-deception. But Zen is a proven method of attaining enlightenment, and in this method there are bodily exercises and physical postures as well as meditations. Indeed, it is because they are offered a *method*, a way towards enlightenment, that many of the serious disciples have taken the road of Buddhist meditation.

YOGA

It is the same need for method and for detailed guidance which has led others to follow the path of Yoga. In fact, both Jainism and Buddhism probably derive from an ancient tradition of Yoga, a form of contemplation of the eternal within, in order to escape the cycle of death and rebirth. Although Yoga is often thought of as a form of physical culture, it is in fact also a philosophy and way of life closely allied to another classic system of Indian thought, Samkhya. But Yoga developed a belief in a supreme Self, or God, an object of contemplation, though it did not seek 'union' with him so much as isolation—from God as from all matter. Through the practice of Yoga, the adept attains a state of perfect peace, and description of its techniques occurs in the Yoga-Sutras of Patanjali, 196 statements written about the time of Aristotle (400 B.C.).[24] The disciplines of Yoga have been popularized in the West in a wide variety of books, though the underlying philosophy has not been conveyed. Recently, however, it is the philosophy too which has been sought.

The increased popularity of Yoga is closely allied to the rediscovery of the body. By concentrating on purely physical positions, a new type of consciousness is achieved. No longer is the mind identified with the self, no longer does the person live entirely at the 'head level'. Now the lungs and the heart become the centre of one's being, and there is a real sense of escape from the tyranny of mind and brain. In the new Yoga scene in London, a variety of approaches are evident. In most centres, there are classes in *Hatha Yoga* involving physical postures, chanting and meditation. One of the most popular groups is the Kundalini Yoga Centre and this has apparently drawn many students from the drug culture.[25] *Kundalini Yoga* is believed to be more rapid in results, and there is an emphasis on dynamic exercises and breath control, the aim being to raise the Kundalini or serpent (sexual) power from the lowest to the highest chakras. While some centres may only be concerned with physical health, there is usually a stress on *Bhakti Yoga* (devotion to God) and on *Raja Yoga* (God-realization through meditation). Yoga practices may also be found in combination with Christian contemplation and with various occult teachings.

THE MAHARISHI AND 'TRANSCENDENTAL MEDITATION'

Others pursued the path of meditation in the hope of attaining pure awareness, and of aiming at the source of all thought. The Maharishi Mahesh Yogi hit the youth spiritual scene at exactly the right time, soon after the Beatles had used LSD. Their temporary involvement with Maharishi made his name and smiling features well known throughout the country. Since then there has been a tremendous upsurge of interest in Transcendental Meditation (TM) throughout the West. Maharishi International University has been set up in Switzerland and organizes regular symposia on Creative Intelligence. In 1971 there were over four hundred student groups in the United States involved with TM, and the first university course in the Science of Creative Intelligence opened at Stanford in the winter of 1969, and drew over 350 students.

TM is defined as 'a natural technique which allows the conscious mind to experience systematically finer states of thought until it arrives at the finest state of thought and transcends it, arriving at the source of thought, the state of pure awareness, the field of pure intelligence'. The science of Creative Intelligence 'derives from the teachings of Maharishi Mahesh Yogi in the Western world during the last decade', and is 'the knowledge of the nature, origin, range, growth and application of creative intelligence'.[26]

It is claimed that Transcendental Meditation as a mental technique arose out of the ancient Vedic tradition of India and is a spontaneous natural process. Followers of Maharishi practice TM twice a day for 15 to 20 minutes. There is no personal counselling. A good deal of stress is laid on the relationship between TM and the incidence of drug abuse. Out of 1,862 subjects aged from 14 to 78 (half of them, in fact, aged 19 to 23), a large number reported decrease in drug use as a result of TM. Before the practice of meditation began, 80 per cent used cannabis of whom 28 per cent were heavy users. After six months' practice of TM, only 37 per cent did so and only 6·5 per cent were heavy users. After 21 months, only 12 per cent used cannabis, the majority of them only lightly. Again, before beginning TM, 48 per cent of the subjects used LSD, of whom 14 per cent were heavy users, but after three months only 11 per cent took the drug, and after 21 months only 3 per cent did so. So a teacher of TM told an International Conference of Narcotic Enforcement Officers that TM offered 'an effective non-chemical alternative to drug abuse for many people', and the State of Michigan Governor's Office of Drug Abuse claimed that the examination of TM was 'a necessary ingredient to every drug abuse education effort'.[27] However, critics have argued that claims of reduced drug abuse must be treated 'with utmost scepticism', because adepts must abstain for 15 days from all drugs before beginning TM, and therefore it is unlikely that there would be many chronic users.[28]

There are now a considerable number of studies of Trancendental Meditation and Creative Intelligence. Research units at the Universities of Cincinatti and Texas (Austin), at Stanford Research Institute at Palo Alto, California, at Harvard and at Centre College, Kentucky, have been examining EEG data and the effect of meditation on heart rate, oxygen consumption and skin electrical resistance. The most detailed research is that by Dr R. Keith Wallace at the University of California at Los Angeles. Wallace worked with 27 students who had been meditating from between six months and three years. Each one would sit in a chair with eyes open 5–15 minutes, then with the eyes closed 10–20 minutes, then meditate 20–40 minutes, and finally sit with eyes closed 10 minutes and open 5–10 minutes. From his observation, Wallace claimed that the brain wave patterns during meditation showed these subjects to be awake and restfully alert, but their metabolic rate had slowed down to a level below that of the deepest sleep. For instance, oxygen consumption showed a mean decrease of 20 per cent, cardiac output decreased on average by 25 per cent—compared with 20 per cent during sleep. It seemed clear that the practice of meditation released the muscles and blood vessels and brought about very important changes in body chemistry.[29]

So, argues Wallace, Transcendental Meditation should be considered as a fourth level of consciousness through which an individual may be led to his true and best self. The basic principle is turning attention inwards to the subtler levels of thought, and ultimately to the source of all thought. This, of course, is also the aim of Yoga and of Zen, but the method is different. Dr Demetri Kanellakos of the Stanford Research Institute contrasts TM with other popular methods.[30]

> Most techniques of self-realisation, including such Western techniques as psychocybernetics, self-hypnosis, psychoanalysis and biofeedback require some form of concentration, contemplation, suggestion, control, belief, intellectual understanding, or at least faith in the efficiency of the system—in short, some effort. Such practices tend to keep us in the wakeful state. TM, on the other hand, requires no effort or strain of any kind, and no special belief.

The psychological changes which occur are unlike those which are present in the states of wakefulness, sleep and dreaming, and Wallace and his colleagues tabulate the character of the four states of consciousness in this way.

		THOUGHT AND EXPERIENCES	
		yes	no
SELF-AWARENESS	yes	wakefulness	transcendental
	no	dreaming	deep sleep

Thus activities are performed in the waking state. In the state of sleep, there is the work of restoring and rejuvenating. In dreaming, the mind is kept in function, and psychosis may occur if dreaming does not. But in the transcendental state, there is self-awareness, as in waking, but an absence of thought and experiences, as in deep sleep. All four states are necessary, it is argued, for healthy human life. Through TM, more of the sensitive nervous system is available for conscious use. Thus it may increase the understanding of literature, or may improve the vision. There is a release of strain as the physiology settles down and stress is released painlessly.

The spread of TM has been most marked, like most similar movements, in the United States. 1967 was the year when Maharishi's name became widely known, largely through the devotion of the Beatles, and later they were followed by Shirley Maclaine and Mia Farrow. The Beatles later explained that they had 'made a mistake' in their adoption of Maharishi,[31] but large numbers of young people have continued to express interest. Maharishi himself was born in 1911 and took a degree in physics at Allahabad University. After spending a number of years in retreat in the Himalayas, he began to teach his own method of meditation at Madras, and made his first visit to the West in 1959. By 1972 TM was being taught in the United States Army Staff College and at three American Army bases. On 16 February 1972, Major-General Franklin Davis suggested that the Army might pay for soldiers to attend meditation courses.[32]

The explosion of interest in TM inevitably was greatest in the American universities. In 1972 at least ten offered degree courses in TM. In Germany too there were reported to be some thirty thousand meditators, and the German Government appealed for a TM tutor to join its staff of a hospital for drug users. In Sweden, an introductory booklet on meditation courses and centres is given to high school and technical school children. A 1972 estimate of meditators for the United States was around 250,000 including one per cent of the student population, and it was claimed in February 1972 that ten thousand more were learning the technique each month. In Britain there were at this time 135 teachers, at least twenty thousand meditators and three hundred new meditators each month. Ten centres are planned for London alone. While some would see TM simply as a technique to aid relaxation and psycho-physical health, Dr Evan Harris Walker, a theoretical physicist with the United States Army Research and Development Centre, Aberdeen, makes a more impressive claim: 'a scientific theory of consciousness as an independent real entity has been formulated. It now appears that research under way offers the possibility of establishing the existence of an agency having the properties and characteristics ascribed to the religious concept of God.'[33]

THE REDISCOVERY OF SUFISM

There are now a very large number of meditation schools and teachers. Some belong to the Hindu tradition while others are more Western and syncretistic. One guru with a large following among the young is Pir Vilayat Inayat Khan of the International School of Esoteric Studies, head of the Sufi Order. Pir Vilayat stresses the relationship between meditation and ordinary life: 'We are opening up our minds, and may I say also our souls, to cosmic dimensions.

We are trying to attain a state where we are able to maintain the same consciousness we can attain in the course of meditation whilst dealing with very material and practical problems.'[34] Through meditation we seek freedom from mind and body, and the attainment of the infinite spirit.

> We want to free ourselves from the limitations of our ordinary experience and become free and accomplished human beings . . . The first step is to free ourselves from the tyranny of all thoughts and impressions, so that we may be able to grasp the essence of our being which is impossible when our mind is cluttered with thoughts. . . . The first attitude is to imagine that your body belongs to the earth, has unfolded itself out of the earth, will return to the earth, and in this manner you can cease to identify yourself with the body. Think of it as the product of the impersonal forces of nature and part of the same elements that compose plants, animals, minerals and everything we know as physical. Contrast this evanescent part of yourself, that is permanent and not subject to change or decay—not individualized and therefore infinite. It is the totality of the Spirit, it is Purusha.[35]

Pir Vilayat lays great emphasis on joy and the sense of release which identification with the Spirit brings,

> The discovery which takes place by identifying oneself with Purusha instead of Prakriti is so overwhelming that it should bring about a sudden flash of intense illumination and joy. Joy that occurs as a consequence of being freed from the limiting powers of the body and the mind. Here we discover ourselves as eternal, unchangeable, supreme, detached, serene, independent —all is perfect peace—That am I. In the consciousness of this state there is a power that overcomes the restlessness of the mind, the agitation of the nerves, the doubts of the soul and the anguish of the heart.[36]

Through the use of symbols, beginners are guided in an easy meditation technique, but later there will be dancing and maybe art and sensitivity groups.

Sufism was in origin the mystical growth from Islam. The sufi was 'one who wears *suf*' (wool), a sign of his commitment to simplicity and austerity. But as the Sufi movement developed it tended to stress inner illumination more than asceticism. It was a tradition which was deeply rooted in Islam and sought its support in the Koran, though the development of Sufism was strongly influenced by non-Islamic traditions, including Hinduism, Christianity and Neo-Platonism. In the eleventh century, al-Ghazzali's writings helped to establish the Sufi mystical path as an integral element in Moslem theology; today, however, much Western Sufism has become detached from its religious and cultural beginnings.

Indeed, it is a central claim of many contemporary accounts of the Sufi path that 'though commonly mistaken for a Moslem sect, the Sufis are at home in all religions'.[37] Sufism is seen as the secret teaching within all religions. On the other hand, it has been pointed out that 'authentic presentations of Sufism in modern Western media are rare'.[38] There appear to be three types of writing on Sufism in the West. First, academic studies by orientalists, including translations of Sufi texts.[39] Secondly, highly esoteric material in which Sufi teachings are mixed with a variety of magical and occultist ideas. Thirdly, authentic accounts of Sufism such as those by Schuon,[40] and Burckhardt.[41] In Islamic thought, there is a kind of Sufism in every spiritual tradition, but it is impossible to follow a Sufi path in a religious vacuum, since it is necessary to have initiation by a spiritual master, the grace of the revelation itself, the discipline linking the soul with the tradition, and knowledge of doctrine. Sufi doctrine includes teaching about the nature and structure of the universe, about the human soul, and about the end of man. There is a stress on two fundamental doctrines, the Transcendent Unity of Being, and the Universal or Perfect Man. All things are seen as theophanies of the Divine Names, deriving their existence from the One Being. Man reflects the Divine Names consciously, and the attainment of holiness means the realization of the state of Universal Man. Sufism is therefore concerned with the integration of Man, with the realization of the One.

The more one examines Sufi doctrines, the clearer it becomes that to separate Sufism from Islam is an impossible task. One of the leading exponents of the Sufi path, Seyyed Hossein Nasr, has pointed to the present search for inner peace which has caused 'a whole army of pseudo-yogis and spiritual healers to establish themselves in the West'. He goes on:

Men now feel instinctively the importance of meditation and contemplation but alas only too few are willing to undergo the

discipline in the fold of an authentic tradition which can alone
guarantee them access to the joy made possible through the contemplation of the celestial realities. Thus they turn to drugs or
self-realization centres or the thousand and one 'pseudo-masters'
from the East—a veritable revenge upon the West for all that was
done to Oriental traditions during the colonial period.

Nasr is concerned about the harm done to the cause of Sufism in
Europe by certain pseudo-Sufis who 'detach Sufism from Islam
thereby turning it into an occultism devoid of any spiritual interest
and in most cases psychically dangerous'. On the contrary, he
insists that 'because Sufism is the esoteric and inner dimension of
Islam, it cannot be practised apart from Islam'.[42] Nevertheless, the
search goes on among the young for a Western Sufism, adaptable
to their syncretistic and occult interests.

'HARE KRISHNA'

In a lecture given in Oxford in 1926, Radhakrishman claimed that
'after a long winter of some centuries, we are today in one of the
creative periods of Hinduism . . . . Leaders of Hindu thought and
practice are convinced that the times require, not a surrender of
the basic principles of Hinduism, but a restatement of them with
special reference to the needs of a more complex and mobile social
order.'[43] Many Eastern writers have attempted to create expressions
of Hinduism which will be meaningful to the West, but the movement which has caught on most quickly among the young has been
the International Society for Krishna Consciousness set up by
Swami A. C. Bhaktivedanta. The Krishna Consciousness movement
hit American cities in 1966, and its founder's translation of the
Bhagavad-Gita contained appreciations by Allen Ginsberg, Denise
Leverton and Thomas Merton. The journal of Krishna Consciousness, *Back to Godhead*, is sold in the streets of many Western cities
and is described as 'the only magazine in the Western world to
present the authorized, transcendental science of God realization
known only to the saints of India's unbroken disciplic succession'.
Readers are urged to explore the great science of Krishna Consciousness and to voyage 'back to our original existence of pure bliss', that
is, back to Godhead. But the movement is best known for its chanting
of the Hare Krishna Mantra, for Swami A. C. Bhaktivedanta had
said: 'The recommended process for God realization in this age is

chanting of the Hare Krishna Mantra: Hare Krishna, Hare Krishna, Krishna, Krishna, Hare Hare/Hare Rama, Hare Rama, Rama Rama, Hare Hare.' In obedience, the disciples leave their temples daily and chant the Mantra through the streets. In London's Oxford Street, they are now well-known figures.

Krishna Consciousness is seen as 'a process of self purification' which is undertaken under the guidance of a spiritual master and in obedience to the scriptures. The devotional life involves chanting, attending talks about the Pastimes of Krishna, and taking foodstuffs which are prepared for and offered to Krishna, the supreme Personality of Godhead. The state of Krishna Consciousness itself is described as a 'normal ecstatic state' and it is claimed that 'by chanting and by engagement in the service of Krishna, anyone who takes part will experience the state of "Samadhi", ecstatic absorption in God-consciousness, 24 hours a day'.[44] The actual process of chanting is fundamental. 'Chant these words', say the disciples, 'and your life will become sublime.' The Hare Krishna Mantra is seen as 'the Great Mantra' which awakes God-consciousness in those who use it. It is also known as the 'Mantra of the sixteen names' and is found in the Kalisantara Upanishad. The Krishna Consciousness devotees claim that 'this combination of sixteen syllables is scientifically formulated to bring about a state of spiritual joy. The Mantra is a purifying process which cleanses the mind and senses. Repetition of any other combination of syllables will not produce the same effect.'[45] So the work of propagating the Great Mantra is central to the followers of Krishna Consciousness. 'The movement's work is done by preaching and bringing the ecstatic sound vibration to our brethren in the streets of all the major cities of the world. . . . The Krishna Consciousness is a movement that will bring universal peace and divine love to every being on this planet.'

The life-style of the Radha Krishna Temple in London has been described as 'spiritual communism'. Money for food comes from the wages of those married devotees who are allowed to live outside the temple and who have full-time jobs, from contributions given during the street chantings, from sales of incense and Krishna lights, and so on. In the temple itself the day is governed by traditions based on the Vedas and the Gita. The cult activity begins soon after 4 a.m. with ritual offerings to the images of Krishna: incense, fire, water, a handkerchief and a flower are offered, and the image is fanned. Domestic duties follow, and then before the breakfast of fruit and cereals, there are prayers and readings. Lunch is preceded by a lunch offering to Krishna. The afternoon is taken up with chanting in public, and there are further ritual offerings. The life in the temple is one of rigid spiritual disciplines, or *bhakti yoga*, total devotion, and beyond this is the hope of perfect spiritual health for ever.

The beliefs of the International Society for Krishna Consciousness have been summarized as follows:[46]

1. The Absolute truth is contained in all the great scriptures of the world, the Bible, Koran, Torah, etc. However, the oldest known Revealed Scriptures in existence are the Vedic Literatures, most notably the *Bhagavad-Gita* which is the literal record of God's actual Words.

2. God, or Krishna, is eternal, all-knowing, omnipresent, all powerful and all attractive, the seed-giving Father of Man and all living entities. He is the sustaining energy of all life, nature and the cosmic situation.

3. Man is actually *not* his body, but is eternal spirit, soul, part and parcel of God, and therefore eternal.

4. That 'all men are brothers' can be practised only when we realise God as our common ultimate Father.

5. All our actions should be performed as a sacrifice to the Supreme Lord . . . 'all that you do, all that you eat, all that you offer and give away, as well as all austerities that you may perform, should be done as an offering unto me'. *Bhagavad-Gita* IX, 27.)

6. The food that sustains us should always be offered to the Lord before eating. In this way He becomes the offering and such eating purifies us.

7. We can, by sincere cultivation of bona fide spiritual science attain to the state of pure, unending blissful consciousness, free from anxiety in this very lifetime! And the proof is in the practice.

8. The recommended means of attaining the mature stage of 'Love of God' in the present age of 'Kali' or quarrel, is to chant the Holy Name of the Lord. Any Name of God will do, but the ecstatic method, the easiest method for most people, is to chant the Hare Krishna Mantra.

What do these young followers of Krishna mean by 'God'? According to the Vedic literature, God or Krishna is the Personality in whom is contained the fulness of six attributes: beauty, strength, knowledge, fame, wealth and renunciation. The word 'Krishna' itself is Sanskrit and means 'all-attractive'. Krishna is 'the one who steals the heart', 'the supreme personality of Godhead'. Krishna appeared on earth some five thousand years ago, and later reappeared in the fifteenth century as Lord Sri Krishna Chaitanya Mahaprabhu to revive the lost art of Krishna Consciousness. The message of Krishna was that the absolute supreme personality of Godhead could descend into the transcendental sound vibration. Through chanting, the heart is purified from internal impurities, and the Krishna energy is awakened. It is claimed that in reality all human beings are Krishna Conscious beings, but that long ages of move-ment from one body to another has led to an identification with the material body. The aim of Krishna Consciousness, on the other hand, is to be freed from the pangs of material existence, and to revive the lost relationship with God, to become truly *awake*. What does it mean to be awake? It means to recognize that *I* am not synonymous with *My Body*. *I* am *consciousness*, *I* am pure *soul*.

The followers of Krishna Consciousness quote with approval Plato's observation that 'the body is a source of endless trouble to us' and his claim that 'in the present life . . . we make the nearest approach to knowledge when we have the least possible intercourse or communion with the body'.[47] The body is seen as 'foolishness'. Sense gratification is deplored, and there is a stress on control in the area of sexuality: unless there is control of sex life, there can be no spiritual advance. So within the marriage relationship there is a demand for austerity and the minimizing of sense gratification. In fact, sex is viewed as an impediment to spiritual growth. 'This does not mean completely forget sex life. It is not forbidden. If you can forget it, good. . . . To become a great soul is to completely forget about sex.'[48] Swami A. C. Bhaktivedanta disapproves of boys and girls mixing together on the grounds that 'it is not very efficacious for spiritual life' and therefore 'should be restricted'.[49] On the other hand, Hayagriva writes that although 'strong sexual passions are often considered impediments to spiritual life', they can easily be transformed, and lust for sex can be channelled into love for Krishna, 'the Reservoir of all pleasure'.[50]

Members of the International Society for Krishna Consciousness reject the use of alcohol and other drugs. On the other hand, many young people from within the psychedelic drug culture have attached themselves to the movement. Their rejection of the use of psychedelic drugs is the direct result of the fundamental belief that 'our natural state of consciousness is one of ecstasy',[51] and therefore that chemical alteration of consciousness is unnecessary. Men exist externally in *Samadhi*, union with God, and it is ignorance which prevents realization of this. Drugs do not lead to the natural state of freedom and bliss, but rather to reliance upon and bondage to a material substance, and the LSD users who have come to the society did not impress the disciples of Krishna; rather did they find them 'generally confused, disorientated and badly in need of help'. Moreover, 'their conversations have not indicated them to be enlightened beings'. Krishna Consciousness, however, enables one to 'stay high forever'.

MEHER BABA

The search for a permanent, non-chemical 'high' led other young seekers to Meher Baba. Unlike many of the teachers, Baba had been around the spiritual scene for many years before the LSD culture rediscovered him. Born in 1894 to Zoroastrian parents in Poona, Baba (then known as Merwan) studied the works of Hafiz, the Persian poet. At the age of 18, he encountered a perfect master Hazrat Baba Jan, a woman of 110, who kissed him between the eyes. As a result of this meeting, it is claimed, a tremendous spiritual current entered him, and several months later he was lifted out of awareness of his physical body, and attained 'God-Consciousness'.

For a while he led an itinerant existence, meeting other spiritual masters, one of whom, Sri Upasani Maharaj, whom he met in 1915, brought him back slowly to normal consciousness. But his experience of 'God-Consciousness' was not interrupted and at the age of 28 in 1922, he assumed the name of Meher Baba, Father of Compassion. In 1924 he established headquarters near Ahmednagar, and around him a community of seekers and visitors grew up. Three years later he ceased writing, and on 10 July 1925 entered a state of total silence, which continued until his death in 1969. Until 1954 he communicated with people through an alphabet board, and led a life of celibacy and asceticism, with long fasts and periods of seclusion. On one occasion, Baba retired into the cave of St Francis in Assisi, and claimed 'A meeting was held when all the saints and masters from the sixth and seventh planes of consciousness saw me, and we mapped out the spiritual destiny of the world for the next two thousand years.'[52]

The followers of Meher Baba believe that he was God in human form, the Avatar of the twentieth century. He claimed that in each age—a period of 65 to 125 years—there were only five 'perfect Masters', the name given to those who had attained *self-realization*. In addition to the Masters, there are some seven thousand individuals who are members of the spiritual hierarchy, individuals who are on the subtle and mental planes of consciousness. But at the end of 11 ages, a period of some seven hundred to fourteen hundred years, the Perfect Masters request God to descend in human form. So, claimed Meher Baba, 'I am the God of all Gods. I am Sakshat Paramatma. I am the ancient one.'[53] 'In the God-Man, God reveals Himself in all His glory, with His Infinite Power, Unfathomable Knowledge, Inexpressible Bliss and Eternal Existence.'[54] But surrender to the God-Man is possible only to the very advanced.

In 1931 Baba visited Britain, and between 1932 and 1958 made several other visits. There were hostile press reports in 1932. *John Bull* announced 'All Britain Duped by Sham Messiah. Apart from the financial aspect of this cult—and money has been freely collected from misguided followers for years—the menace to the minds of simple people cannot be exaggerated.'[55] In spite of hostility, however, there were people who accepted Meher Baba as the Ancient One, who, it was claimed, had come, 'not to teach but to awaken', to push humanity spiritually into the future. Baba prescribed no methods, mantras, yoga or ritual. His message was incredible in its simplicity: love and service. 'I will teach you how to move in the world yet be at all times in inward communion with men as the Infinite Being.'[56] In 1947 the publication of Jean Adriel's *Avatar* increased the knowledge of Baba in the Western world, in which she referred to Baba's 'catalytic effect upon consciousness': he brings into the open the negative aspects of men's minds, the Karmic fetters which, through Baba's guidance, can then be removed. Baba himself saw the aim of his work to be 'elimination of the ego', that is, the false ego, and the introduction of a 'direct journey to God'.[57] Those who sought the truth through rituals were compared by Baba to travellers in a goods train which was from time to time detained indefinitely; those who used meditation and service to humanity were like travellers on the ordinary stopping train;

but those who surrendered to Baba were able to travel express and
direct in the shortest possible time. Baba spoke of a day when he
would break his silence and 'utter that Original Word'. His Avataric
form was seen as 'the last incarnation of this cycle of time', but
when his silence was broken, the impact of his love upon the world
would be universal and would enable men to know their true self-
hood.

During the 1950s and 1960s, Meher Baba was very concerned
with the attainment of human brotherhood and the threat of imminent destruction. He claimed that constructive and creative forces
were operative for the redemption of humanity, for man's liberation
from egoism and the slavery of illusory values. When true understanding was achieved, wars would disappear, and a new humanity
would emerge. Baba connected the appearance of this new humanity
with the return of mysticism: 'When spiritual experience is described as being mystical, one should not assume that it is something
supernatural or entirely beyond the grasp of human consciousness:
all that is meant is that it is not accessible to the limited human
intellect, unless it transcends its limits and is illuminated by the
direct realization of the Infinite.'[58] In Baba's teaching there is an
emphasis on seven realities: existence, love, sacrifice, renunciation,
knowledge, control and surrender. In order to attain God-realization,
the individual needs to perceive these realities, and the spiritual
discipline of Bhakti Yoga is taught in its three stages: the first is
ritualistic worship, the second constant remembrance of God by
continuous mental or physical repetition of any name of God, and
at the third stage the disciple is concerned with divine love and
longing, and has penetrated beyond thought. Yet Baba denied
that he was attached to any one spiritual path, and on 17 June
1952, he dictated the following words at Myrtle Beach, South
Carolina:[59]

Meher Baba is equally connected with Islam and its Sufism,
Christianity and its Mysticism, the Orient and its Vedantism,
broad Buddhism, practical Zoroastrianism, Jainism and many
other such *isms* which all speak the same divine truth and lead
to the same divine paths. He has to awaken the followers of these
paths to the real meaning of these *isms* in their true spirit by
reorientating these *isms* and in this capacity He has reorientated
Sufism in the charter to be universally adopted.

So in 1952 Baba devised a charter for a contemporary form of Sufism, and a group based in San Francisco assumed the name Sufism Reoriented and began to publish his works. Sufism Reoriented claims to provide a system of inner training for those who wish to move beyond the forms of religion and reach the inner heart of spirituality. The Sufis regard the world as their school in which they have to learn to live a divine life, and Sufi training teaches detachment in the midst of this world. The aim of spiritual progress is 'to find the true centre of experience and reorganize his life in the truth. This entails the wearing out of the ego and its replacement by Truth-consciousness. The disintegration of the Ego is a condition of realizing the Truth.'[60] Baba saw the ego, the affirmation of separateness, to be 'the chief hindrance to the spiritual emancipation and enlightenment of consciousness'.[61] This sense of separateness is overcome only through the experience of love and the longing to become one with the Beloved.

It was in 1966 that Sufism Reoriented issued a pamphlet entitled *God in a Pill? Meher Baba on LSD and the High Roads*, and it was this pamphlet which was to make the Avatar well known within the psychedelic drug culture. Baba was introduced as 'the best non-acid authority available to compare the results of chemical stimulation of the deeper layers of being with those produced by techniques known and used throughout time by spiritual teachers'.[62]

His observations on LSD came as a result of a visit to Nepal in 1965 by a young enthusiast who journeyed on to consult Baba. Allan Y. Cohen has described his visit as 'a pilgrimage which became a focal point for the downfall of the psychedelic fantasy'.[63] Certainly, the advice came as a surprise to many young drug users.

For Baba psychedelics were 'harmful—physically, mentally and spiritually'.

All so-called spiritual experiences generated by taking 'mind-changing' drugs such as LSD, mescalin and psilocybin are superficial and add enormously to one's addiction to the deceptions of illusion which is but the shadow of Reality.

No drug, whatever its great promise, can help one to attain the spiritual goal. There is no short-cut to the goal except through the grace of the Perfect Master, and drugs, LSD more than others, give only a semblance of 'spiritual experience', a glimpse of a false reality.

The experience of a semblance of freedom that these drugs may temporarily give to one is in actuality a millstone round the aspirant's neck in his efforts towards emancipation from the rounds of birth and death.

The experience is as far removed from Reality as is a mirage from water. No matter how much one pursues the mirage one will never reach water, and the search for God through drugs must end in disillusionment.[64]

Baba concedes that experiences gained through LSD may be experiences of shadows of the subtle planes, that is, the planes of emotion and energy. But, he insists, 'the user of LSD can never reach subtle consciousness in this incarnation despite its repeated use'. For the experience of real spiritual consciousness, surrender to a Perfect Master is necessary. What is a Perfect Master? He is a God-realized being who has completed the cycle of evolution and involution through which consciousness is developed, matured and perfected, and who subsequently chooses to return and participate actively in creation in order to lead others to the perfection of consciousness.

Baba identifies four stages of experience of consciousness: gross consciousness, subtle consciousness, mental consciousness and God consciousness. The experience is higher according to the reduction of the burden of impressions (Sanskaras). But there is also a state which he calls 'perverted consciousness', when induced experiences, for example, those gained through drugs, are indulged in, and become a source of delusion:

The experiences derived through the drugs are experiences by one in the gross world of the shadows of the subtle planes, and are not continuous. The experiences of the subtle sphere by one on the subtle planes are continuous, but even these experiences are of illusion, for reality is beyond them. And so, though LSD may lead one to feel a better man personally, the feeling of having had a glimpse of reality may not only lull one into a false security but also will in the end derange one's mind. Although LSD is not an addiction-forming drug, one can become attached to the *experiences* arising from its use and one gets tempted to use it in increasing doses, again and again, in the hope of deeper and deeper experiences. But eventually this causes madness or death.[65]

Baba does not deny that 'to a few sincere seekers, LSD may have served as a means to arouse that spiritual longing which has brought them into my contact' but he argues that once this purpose is served, further ingestion would be both harmful and pointless. To Baba-lovers, the Avatar is not a teacher but an awakener through whom men can become one in love. 'I have come to sow the seed of love in your hearts so that in spite of all superficial diversity which your life in illusion must experience and endure, the feeling of oneness through love is brought about amongst all nations, creeds, sects and castes of the world.'[66]

. . . AND MORE GURUS STILL

In 1971 a 14-year-old Guru, Maharaj Ji, became a prominent figure in sections of the youth spiritual scene. Known to his disciples as 'Lord of the Universe' and 'Prince of Peace', Guru Maharaj Ji's claims are propagated through the Divine Light Mission which, towards the end of 1972, claimed five million followers in India, forty thousand in the United States, ten thousand in Europe, six thousand in Britain and six hundred in Japan.[67] Devotees of Guru Maharaj Ji call him 'the Messiah' and see in him the source of 'Knowledge' and of 'divine light'. There is no creed, no dogma, no moral codes, no set times of meditation, but a listening to the sound within. The first Western girl to receive 'the Knowledge' simply described it as 'knowledge of one's own true self, the true nature of one's soul'.[68] Guru Maharaj Ji—his full name is given as Balyo-geshwar Param Hans Satgurudev Shri Sant Ji Maharaj—is the son of one Param Sant Satgurudev Shri Hans Ji Maharaj, who died on 19 July 1966. Among the Guru's aims is that of 'uniting all religions'.[69] During 1972 his following increased in British cities, and young refugees from drug use sought after 'the Knowledge'.

One former member of Divine Light described how he joined the movement while he was using LSD. But he found a permanent 'high' through taking 'Knowledge'. He was shown four techniques of meditation. First, the Light—placing the forefinger tips between the eyebrows, then putting the thumb and middle fingers under the closed eyes, then forcing the eyes to focus to the point where the forefinger is by pushing the eyeballs slightly inward. Secondly, music—pushing the thumbs tightly into the ears, and waiting for the music. Thirdly, nectar—pushing the tongue up past the throat to channels where the 'Divine Flow' is said to be. Fourthly, the Word

—breathing heavily and slowly. However, this young devotee was not impressed by the apparent wealth of Guru Maharaj Ji whom he called 'the best con man probably for centuries', and was cynical about the financial aspirations of the movement:

> When Divine Light Mission first came to Britain it was described as Spiritual Revolution. It was started long before the Jesus Freaks and others came on the scene. Divine Light Mission were really hip at first—long hair, beards, saffron robes, the lot. Then one day this year, one of the hip Indian Mahatmas came back from India with his hair and beard cut, and a Saville Row suit, nice shiny black shoes, even socks.[70]

The writer believed that Divine Light was 'the fastest growing organisation in the world'. His worries about the finances of the Mission seem to be shared by the Indian Government, who announced an inquiry in November 1972, as a result of customs seizures of money, watches and jewels from the Guru's aeroplane.[71]

The Eastern mysticism of the counter-culture is expressed musically in the work of Quintessence, a group consisting of flute, guitars and drums, whose music owes much to the influence and spiritual atmosphere of North Morocco, of Tibet and Japan as well as of India. Quintessence saw music as 'a very spiritual thing', a holy work, and their musicians were people whose religious and philosophical ideas were moving in the same directions. Some have compared their work to trance music and to whirling dervishes; their music in fact represents a deep sympathy with Eastern lifestyles and particularly with Hindu religious ideas. Their early records were made under the spiritual supervision of their guru Swami Ambikananda, who taught them their chants and was a guide and support.[72]

There are, of course, many more gurus and teachers springing up all the time, and new centres open and close frequently. The rediscovery of the East has been a central element in the spiritual quest of the young. Often, it is superficial and idiosyncratic, but more people than is often realized have studied the Eastern teachings at a deep level. Not all have been content, however, with the teachings as they stand, and we need therefore to examine another facet of the quest—the more general search for an inner truth behind all religions, resulting in the creation of new occult and magical life-styles.

5
Mysticism and Magic

CONSCIOUSNESS AND MAGIC

It would be utterly mistaken to view the revival of interest in Eastern mysticism as a fringe phenomenon unrelated to Western research into consciousness and personality. Since William James claimed that our normal waking consciousness was simply one special type, and that there were 'potential forms of consciousness entirely different', there has been a great deal of study and interest in this area. But it was not a sudden development, for other psychologists contemporary with James were little concerned with the matter, and his work was dwarfed by the development of psychoanalysis. Freud and his successors have been accused of viewing human personality as a glorified hydraulic pump and the psychoanalyst as an effective plumber who would steer the sexual flow of energy into respectable channels. Certainly Freud was considerably influenced by the physical sciences, and minimized the importance of consciousness. Moreover some behaviourists denied its existence altogether, while others connected consciousness exclusively with 'mind' as against 'body'. On the other hand, the Eastern traditions which have been rediscovered are profoundly concerned with levels and types of consciousness. Hindu writers may identify several different 'chakras' or centres of consciousness in the body, while Buddhists may see a progression through stages of consciousness towards 'oneness'. But in the West, unusual states of consciousness tend to be regarded as pathological, and so researchers into alterations in consciousness have tended to gather their data from the mentally ill. Indeed, it is common to describe creative genius as madness. The search for an alternative approach in the East is one facet of a disenchantment with conventional Western models. The philosophy of mind was seen to be inadequate. There was a loss of insight, of poetry, of creativity.

D

Recently, however, various writers and thinkers have suggested that man is entering a period of enlarged and evolving consciousness. Such thinkers as Marshall McLuhan and Teilhard de Chardin have clearly made a major impact on our thought. McLuhan saw the power of electricity to be fundamental. Teilhard believed that man as he had evolved had reached a pinnacle of physical complexity and of centredness of consciousness. Evolution was seen as an ascent towards consciousness, and the future of consciousness was to become more and more complex. Teilhard also introduced the idea of love as the unifying factor in the evolutionary process. Others have pointed to the subversive effect of the changes on the present social order: 'the new Enlightenment . . . is altering the *unconscious apparatus of the individual* even before it can be articulated consciously as a social theory or a commitment to political convictions'.[1] So the individual's acceptance of and obedience to institutions, authorities and values is being dissolved. The consciousness revolution has political consequences. Timothy Leary has claimed that 'in the last six or seven years a small group of us . . . has brought about a change in the consciousness of the United States'.[2] Whether he is responsible for the changes or not, there is no doubt that they have occurred.

During 1969 in particular the concept of a 'mind revolution'—involving a mental and spiritual break with the mainstream culture —became familiar in the Underground. A writer in September of that year predicted that 'this winter is going to be quite a scene' as 'the collapse of our culture continues apace'. The real revolution, he argued, was in the mind of man. 'A safe prophecy is that very soon the persecuted will not be the militant revolutionaries (who will be locked in the mortal combat of their choice) but the groups of people who have begun to LIVE revolution by sharing together their own inner knowledge in community.' The necessary break with the status quo was seen as closely connected with the use of psychedelic drugs: 'In the present cultural scene, conditioning is so powerful and the language-cage so inhibiting, that only acid and the explorative use of hashish have any chance of altering the experiential level of the individual in any significant group way, and this is, in fact what has been happening. Of course, the very exceptional individual gets there by his own searching, but given the social pressure in our society such a possibility is very rare.'[3]

There were some individuals, including people held in great

respect in the spiritual sectors of the counter-culture, who were not happy with the total rejection of psychedelics by the spiritual seeker. Lisa Bieberman, who published a bi-monthly bulletin from the Psychedelic Information Centre in Cambridge, Massachusetts, argued that the fact that LSD use had become 'demonic' in such areas as Haight-Ashbury was no valid argument against its legitimate use. The devil, she says, is a fallen angel.

> I too have observed the demonic aspect of the LSD scene. . . . If LSD is meant to open a man to God, then the demonic is exactly what one would expect from its perversion. I have seen the misery. It is terrible to behold. Which is all the more reason why it must be answered with something more to the point than Baba or Maharishi. Not that these are not preferable to insanity. But they are a poor thing to settle for. If, as I believe, God gave us phanerothymic drugs in this skeptical age for our conversion, then the Church had better take notice.[4]

'Phanerothymic' is Lisa Bieberman's alternative term to 'psychedelic'. She argues for the use of phanerothyme as a sacrament, and issues six instructions for such use: don't take it too often (not more than once in three months); do use it at least once a year; place the setting and group carefully; take it reverently; ask God's guidance before, during and after use; and, if phanerothyme gives a *clear* directive, follow it. Superficially her position is like Leary's. She calls it a 'western approach to the religious use of psycho-chemicals', for she believes that the experience 'is closer to the Western Judaeo-Christian heritage than to the oriental philosophies which are most often invoked to interpret the drug experience'.[5]

Lisa Bieberman points to the disillusionment not simply with psychedelic drugs but with many of the philosophies and cults which have followed them. But, she claims, the one fact which rarely occurs to the LSD user is that the fundamental values of his own religious culture may be reinforced and confirmed by the drug experience, and it is in this direction that she looks, to the Judaeo-Christian tradition, and more specifically, to the Quaker meeting. Within such a devout, quiet religious context, she advocates the use of psychedelic drugs as a means to achieve a state of mental and spiritual clarity, and she rejects the swing towards the East and the accompanying disenchantment with Western society.

However, the movement towards Christianity, even of a Quaker type, has not been very pronounced in the psychedelic culture. The Eastern trends have dominated the spiritual revival, but they have tended to be confused with a great deal of syncretistic Western material. Rarely have Eastern traditions hit the counter-culture in a 'pure state', but have rather carried with them, or accumulated, elements derived from occultism, theosophy, psychic and spiritualistic movements, astrology, and so on. Magic and the occult have become 'an integral part of the counter-culture'.[6] Some have described the growth of the occult in terms of a straightforward progression from psychedelic drugs to occult interests, occultism being thus a by-product of drug abuse. But this is to misread the evidence and to exaggerate the role of chemicals. The occult revival is part of a developing search for the inner world, for consciousness, for spirituality: the use of chemicals is merely one facet of this search, associated with one crucial historical phase of the search, but for many today it is a facet which is of mainly historical interest.

But the use of drugs to achieve consciousness alteration is also a facet of the scientific study of extra-sensory phenomena which has been developing since the end of the last century. Drug-induced states are not the only types of altered consciousness which have been studied; the early interest in telepathy and psychical research led to the founding of the British Society for Psychical Research in 1882, while American studies were given a certain boost by the work of James. Today some twenty states of consciousness have been identified: the dreaming state, the sleeping state, the hypnagogic state (which occurs between wakefulness and sleep), the hypnopompic state (which occurs between sleep and wakefulness), the hyper-alert state, the lethargic state, states of rapture (including those induced by sexual stimulation, frenzied dances, rituals, and so on), states of hysteria, states of fragmentation, states of regression, meditative states, trance states, hypnotic dream states occurring during trance, daydreaming states, internal scanning (the awareness of bodily feelings in the organs, tissues, muscles, and so on), stupor, coma, stored memory, 'expanded consciousness' of various kinds, including drug-induced states, and finally the ordinary waking state. The area of consciousness 'expansion' is the area which has attracted particular interest in the current exploration of 'inner space', and there has been a coming together of the mystical and scientific categories. It is increasingly argued today that 'the experience of higher states of consciousness is necessary for survival of the human species'.[7]

At the present time, therefore, large numbers of young people use psychedelic drugs as a means towards what R. D. Laing has called 'meta-egoic' experience. Such an experience is one which goes beyond the horizons of ego consciousness, the conscious state in which men experience the world and themselves within a framework of certain structures of space and time. 'The "ego" is the instrument for living in *this* world. If the "ego" is broken up, or destroyed (by the insurmountable contradictions of certain life situations, by toxins, chemical changes, etc.) then the person may be exposed to other worlds, "real" in different ways from the more familiar territory of dreams, imagination, perception or phantasy.'[8] For Laing, 'true sanity entails in one way or another the dissolution of the normal ego'.[9] It is through such a process that one begins to experience the transcendent. 'The creation of a new consciousness', claims Charles Reich,[10] 'is the most urgent of America's needs. . . . Consciousness III is an attempt to gain transcendence.' What Reich calls Consciousness III is in fact the contemporary quest for liberation, for self-awareness, for a new community, and for 'revolution by consciousness'.

The journey from the psychedelic drug scene through Eastern mysticism to a search for one's personal consciousness may be accomplished in a very short period! Thus one schoolboy wrote in an Underground paper in 1972:[11]

> I am one of those who came upon Hesse, Ginsberg, Kesey, Leary, Snyder, The Grateful Dead, etc., independently and in isolation . . . and then went on to drop acid and to affirm commitment to the hip culture or whatever you want to call it. I'm one of the ones who made it to the Pink Fairies and receive free copies of *Friends* as it then was and delighted to see that alienation from the majority was in fact common to a much wider body of people than previously imagined. . . . Since then I've been through the post-acid search for faith—oriental, Zen, even Christianity, and the heavy political trip and now coming out the other side I'm more aware that in fact the two are inseparable; a man's actions are based on his beliefs.

This sort of language is vastly different from the schoolboy rationalism of the last decade. The multiplication of mystical sects in the youth culture suggests that 'we live in an age of marginal mystical recrudescence, a world where Humanists seem positively archaic'.[12] American writers stress that it is Eastern influences which dominate the revival of religious interests among the young. 'This new American religion is essentially Oriental rather than Western, non-rational rather than rational, occult rather than prophetic, and emotional rather than intellectual.'[13]

It is this 'new American religion' which figures in the Underground press. So John Wilcock, the editor of *Other Scenes*, when asked about the interests of his paper, included the comment:[14]

> I like to have religion, as today exemplified by all possible religions. The Universal Life Church, which is like a gimmick, really, but nevertheless it's a religion, and mysticism and all the other religions that people are interested in, like astrology, and almost everything except the orthodox Christian and Jewish, almost everything except the orthodox Western religions. There's a great deal of interest in all the Eastern religions, and all aspects of religion. As I say, things like astrology. So that's religion.

The Underground religious culture has even included the revival of old pagan religions. The Pagan Movement describes itself as 'an anarchistic pancultural society' for those who worship the Goddess and Gods of nature.[15] An enormous number of Occultist groups has sprung up. So when in 1967 fifty thousand anti-war demonstrators besieged the Pentagon, among them were 'witches, warlocks, holymen, seers, prophets, mystics, saints, sorcerers, shamans, troubadours, minstrels, bards, roadmen and madmen'.[16] The British Underground papers concern themselves with Druids, Stonehenge, Blake, flying saucers, and a whole panorama of mystical and magical figures. As one looks at the Underground press as a whole, Roszak notes, 'one is apt to find their pages swarming with Christ and the prophets, Zen, Sufism, Hinduism, primitive shamanism, theosophy, the Left-Handed Tantra'.[17]

In the evolution of the Haight-Ashbury psychedelic subculture, one of the most striking features was the movement from LSD to magic. Most of the young people in the psychedelic movement were doing well in the 'straight' world. 'However, upon entry into the psychedelic scene, repeatedly taking LSD in a psychedelic information environment which reinforced their visions, perceptual alterations, and cognitive functions, they developed a magical belief system. A belief in astrology, astro-projection, mental telepathy, telekinesia, and parapsychic phenomena of all kinds was so great that it motivated their lives.'[18] Smith noted a ten-fold increase in births during February because mothers wanted children born under the sign. Astrology became a major force in people's lives, and they would alter an entire week's activities because their 'sign was bad'.

> Recently several individuals left Haight-Ashbury because 'the world was going to end' following its fragmentation by a passing meteorite. Mental telepathy and ESP are commonly practised, and one individual at the Haight-Ashbury Clinic, for example, was convinced that he could 'put the evil eye' on people who offended him. All of these magical concepts are characteristic of primitive religion, and yet, as indicated by demographic studies, a majority of these young people were Caucasian and from middle-class homes with little background in such magical concepts.[19]

Smith identified the absorption with magic and astrology as an important element in the 'psychedelic syndrome', and his research in the communes in North California has reinforced this view. There is a good deal of deranged mysticism in the communes, some of which was superficially manifest in the publicity which surrounded the Sharon Tate murder. Often it is the 'flying saucer' mythology which dominates the movement—the spot chosen for setting up the commune will be the place where the astro-magnetic rays enabled the saucer to land. Parents in the communes will give their children names derived from astrology, Eastern metaphysics and psychedelic mysticism, for example, Oran, Morning Star, Rama Krishna, Ongo Ishi, Star, and Ora Infinitya. But the interest in mysticism in general has not been restricted either to communes, or to those still within the psychedelic movement; a mystical path has indeed frequently been sought following a dissatisfaction with the limitations of psychedelic drug experience. So during 1967-8 one saw in London the beginnings of the emergence of a mystical/ magical complex, composed not only of the followers of Eastern disciplines of the type described in the previous chapter, but also of more syncretistic groups who drew upon a wide range of traditions. One of the best known centres for the early mystical scene in London

was Gandalf's Garden in Chelsea, and many of its ideas were
propagated through a journal of the same name.

GANDALF'S GARDEN

Muz Murray, who founded Gandalf's Garden, was a young man
with an atheistic background, who had started to read Western
philosophers and Zen writings while at art college. He spent seven
years hitch-hiking round Europe, the Middle East and Africa, and
in Cyprus in 1964 he experienced a state of mystical awareness.
It was as if an arm was pressing his brain out of existence, as if a
whole new universe was being poured into his head. At this point
Muz had not touched psychedelic drugs, but he subsequently
related his own experience to what seemed to be happening to many
young people during the LSD summer of 1967, and on returning to
England in that year became worrie l at the degree of aggression and
paranoia within the Underground. He found, as he went around
events and happenings, that people attached themselves to him and
poured out spiritual problems. Many of the descriptions of drug
experiences which were recounted to him sounded similar to his
own natural mystical experience of 1964, and so he took a large
dose of LSD. In a talk given in 1970 he described the results and
his interpretation:

> I went totally out of awareness of this world's existence, experi-
> enced the creation of the planet, my whole previous life-cycle as
> a plant, cellular consciousness, consciousness of atoms and
> molecules, and delving into realms and dimensions where man,
> at this stage of existence, has no right to delve. I was very close
> to going insane. Only through my previous experience was I able
> to understand some of the realms which I entered through LSD.
> I found that LSD only releases what is in one's subconscious,
> all one's past experiences: it cannot take you into future experi-
> ences as a natural mystical illumination will. A natural mystical
> experience takes you vertically: the LSD experience takes you
> horizontally.[20]

Muz Murray believed that large numbers of young people were
becoming confused and disoriented because they were unable to
control the drug experience and to integrate it into a spiritual life-
style. If it were possible to provide methods of control, such as
Yoga, breathing or meditational exercises, then this would be an

important service to the new mystical scene. It was out of this ferment that Gandalf's Garden developed, and the response to it was far greater than its creators had anticipated. Large numbers came to the Chelsea centre to hear famous Yogis, Zen Buddhists, Young Sufis and others; rules of silence were designed for those who lived in the community, and there were times of corporate meditation. But for many who could not come to the centre itself, it was through the magazine that ideas were circulated. Muz and his companions strongly held that there was an upsurge of mystical consciousness throughout the planet in the higher civilized countries, and they related this to the movement of the planets from Pisces to Aquarius. There were influences from outer space, densities of particles falling more heavily than before, and these were affecting men's minds and spirits, raising their vibrations to a higher level. As a result more people were experiencing 'cosmic consciousness' and more psychics and mystics were appearing.

So *Gandalf's Garden* magazine became a vehicle for the expression of the early London mystical scene. The influence of Tolkien's *Lord of the Rings* was evident in its choice of hero. Gandalf the White Wizard was seen as the 'mythological hero of the age'.

> In the land of Middle Earth under threat of engulfment by the dark powers, Gandalf unites the differing races, mistrustful of each other through lack of understanding and communication, in a final effort to save the world. The crusader spirit in Gandalf is echoed in the cry of the Now Generation seeking an alternative to the destructive forces of today's world, by spreading human love and aid, for the unity of all the peoples of the Earth.[21]

Gandalf's Garden, however, was seen as more than a journal or a centre: it was 'the magical garden of our inner worlds . . . soulflow from the pens of creators . . . a wellspring of love'. These young seekers urged their followers to cultivate their inner gardens and to emulate the Soul Wizards of the East who sat in silence and contemplation. Those who came to Gandalf's Garden were led by common vibrations. Posters saying 'Gandalf's Garden grows here' were distributed so that sympathetic souls could proclaim themselves. The movement used the description 'Overground' for they saw themselves as searchers for a celestial city. Their revolution was a spiritual revolution, the creation of 'a new vision of what we are and where we want to go'.[22]

A typical issue of *Gandalf's Garden* might include articles on Eastern mystics, on the Sufis, on palmistry, on communes or even on black magic, plus advertisements for groups such as Swedenborgians and Theosophists as well as for current LPs. Throughout the magazine was a strong sense of changes in consciousness, a sense which Muz Murray frequently articulated:

> When the same thought awakens in a million evolving minds, that same idea makes a mental imprint on the psychesphere of this planet, and the world begins to slowly move in that direction. Thoughts are catching in the individual cells of the new World Brain. . . . On the edge of the Aquarian Age we are drawing into the swing of great cosmic events. The long awaited long-lost Dawn of Consciousness is at last glimmering in the minds of New Age Man-to-Come. Something is happening to the Planetary Consciousness. . . .[23]

Other writers stressed the sense of affinity with the East. 'The people of the East are our friends,' wrote Jim Griffin. 'We are more like them than we are like the average Westerner, and because they are much closer to the truth, they can be turned on much easier.'[24]

In the summer of 1971 Gandalf's Garden ceased to publish its journal and split into a number of 'seed centres' throughout Britain, the central one being near Norwich. The original Gardeners from the Chelsea centre had moved to different parts of the world—one to an ashram in the Himalayas, others to various parts of Britain. Muz himself went to the East, saying,

> In England I should still be caught up with the needs that are in the air, no matter in what isolated retreat I found myself. And therefore I know the stimulus of a totally different mental climate is necessary to overcome the pulls of the past. Such is the vibration of the East. And there I shall have time to assess. *I do not go Eastwards to seek anything else, since I am well aware that Britain and South America once again are becoming the mystical-spiritual centres of the world.*[25]

So, in Britain, the 'Friends of the Garden' established their 'seed centres' to be 'gatherings of people who are not restricted by or to any one spiritual viewpoint, religion, sect or path, and who are open to the totality of things to be discovered in this incredible state of existence, whether it be from the intuitive mystical experience or the aware scientific investigation of the Cosmos'. In 1971 there were centres in Norwich, Edinburgh, London, Glasgow, Leeds, Portsmouth, Bath, Cambridge, Hull, Salisbury and Manchester, and centres planned for Coventry, Oxford, Bristol, Hove, York, Cheltenham and Colchester.

THE OCCULT REVIVAL

In America the movement towards the occult intensified after the decline of the psychedelic culture. The first Festival of the Occult Arts occurred on 19 April 1970 at Fillmore East. In 1970 also the first B.A. in Magical Studies was awarded at the University of California, Berkeley. By this time occultism was a profitable concern, and free zodiac cups were being offered on TV commercials. *Cooking with Astrology* was given to those who bought a particular brand of bacon, while occult games were reported to be the biggest hope of toy manufacturers for the coming decade. For five dollars, the 'Mystery Zodiac' featured a spinning plastic wizard with a magnetic wand. Occult equipment became common in the 'head shops'. Soon PanAm were offering a $629 'Psychic Tour' of Britain including a visit to a psychic healing centre, a seance, and a day at Stonehenge with the Chief Druid.[26] Shops such as the Samuel Weiser Bookshop on Broadway became important resource points for occult information, while in one shop in Los Angeles a slogan warned, 'Shoplifting plays hell with your Karma'. 'A wave of fascination with the occult is noticeable throughout the country', claimed *Time* magazine.[27]

In Britain too the occult revival has involved a number of bookshops and booksellers. Atlantis Book Service deals in occult books by mail order, and Atlantis Bookshop in Museum Street near the British Museum in Central London is a well-stocked centre for such literature. There are books on werewolves, witchcraft and astrology, and a directory *The Aquarian Guide to Occult London*. There are magazines like *Man, Myth and Magic*, the first issue of which sold eight hundred thousand copies. The best known bookshop is certainly Robinson and Watkins in Cecil Court, off Charing Cross Road, London. Here the emphasis is on mysticism in its widest sense, though there is a large collection of occult works. Not far away, in Soho, a young couple opened a shop called Dark They Were and Golden Eyed. In Cambridge, Cokaygne Bookshop includes works on the ancient mysteries, on sorcery, and on most occult subjects. As well as the shops which specialize in occult literature, a number of popular books have sold widely in general bookshops—William Blatty's novel *The Exorcist*, for instance, has been a best-seller in the United States. Films such as *Rosemary's Baby* have also had some influence.

The occult shops and centres in the United States and in Britain are frequently run by people who are very unsympathetic to 'black magic' and who are concerned that only true occult methods should be followed, though witchcraft candles shaped like cats or devils may be sold. Other shops may concentrate more on exploring Eastern religions, and these will often attract people who have moved from LSD towards a search for non-chemical 'highs'. As well as literature, pop music has been an important influence, with LPs like *Signs of the Zodiac* and Louise Huebner's *Seduction Through Witchcraft*, one of the tracks of which was 'Orgies: Tools of Witchcraft'. There are rock groups with names like Electric Lucifer and Black Sabbath, while the most successful occult rock record was Dr John the Night Tripper's 'Gris-Gris'. The Devil too has been a favourite theme in some areas of youth occultism, and on 6 December 1969 when the Rolling Stones played at Altamont, California, some Hell's Angels stabbed Meredith Hunter to death while Mick Jagger was singing 'Sympathy for the Devil'.[28] But other facets of the revival have been quieter and less dramatic. It is possible to identify a number of fairly distinct areas in the occult revival: astrology and the Zodiac; spiritualism; occult forms of Eastern mysticism; witchcraft and Satanism; and the revival of ancient mystery religions and myths.

ASTROLOGY AND THE ZODIAC

The first and most spectacular increase has been in the field of astrology. The 'dawning of the Age of Aquarius'—which, according to the *Dictionary of Mysticism*, began in March 1948—has been celebrated in *Hair* as a time when 'peace will guide the planets and love will steer the stars'. Devotion to the stars has now reached enormous proportions in the United States where personal horoscopes are dispensed by telephone and by computer. It has been claimed that astrology columns which are included in twelve hundred of America's 1,750 daily newspapers have a total readership of some forty million, while astrology magazines sell about two million copies monthly. Dell's *Horoscope* sells half a million and

Fate, 115,000. A survey in the 1950s by the German Institute of Public Opinion found that 29 per cent of a national sample believed that the stars were connected with the ordering of human destiny.[29] A doctor in Czechoslovakia has devised an astrological method of birth control and relates the birth of defective children to bad planetary conjunctions. His Astra Research Centre for Planned Parenthood received financial aid from the Czech Government in 1968, and gynaecologists elsewhere in Eastern Europe have pursued the study. The theory behind it is that a mature woman is more likely to conceive during the same phase of the moon which existed at her own birth, and prediction of a baby's sex also is related to the position of the moon. Other studies have attempted to connect criminal activity with the full moon.

In Britain the interest in astrology has gathered momentum: the Aetherius Society continues to pray for earth on the advice of interplanetary agencies; the rock group Magick dedicate their music to the archangel Michael. But it has been in the United States that astrology has gained most influence among young people. On 4 February 1962, according to occult astrologers, the sun, moon, Mars, Venus, Jupiter, Mercury and Saturn were all in Aquarius, and it has been argued that the Messiah of the space age may have been born on that day, for there were similar portents at the birth of Christ. So has arisen a counter-culture astrological tradition in which the new search for consciousness, the interest in psychedelic drugs, and the revival of mysticism have fused together. More young people have begun to take interest in such well-established centres as the First Temple of Astrology in Los Angeles or the Church of Light in the same district, both groups originating in the early years of the century.

SPIRITS, PSYCHICS AND HEALERS

Secondly, there has been a revival of spiritualistic and psychic groups. In the United States, the Association for Research and Enlightenment has attracted large numbers of young students of one of the most powerful modern psychics, Edgar Cayce. Cayce's meditation techniques are studied and there is a great interest in his methods of healing. Cayce taught that healing powers could be raised within groups, and he claimed that he could diagnose patients from many miles away while he was in a self-induced trance sleep.

Another famous psychic, Eileen Garrett, had set up the Parapsychology Foundation in 1951, and its New York office contains an
enormous library of paranormal literature. Societies involved with
psychical research continue to flourish, and more young people are
becoming involved. The influence of the late Bishop James Pike,
whose spectacular seance on American TV in 1967 brought spiritualism back into prominence, has been quite considerable among
Christians in the United States. In addition to spiritualism, there
has been a good deal of interest in ESP and telepathy, and in the
study of techniques for exercising psychic gifts.

In London, the College of Psychic Science in Kensington, which
publishes a journal *Light*, exists to investigate psychical phenomena and to attempt to relate them to contemporary scientific
knowledge. Other groups, such as the Spiritualist Association, are
concerned more with the practice of mediumship, while the Christian
Spiritualist League practises spiritual healing and clairvoyance.
The Churches' Fellowship for Psychic and Spiritual Studies is a
rather different kind of group, involving some highly reputable and
responsible persons, which has been concerned with the study and
evaluation of a wide range of spiritual phenomena. Many of these
bodies, both spiritualist and purely research groups, have existed
for a long time, but today more young people are actively involving
themselves with the spirit world. Practices such as seances, ouija
boards and glass turning have increased in popularity, and there
have been reported cases of physical as well as psychological damage
as a consequence of such practices. Mediumistic healers such as
Harry Edwards have attained great popularity. Edwards himself,
President of the National Federation of Spiritual Healers, is reported
to receive ten to twelve thousand letters each week, and he claims
the power both of 'absent healing' and of 'spirit travelling'. He and
other healers have received some support from Christians, and there
are a number of Christian healers, the best known being Oral Roberts,
whose powers may be seen as being 'of a mediumistic rather than a
charismatic nature'.[30] Although he has received support in the past
from Billy Graham, Oral Roberts has been heavily criticized for his
healing methods.[31]

OCCULT MYSTICISM

Thirdly, the interest in Eastern mysticism has also developed an
occult aspect. There has grown up a considerable interest in the

I Ching, an ancient Chinese oracle used by manipulating 49 yarrow stalks or by throwing three coins six times. From this a hexagram is constructed, and reference is then made to the volume *I Ching* or *Book of Changes*, which has been called 'the experimental basis of classical Chinese philosophy'.[32] By using it, it is hoped to reach some understanding of synchronicity and of the role of chance within the cosmos. Jung was responsible for introducing the first Western translation of the *I Ching* to a wide audience. Today the volume is one of the most popular in the counter-culture mystical world, and the young participants hope to discover correct courses of action by their use of sticks and coins. In New York and Los Angeles there is an International I Ching Studies Institute and Khigh Dhiegh, its founder, runs courses on I Ching as a means to the understanding of consciousness. The Taoist conception of Yin and Yang, the mother and father of all cosmic events, is interpreted as the eternal cycle of opposites, and related to the understanding of physical and psychical in man. The individual psyche is seen as linked to the whole pattern of action in the cosmos.

Equally popular are Tarot cards. The Tarot is a book of emblems based on relations between the stars and man. There are many varieties of Tarot. Of the 78 cards in a pack, the first 22 symbolize man's initiation, the first ten Trumps being his fall, and the other 12 his path to becoming an adept. The remaining 56 cards are similar to ordinary playing cards, with different emblems representing worldly glory, affections, suffering, fortune, and so on. Occult tradition claims that Tarot was invented around A.D. 1200 by a gathering of scholars in Egypt, and there are certainly references to Tarot cards at the end of the fourteenth century in France. The cards are used as windows into another world, as part of a method of divination and fortune telling. But they may also be used as instruments of meditation on the cosmic processes. In Los Angeles there is a Temple of Tarot and Holy Qabalah where the chapel is decorated with paintings of the emblems.

Both the I Ching and Tarot are based on a mystical interpretation of numbers, and this concern with numerology and charts, with codes and symbols, has been an underlying feature of much counter-culture mysticism. Numbers are seen as occult symbols of human destiny. One approach which is found in association with Tarot cards is based on the Jewish Kabalah, a system which centres around the Tree of Life interpreted in relation to the human body. The Kabalah system of cosmology is similar to some Gnostic and Neo-Platonist writings. Its literal section teaches three methods of interpreting the numerical value of words: Gematria which traces the symbolic connection between words with similar totals, Notarikon which takes each letter of a word and makes it into a sentence, and Temurah which finds hidden meanings in the shapes of letters. This kind of mathematical occultism was taken very seriously at different historical periods. But the Kabalah is more than numerology: it is concerned with a doctrinal interpretation of the Holy Tree, or ten Sefiroth with 22 paths linking them. There are many other systems and techniques based on numbers and mystical interpretations of numerical relationships, and a whole area of interest in astrological numbers, in the pyramids, in palmistry, and so on. But much popular occult writing is more general than this, and seems to draw on a confused assortment of secret teachings, masonic and similar rituals, as well as psychic, spiritualistic and oriental ideas.

A good example of the kind of literature which reaches the occult market is *Occult Gazette*, published by the School of Universal Philosophy and Healing, whose Principal is one Gladys I. Spearman-Cook of Kensington. Mrs Spearman-Cook holds Mind Development Classes which deal with such subjects as mind, hierarchical sperm, the glorified atom, molecular divinity, re-genetics and ascension. In her paper, she expresses belief in living fire and in 'spiritual communism'. In a letter addressed to the Pope on 25 January 1970, she wrote:[33] 'I quite agree with you that women cannot become priests, because they are not the recipients of the God-Fire. They deal with the magnetic fire, therefore they cannot sperm the Earth with the Divine Christos Blood. The only way they can do this is by becoming "married up" to Divinity. Then they still cannot sperm the Earth with Fire, but can give over Royal Divine Wisdom.' She went on to explain further that the priest's role was to 'sperm the congregation with Divinity' and that he could only do this when 'the whole of his spermatic waters are raised up the spinal rod, and all is centred in the Middle Commissure, on mind centralisation'. Elsewhere in the newspaper one reads a good deal about atoms born from the powers of outer world space, about the hierarchical fires which give new life to the sick, about theocratic consciousness, and related topics.

SATANISM AND WITCHCRAFT

Fourthly, one must consider the revival of Satanism, witchcraft and so-called 'black magic'. It is in this area that most anxiety has been expressed, and it is clearly one in which the emotions can easily run wild. Absurd claims and totally unsupported statements are frequently made, for example, 'in England, a nation which many had thought of as perhaps the world's most rational society, a legislator now claims that a majority of the secondary school students have been in touch with either a witch or a wizard'.[34] While few people would be likely to believe nonsense of this kind, probably many would be inclined to overstate the degree to which Satanism has actually spread among the young. One well-informed writer on the Underground scene in America and Britain has recently claimed that 'black magic has such a sparse following that sensationalists writing for a vicarious audience would certainly be disappointed'.[35] This is probably a reliable judgment. Nevertheless, it is obvious that both black magic in the strict sense, as well as the more frequently encountered phenomena associated with demonic possession and witchcraft, have increased among young people. Those involved are a minority, but there is certainly cause for concern.

In San Francisco the Church of Satan, founded by Anton Szandor La Vey in 1966, presents an inverted form of the Christian teachings. 'Blessed are the strong, for they shall possess the earth.' 'If a man smite you on one cheek, smash him on the other.' Satan is seen as a symbol of human self-assertiveness and of animal nature. La Vey claims some ten thousand followers, but many more have read his gospel expounded in *The Satanic Bible* and *The Compleat Witch*. As his Church is registered in California as a religious body, he has been able to perform Satanic weddings and funerals. La Vey, according to Freedland, believes in an ordered society, is opposed to the use of drugs as a magic tool and is unsympathetic to the hippy ethos because of its denial of the ego.[36] There are, however, other groups which include devotion to Satan or Lucifer. The Process Church of the Final Judgment, for example, includes Satan in its Godhead, alongside Christ, Jehovah and Lucifer. The Fraternitas Lucifer, devoted to the service and worship of Lucifer and his doctrine, was set up by an adept of the Right Hand Path. In order to be initiated, disciples must undergo a four-month course

on the occult as revealed to Lucifer, the Prince of Light, Lord of
this World. The order is naturist and pacifist, celebrates ritual and
magic, and believes in reincarnation. In an advertisement in 1971
it stated that ex-Christians were 'ideal' as members.

As the occult movement has grown, so new witches have appeared,
and witchcraft as a religion has revived. Margaret Murray had
argued that witchcraft was the pagan religion of pre-Christian
Europe, and that, as a result of persecution by the Church, it had
become an underground cult.[37] Many contemporary 'white witches'
see themselves as descendants of pagan cults rather than followers
of Satan, though the 'black witches' invoke power from the dark
forces of nature or from Satan himself. It has been claimed that
there are about six to seven thousand practising witches at the
present time, including three thousand in England, two thousand
in the United States, and one to two thousand elsewhere.[38] The
interest in pagan religion in Britain has resulted in the appearance
of magazines such as *The Waxing Moon*, organ of the Pagan Movement, *Insight*, a journal for the occultist issued from Bournemouth,
and *Quest*, issued from West London. In Ealing, Spook Enterprises
apparently know how to exorcise an Egyptian vampire. Occult
handbooks like *The Witches' Almanack* have appeared, and there is
always a ready market for the convert from witchcraft to
Christianity.

THE ANCIENT BRITISH MYTHS

Finally, we have seen the resurrection of ancient mystery cults and
myths connected with the pagan British religious culture. Much of
this revival has been unconnected with witchcraft, and indeed at
certain points it has assumed a Christian or quasi-Christian character.
At its centre is Glastonbury and its mystical traditions. *TORC—
Glastonbury Voices* is one occasional magazine which concerns itself
with the mysticism of Glastonbury, with articles on the origin of
Glastonbury Tor, the summer solstice, and wholefood cooking. In
the groups seeking to revive the ancient British myths, there has
been an emphasis on the spiritual power within these islands, a
favourite theme of Gandalf's Garden. Thus a group called The
Young Britons was described in 1971 as 'a very loosely-knit overground orientated international do your own thing association which
seeks to further the cause of the Alternative Society by awakening
interest and knowledge in the ancient spiritual powers latent in

Britain and using this as an influence for evolutionary good in the world'.[39]

The revival of the Glastonbury legends remains an important aspect of the new spiritual quest. The belief that the first church in Britain was set up by Joseph of Arimathea at Glastonbury is one which many Christians have cherished, though the historical evidence for such a belief is scanty. Associated with this belief has been the idea that Christ himself visited Britain, a legend which appears in Blake's well-known hymn 'Jerusalem'. Joseph, it is claimed, brought with him the cup which was used at the Last Supper and also for collecting the blood of Christ from Calvary, and this cup, the 'Holy Grail', was buried at Glastonbury, possibly in the Chalice Well. Around the grail legends grew the stories of King Arthur, and it is from these stories that a great deal of the Glastonbury mysticism and magic, including the English Tarot cards, derives. In this century it was discovered that Glastonbury was the centre of a zodiac which was marked out around the local countryside in ditches, tracks and old walls. Thus speculators have connected the structures of the Glastonbury zodiac with the Egyptian pyramids and have seen Glastonbury as a pre-Christian source for the transmission of spiritual power. Ideas about 'flying saucers' have been linked with this complex of beliefs. Thus Glastonbury has acquired an even more significant position in the mysticism of the youth culture than it had among earlier devotees, who already had included high church Anglicans and British Israelites.

The interest in the Arthurian legends and study of the historical evidence relating to the Glastonbury area has, of course, existed for many years.[40] But in recent years Glastonbury studies and pilgrimages have acquired a very different character. Thus at the end of 1969 a correspondent wrote:[41] 'Glastonbury has had a remarkable year. Hundreds of young people—hippies, poets, mystics, weirdies and sundry unclassifiables—have hitch-hiked and tramped into the town from all over Britain, Europe and even America since March looking for "vibrations".' Muz Murray of Gandalf's Garden commented on the arrival of the new pilgrims who had caused such dismay and anger among the local residents.

It's my contention that the tor and the giant zodiac imprinted on the landscape around Glastonbury, which has had enough written about it now to hold some veracity, were together the centre of cosmic power in Atlantean days and that at the present time there's an increasing influx of Atlantean souls on this planet, feeling foreign in a strange world and seeking the centres where they intuitively feel the old powers of regeneration. The hip population are those seekers. Glastonbury Tor is such a centre. . . .

The Age of Pisces brought the Word and Faith of the Christ-image, and now the Aquarian Age is of the awakening conscious-ness, and the putting into practice of the Christ spirit, Buddha mind, Ramana Mishra, love, etc. There's a great new heart beating in humanity and the pilgrimages to such places as the tor are the inward breath, the succouring, and the outward breath again into society.[42]

The writings which have been most influential on the recent resurgence of Glastonbury mysticism have been those of John Michell, particularly *The Flying Saucer Vision*, *The View over Atlantis* and *City of Revelation*. Michell believes that the original foundation at Glastonbury represented the Holy City whose coming was prophesied in the Apocalypse. There was once, he claims, a golden age of perfect spiritual knowledge, and an ancient cosmic science aimed to maintain harmony on earth through constant reference to the Temple, the sum of all the forces which form the sacred geometry of the universe. He argues that 'the New Jerusalem, Stonehenge and the original Christian Church at Glastonbury were each born of an identical tradition, a system of knowledge that in some remote age appears to have been universal'.[43] He contends:

It is thus apparent that the Holy City of St John's vision, whose outlines are also found in the sacred precinct of Glastonbury, is not an original product of the Christian revelation, but an image of eternal truth, recognized and adopted by the builders of Stonehenge as the foundation stone of their temple, the model of the cosmic order transferred to earth. The records of sacred history suggest that the type of consciousness associated with gnosticism, and with those aspirations implied in the squared circle symbol of the Holy City, occurs most particularly at the times of transition from one Platonic month to another within the great year, when the influences by which human intelligence was first promoted are again active. St John's Revelation is a work of the early Piscean era; Stonehenge was built at about the beginning of Aries. It is therefore quite in accordance with what might be expected that the plan of the cosmic city should again become visible at the dawn of Aquarius.[44]

THE CURRENT MYSTICAL/MAGICAL/OCCULT SCENE IN BRITAIN

At the present time *Alternative London* alone devotes some 21 pages to mysticism, dividing the groups or traditions into 13 main sections:[45]

1. Hindu-orientated groups—Divine Light Mission, Friends of Meher Baba, Gandalf's Garden, Radha Krishna Temple, Rama Krishna Vedanta Centre, Sai Baba Centre, etc.

2. Buddhist groups—Friends of the Western Buddhist Order, Buddhist Society, etc.

3. Sufi Orders—International School of Esoteric Studies, Sindh Sufi Society, Sufi Movement.

4. 'Other groups'. This section includes the Aetherius Society (which exists 'to propagate Vital Transmissions from the Master Aetherius, the Master Jesus, Mars Sector 6, and other Highly Evolved Cosmic Intelligences'), Centre House, Subud, the Druid Order, Gurdjieff Society, Scientology, Bahai, etc.

5. Teaching, publishing and research groups—School of Economic Science, Krishnamurti Foundation, etc.

6. Meditation groups—TM, Students' International Meditation Society, etc.

7. Spiritualistic groups—College of Psychic Science, Spiritualist Association, etc.

8. Healing groups—Acacia House, Radionic Association, etc.

9. Yoga groups—Sivananda Yoga Centre, London School of Yoga, etc.

10. 'Your own Guru'. This section includes Astrological Association, and use of I Ching, Tarot, Kabalah, etc.

11. Flying Saucers.

12. Witchcraft.

13. English Mysticism.

The contemporary interest in mysticism, occultism and magic therefore presents a complex and confused field. As well as the new growths out of the youth culture, there are a variety of well-established groups and movements which have existed for many years, but have now been absorbed into the post-psychedelic scene. Running through the whole field is a search for direct experience of the supernatural, for techniques which will help to make such experience possible, and for the inner truths which lie behind ritual and dogma. 'It is the technique and condition of openness that the young pursue, sometimes wildly, as they slide from Western dogmatism towards Oriental theologies: the Bhagavad-Gita, sutras and mantras, the Tao, Zen texts. There is in all this a recurring sense of individual discipline and understanding, a weaving of the ideas of karma and reincarnation and detachment and enlightenment—ideas which have vanished from our own traditions in the rubble of dogma, censorship and schism.'[46] Yet this observation must raise the immediate comment that the search is not new. It is very important to consider the background of the current quest, not simply the immediate background of the youth drug culture, but that of earlier involvements with occultism and the esoteric.

EARLIER OCCULT MOVEMENTS

The foundation of the Theosophical Society in 1875 by H. P. Blavatsky released a new world of Eastern, occult and esoteric studies. With the emergence of the Golden Dawn in 1886 and the reorganization of the Brotherhood of Light in 1895, out of which grew the Ordo Templi Orientis, there developed a serious concern with occult magic. Aleister Crowley, who assumed control of the Ordo Templi Orientis, resurrected a Graeco-Egyptian ritual through which he claimed man could enter into full union with his Angel.[47] According to Crowley, 1904 was the crucial date for the revival of magic, for then 'an occult current of cosmic magnitude was initiated on the higher planes'.[48] The beginning of this occult current created the birth-pangs of a new aeon, and according to Crowley this new aeon would establish full Solar Consciousness in mankind. When this had happened, silence would replace speech, and men would possess direct intuitive understanding. But already some men were possessed by this consciousness, and in them the power of creation would be wielded by forces which at present were termed 'occult'. Central to Crowley's theory was the Kundalini or serpent power, the basis of sexual magic. Sex became a means to spiritual attainment, and the Gnostic liturgy incorporated a metaphysical orgasm.

The importance of Crowley in the magical revival has been well described by Kenneth Grant who studied under him and took over from him the Ordo Templi Orientis.[49] In Crowley one saw a number of important elements of the darker occult Gnosis: the use of sex to gain access to invisible worlds, of astronomical symbols within the magical process, of drugs and mantras to energize the 'subtle centres', of pagan rituals, in particular those associated with the Sumerian traditions of Shaitan. Crowley believed that Aizaz, the messenger of an extra-terrestrial Intelligence which in 1904 communicated to him *The Book of the Law*, did in fact represent forces who ruled the earth, and as the new consciousness developed, there would emerge a closer link with these forces. His followers stress that profound consciousness changes are imminent: 'We are on the threshold of profound and far-reaching change. The Aeon of Horus is the Aeon of Magick which *is* Change; but unlike all previous changes in the history of the race this change will be of cosmic magnitude and it will occur in conformity with will, or, alternatively it will terminate abruptly in chaos or disaster.'[50]

The occult rituals and Gnostic beliefs of Crowley are much closer to other occult movements than is often admitted. The view of Crowley as a 'black magic' practitioner, a position which he denounced on a number of occasions, has obscured the closeness of the link between this and other forms of secret doctrine and ritual magic.[51]

Other developments in the nineteenth century had encouraged interest in occult and psychic phenomena. The Fox sisters were experiencing 'spirit raps' in 1848, and there was a revival of spiritualism in the 1850s and '60s, though Margaret Fox in 1888 repudiated her earlier claims. Theosophy was a quite different movement, although H. P. Blavatsky had a strong spiritualist aim in founding the Theosophical Society.[52] Blavatsky claimed to teach a hidden wisdom, *theosophia*, which was the central core of all world religions. Underlying this wisdom religion was 'the secret doctrine' which gave the key to the universe.[53] She believed in Karma and in reincarnation, though Theosophy itself provided no clear doctrinal system. It was seen as 'the accumulated wisdom of the ages', the Gnosis. Later Annie Besant, Rudolf Steiner (who founded Anthroposophy), C. W. Leadbeater, and others developed particular aspects of Theosophical teaching. Besant discovered Krishnamurti in India and brought him to England as a world teacher, a role which he later rejected. So in the early years of this century, there was a clear revival of Gnostic and occult traditions, and the spiritual atmosphere in the period which followed the founding of the Theosophical Society was not unlike that which prevails today in the occult wing of the counter-culture.

In addition, there has been for many years an occult and highly bizarre 'underground church' in the form of some of the irregular episcopal sects known as *episcopi vagantes*. While many of these tiny groups hold more or less orthodox beliefs, a significant section of the movement has been, and still is, involved with Gnosticism, occultism and 'ancient mysteries'. Some of them are very close in ethos to Underground cults. Thus the late Bishop Jan Van Ryswick who hailed from Kensington used to issue *The Avatar Charter of Humanity*, while spiritualistic and occult teachings were propagated from various 'cathedrals' and churches in London, the south coast and elsewhere. The Liberal Catholic Church still combines Theosophical teachings with Catholic ritual, believing that 'neither the ceremonies of the Church nor those of Freemasonry can be understood without the aid of Theosophical teachings'.[54] The Eucharistic action is described in terms of the atmic, buddhic and causal levels of consciousness. One leading *episcopus vagans*, the late J. S. M. Ward, who ran the 'Orthodox Catholic Church', was also a leading international authority on Freemasonry (on which he wrote for the *Encyclopaedia Britannica*), and among his works are books on Freemasonry and on the psychic powers of Christ.[55] The phenomena associated with irregular episcopacy probably constitute the classic example of what happens when the Western Augustinian doctrine of orders degenerates into magic, and the Christian priest becomes isolated from the Church and associated, in some cases, with the possession of occult and magical powers.

While the *episcopi vagantes* have never attracted significant numbers of disciples, the similarity between some of these groups and the mystical ones of the post-psychedelic culture is so striking, that some of their characteristics are worth examining in more detail. The clearest example of a Gnostic episcopal sect in Britain is the Pre-Nicene Catholic Church, established in the 1950s by one Richard John Palatine, who was consecrated on 25 September 1953 as its presiding bishop.[56] This sect claimed that its apostolic succession was derived through eleven lines, encompassing a variety of Eastern as well as Roman Catholic, Old Catholic and Anglican antecedents, all of the lines being linked in the person of one *episcopus vagans*, the man who consecrated Palatine. Linked with the Church and inseparable from it are the Brotherhood of the Illuminati, the Ancient Mystical Order of Fratres Lucis, the Brotherhood of the Pleroma, and the Pre-Nicene Foundation, and all these constituent bodies were part of the Sovereign Imperium of the Mysteries, which was incorporated under the Mysore Societies Registration Act No. 3 of 1904 as well as in Sacramento, California.[57] This group issued *Lucis Magazine* and offered courses on 'the art of illumination'. Palatine was described in its literature as 'an illumined lecturer, writer and teacher' and as 'one of the truly illumined and spiritual exponents of occult philosophy and spiritual training in the world today'. [58] Through *Lucis Magazine*, it was claimed, 'we will co-ordinate the Masonic, Theosophical, Rosicrucian, Hermetic, Spiritualist, Alchemist, New Thought, Healing, Mysticism, Gnostic and Esoteric Christianity, the underlying truths in the present Christian Religion and their relationship to the Eternal Truths of God'.[59]

The story of the Brotherhood of the Illuminati and its links with earlier occultism has been told by Palatine in a booklet which, among other aims, claims 'to show the Reader how he or she may work with the forces of light to combat the spread of International Communism and kindred forces which seek to keep mankind in chains'.[60] In this booklet, he expresses a belief in cyclic manifestations of Gnosis, and describes the foundation of the mystery schools, the Gnostics and Manichees, the Knights Templar, and the creation of the Fratres Lucis in Florence in 1498. The Brotherhood of the Pleroma claims to incorporate the main elements of the Holy Grail, Templars, Rosy Cross, Alchemist, Hermetic, Masonic, Gnostic and Mystery Religions. The Order of the Illuminati had originally been formed in 1776 by Adam Weishaupt and was thoroughly Masonic. As the order grew, it influenced various Masonic and Rosicrucian groups in Europe. After a series of political complications, during which the Illuminati were banned in Bavaria, the Order was revived in 1880. At this time one John Yarker was the head of the Rites of Memphis and Mizraim in England, and he became head of the British section of the Illuminati. The Rites of Memphis and Mizraim had been set up in 1839 by a French Mason, but had never been officially recognized by the Grand Lodge of England. In 1902 the newly created Ordo Templi Orientis, later to

become notorious through the activity of Crowley, claimed to open
up all Masonic and Hermetic secrets through the teaching of sexual
magic. Crowley became a fifty-second Initiate of the Rites of Memphis and Mizraim.[61]

There is thus a direct link between the occult wing of Freemasonry, the magic of Crowley and the Gnosticism of the Illuminati. Yarker before his death in 1913 placed the Illuminati under
the protection of the Ancient and Universal Pan-Sophic Rite of
Freemasonry and transmitted authority over it to one Herbert
James Monzani-Heard, an *episcopus vagans* who died in 1947, and
in 1952 Palatine became the Archon of the Fratres Lucis with the
Brotherhood of the Illuminati as its outer section. In 1959 as a result
of confusion with another organization, the Royal Court and Order
of the Illuminati, Palatine's group changed its name to the Brotherhood of the Pleroma. The group also claimed affinity with the ancient
Fraternity of the Rosy Cross, though it repudiated modern Rosi-
crucianism.

The teaching of this group was occult and Gnostic. 'This system',
claimed one of its booklets, 'is nothing less than the revival of
Gnosticism and the Pre-Nicene Religion, adapted in all respects to
modern thought and scientific knowledge of the Western world.'[62]
The aim of the Brotherhood was to reveal the Christian Gnosis and
'to prepare receptive minds for the next manifestation of the
Christ among mankind'. There was also a belief that a 'new revelation' would be given soon, 'namely in 1975 when the Messenger
from the Communion of Saints will make himself known again to
mankind'.[63] One of the Sons of God, it was held, always appears at
the end of an age. In order to prepare for his coming, students of
the monthly monographs would be guided in the 'inner Illumination of the Soul' as well as 'an extensive knowledge of the Solar
System'.[64] It was taught too that we have entered the Aquarian
Age and that the Secret Brothers have appeared to re-educate mankind in the inner Truth or Gnosis.

There were a number of similar groups in the 1950s and 1960s
who propagated this type of Christian Gnosticism. The Age of
Aquarius was a favourite theme of another *episcopus vagans*, C.
Dennis Boltwood, who ran a college in Tottenham. He prophesied
that 'the Aquarian Age is the beginning of the Kingdom of Heaven
on Earth. The North Pole axis of our Earth-Planet is passing from
the coils of Draco at the rate of fifty million miles a year to the Con-

stellation of Cepheus, the symbolic figure of the Christ—enthroned with sceptre in his hand and crowned with the Ruling symbol of Righteousness.' He believed too that 'the whole cell structure of the human mind must prepare to receive accelerated vibrations', and he saw redemption in terms of planetary vibrations and influences.[65] Other sects combined Catholic ceremonial with spiritualism and beliefs in reincarnation. W. B. Crow (known in religion as His Holiness Mohoran Mar Basilius Abdullah III, Sovereign Prince Patriarch of Antioch), a former Theosophist who lectured in biology at Leicester, ran the Order of the Holy Wisdom, which he described as follows:[66]

> Being absolutely universal (that is truly Orthodox and Catholic), it has access to the divine wisdom of Theosophy embodied in the symbols of all nations. It utilizes the knowledge passed on in the great streams of sacred tradition, not excluding those of the so-called Primitive Religions, those of the Far East, the Brahmanic-Yogic, Ancient Egyptian, Zoroastrian-Magian, Kabalistic, Gnostic-Masonic, Gothic-Rosicrucian, Druidic-Bacchic, Chaldean, Buddhist-Lamaistic and Islamic-Sufic. The Order has for its special object the establishment and maintenance of a planetary and zodiacal temple of the Universal religion, the preparation and initiation of suitable candidates and the celebration of the ancient mysteries in their pristine form.

There were many similar religious sects hidden away in the side streets of various cities and towns in the 1950s, and the language and theology which they often expressed show close similarities to much in the current search among youth. But one man has been of outstanding importance in providing a weighty intellectual basis for the revival of Gnosticism: the late Swiss psychiatrist, C. G. Jung. Through his fascination with alchemy, Jung felt that he had stumbled upon the historical counterpart of his own psychology of the unconscious, and he came to believe that there was an intellectual chain which ran back to early Gnosticism.[67] In his *Modern Man in Search of a Soul*, Jung wrote of '. . . the widespread interest in all sorts of psychic phenomena as manifested in the growth of spiritualism, astrology, theosophy and so forth. . . . We can compare it only to the flowering of Gnostic thought in the first and second centuries after Christ. The spiritual currents of the present have, in fact, a deep affinity with Gnosticism.'[68]

He went on—in 1933!—to speak of Gnostic churches, Theosophy and Anthroposophy (which he called 'pure Gnosticism in a Hindu dress') and of Kundalini Yoga. Later he wrote an important commentary on *The Tibetan Book of the Dead*, and papers on Yoga, Zen, the *I Ching*, and on the myths and symbols of Christianity. It is probably true to say that Jung's writings contain in germ most of the material of the present occult revival.[69]

What has appeared in our day is clearly a new Gnosticism. Historically Gnostic movements have been characterized by three features. First, a stress on the acquisition of secret knowledge, *gnosis*, which is hidden from all but a group of initiates, and through possession of which salvation comes. The acquisition of knowledge about the human soul—Origen speaks of 'certain secret principles' by which the soul enters the body[70]—and the use of mathematical and numerological concepts were characteristic elements. Secondly, a division of the world into the Illuminati, the initiates, those who are 'in the know', and the common herd, the rest of mankind. Thirdly, a location of the origin of evil in the material creation, so that salvation involves deliverance from the tyranny of matter. Indeed, the *gnosis* is not so much knowledge of God as knowledge about the structure of the higher world. To acquire knowledge is the essential fact of life.[71] 'He who knows is a being from above.'[72] Through such knowledge the Gnostic comes to self-knowledge.

> And once we have mentioned self-knowledge, we can go on to say that this is the chief gnosis of all. The Gnostic is a Gnostic be-cause he knows, by revelation, who his true self is. Other religions are in varying measure God-centred. The Gnostic is self-centred. He is concerned with mythological details about the origin of the universe and of mankind, but only because they express and illuminate his understanding of himself.[73]

One sees all these characteristics, to a greater or less degree, in contemporary occult movements—behind them all is a concern for self-knowledge, for exploring 'inner space', and for attaining to a new consciousness. Yet only a minority of young people within the counter-culture have in fact taken an occult or mystical path. For many more, the pressing need is to evolve a new style of community, an alternative society which will express the new consciousness. It is to this society that we shall now turn.

6
New Consciousness
New Community

The accusation that Western society has outlawed the Spirit is by no means peculiar to the counter-culture. For years such criticism has been commonplace in the tradition of poets, literary critics, psychologists, and others. The venerable Cambridge literary guru F. R. Leavis, for example, wrote,[1] 'My own recourse to the word "spiritual" (and all important words are dangerous) is determined by the contemplation of a world in which the technologico-Benthamite ethos has triumphed at the expense of the human spirit —that is, of human life.' C. G. Jung spoke in similar vein in many of his writings. The Western world, he claimed, had lost its symbolic life. D. H. Lawrence too was complaining of the destruction of human values: 'For the truth is, we are perishing for lack of fulfilment of our greater needs, we are cut off from the great sources of our inward nourishment and renewal, sources which flow eternally in the universe. Vitally, the human race is dying. It is like a great uprooted tree, with its roots in the air. We must plant ourselves again in the universe.'[2] In the 1920s Kafka was describing the necessity and the frustration of revolt, and the permanence of guilt,[3] and existentialist writers from Dostoevsky to Sartre portrayed the human situation in tragic prose. T. S. Eliot wrote of 'the waste land', the world of 'hollow men', of decay and dereliction, while in the '50s Colin Wilson told of a 'world without values',[4] and his figure of 'the Outsider' seemed to symbolize the age.

But today it is young people too who are seeing our society as an anti-spiritual force. Caroline Coon, who founded Release, has described the Underground as a new style of self-conception. The need for individuals to achieve self-awareness was, in her view, the basic fact underlying the philosophy of the Underground, and this

philosophy was the direct result of the repressions felt in a materialistic society. The hippy is 'a product of a society whose moral
spirit is lower and more disillusioned than it has been for a long
time'. Against this disillusionment the Underground aimed to
create a group with a mode of living which was a conscientiously
cultivated work of art. Central to its life-style was an emphasis on
'play' and on the intensifying of the present moment, on 'dropping
out' of the occupational structure, on music and art, and on non-
violence.[5] In the search for alternative life-styles, San Francisco
and Berkeley are still seen as pioneering areas. Underground writers
in Britain will talk of visits to Berkeley in such terms as 'an incredible experience', for they find there 'a will to make into reality the
vision that we all share of a better world, a better way of life that has
no comparison anywhere in England'.[6] Berkeley is a frontier city
with a sense of community and of ongoing struggle towards a new
order. It was in Berkeley that students insisted on their right to
organize in support of the Negro Civil Rights struggle, and this
insistence provoked a student rebellion. This support for the Civil
Rights movement brought American students effectively into
politics, and opposition to the Vietnam War intensified their
opposition to the establishment. There was a cultural conflict, a war
of old and new generations. But it was not so much a conflict
between young and old as between those who wanted to preserve
the present order and those who wanted to change it.

It has been against this background of growing protest that the
concepts of *subculture* and *counter-culture* have become widely
known and used in recent years. Both terms, as we saw above, were
originally used in the field of criminology. 'Subculture' was probably used first by Milton Gordon to mean 'a sub-division of a
national culture composed of a combination of factorable social
situations such as class status, ethnic background, regional and rural
or urban residence, and religious affiliation, but forming in their
combination a functioning unity which has an integrated impact on
the participating individual.'[7] A good number of years later, J. M.
Yinger introduced the notion of *contraculture* to mean 'a series of
inverse or counter values' in a situation of conflict. A contraculture
exists, he claimed 'wherever the normative system of a group
contains, as a primary element, a theme of conflict with the values
of the total society, where personality variables are directly involved
in the development and maintenance of the group's values, and

wherever its norms can be understood only by reference to the relationships of the group to a surrounding dominant culture'.[8] By the end of the 1960s the ideas of subculture and counter-culture were no longer restricted to criminology. They stood for a significant trend among whole sections of the youth population of the West. So Roszak in 1968 wrote:[9] 'It strikes me as obvious beyond dispute that the interests of our college-age and adolescent young in the psychology of alienation, oriental mysticism, psychedelic drugs, and communitarian experiments comprise a cultural constellation that radically diverges from values and assumptions that have been in the mainstream of our society at least since the Scientific Revolution of the seventeenth century.'

Roszak has described a continuum of thought and experience which links the sociology of C. Wright Mills, the Freudian Marxism of Marcuse, the Gestalt-therapy anarchism of Paul Goodman, the body mysticism of Norman Brown, the Zen psychotherapy of Alan Watts, and the chemical theology of Leary. As one moves along the continuum, he claims, sociology gives way to psychology, politics to the person, rationality to irrationality.[10] We have seen in earlier chapters that there has been a clear movement among some sections of youth from psychedelic drug experience to involvement with oriental mysticism and with magic. But it would be wildly incorrect to see the process of growth of the counter-culture in terms of an ever-deepening esoteric spirituality. On the contrary, what has been most striking has been the search for new styles of community, and, while there has certainly been an 'escapist' element, and a strong sense of disaffiliation from the majority culture, the dominant trend has not been towards pietism but towards a new style of politics. 'The Alternative Society' became an ideal, and as the apparatus of art, music, and a press was built up, the name 'Underground' became a widely accepted, if always confusing, label for the community sense which had appeared. By 1967 there was a British Underground, and a number of key events heralded its arrival.

One of these was an international congress in July 1967 on the 'Dialectics of Liberation'. It took place at the Roundhouse in Chalk Farm, London, and gathered together all the well-known gurus— R. D. Laing, Paul Goodman, Herbert Marcuse, Stokeley Carmichael, Allen Ginsberg, among others. The purpose of the congress was to demystify human violence and violent social systems, and to explore new forms of action towards liberation. What in fact

developed was a commitment to support of anti-colonialist violence
in the Third World, aided by the thought of Marcuse and Fanon,
while the smaller group of artists and poets pursued more philosophical questions of consciousness, alienation, ecology, contemplation and personal freedom. The Dialectics of Liberation was
a major turning-point in the emergence of alternative life-styles in
Britain. Most of the formative influences on the counter-culture
were present, and most of the ideas which were later to be developed
were also present, at least in germ. The Congress did not aim to
solve any world problems but to initiate a process of thought and
dialogue. The threat of world destruction was central. Stokeley
Carmichael talked of the destruction of humanity by racism,
Gerassi of destruction by imperialistic greed, Gregory Bateson and
Lucien Goldmann of the erosion of man's ecological context,
Marcuse of destruction by repression of natural instinct, and
Laing and Cooper of destruction by illusion and mystification.[11]
All the speakers linked social and political with personal, psychic
liberation: 'the common cause was undeniably there; the same
insistence on revolutionary change that must at last embrace psyche
and society'.[12] The Underground with its search for identity was
coming to see itself as integrally linked with the Third World and
its search for freedom.

How had the 'Underground' come to be? What were its characteristics? A glossary issued in 1969 simply defined it as 'a mental
atmosphere among those who "kick against the pricks" of the
Established structure of society'.[13] Another writer in the same
journal complained that it was 'a sloppy word . . . meaningless,
ambiguous, irrelevant, wildly imprecise, undefinitive, derivative,
uncopyrighted, uncontrollable, and used up'.[14] Richard Neville
wrote that the label 'embraces hippies, beats, mystics, madmen,
freaks, yippies, crazies, crackpots, communards, and anyone who
rejects rigid political ideology . . . and believes that once you have
blown your own mind, the Bastille will blow up itself'.[15] Neville,
however, saw the Vietnam War as the 'One Great Youth Unifier'. In
fact, the origins of the Underground culture go back well beyond the
hippy explosion and the LSD summer to the early 1960s. The word
'Underground' seems to have been used first in New York around
1964 in connection with journals which circulated through totally
different channels to the straight press, and whose concern with sex
and religion made them unacceptable at 'ground level'. Rebel

literature had been issued by such publishers as City Lights and New Directions in America in the late '50s, and it was this same period which produced *Evergreen Review*, the literary medium for much of the beat philosophy. But by the middle '60s the sheer amount of literary material had vastly increased, and this was particularly marked in New York.[16]

Ed Sanders' Peace Eye Bookstore and his Fug Press became the centre for distributing poetry and writing which had previously been unpublishable. Sexual shock tactics were employed both in the titles of Sanders' publications and in the gimmicks used by Peace Eye—which included the sale of collected pubic hairs from New York literary personalities, and a jar of cold cream used by Ginsberg and Orlovski as a lubricant before intercourse, and duly signed on the container! Sanders also was the leader of The Fugs, a rock-folk group, and their performances were decorated with anti-bomb slogans and drawings of Egyptian gods making love. Tuli Kupferberg, another member of The Fugs, launched Birth Press which handled material concerned with sex, drugs and poetry. Out of this period too Andy Warhol burst upon the pop art and film scene with films of orgies as well as of people's facial expressions. But New York was not the only centre of the new style of protest material. From Athens, Dan Richter's bookshop became the focal point of a Mediterranean scene, and there was a good deal of activity in Paris, in Tangiers, and in Germany, while the Provos in Amsterdam hit the public eye in 1966. In England too in the declining days of CND, the Peace Café in Fulham Road was an important centre of beat poetry and activity, and literary figures such as Dave Cunliffe, Lee Harwood, Ian Vine, Spike Hawkins, Miles, and Mike Horowitz were gathering groups around them. Alex Trocchi had arrived in England in 1963 and had collaborated with William Burroughs. Better Books opened a paperback shop in Charing Cross Road, and in 1965 Ginsberg visited London.

All this ferment was, of course, pre-hippy, pre-acid, pre-1967. It was only after the Haight-Ashbury events and the developments of 1967 that the international Underground really exploded. Tom McGrath who launched *International Times* in 1967 wrote one of the most valuable accounts of the new movement to appear at this time.[17] It was, he said, an inner-directed movement, a new way of looking at things, a new consciousness. 'The revolution has taken place WITHIN THE MINDS of the young.' He identified a number

E

of characteristics of the new way: permissiveness and freedom
for pleasure where no harm is done to others; a post-political and
anti-political posture ('this is not a movement of protest but of
celebration', claimed McGrath); a spontaneity ('this new thing is
just people coming together and grooving'); and a happy optimistic
view of man. 'This is a post-existential movement, bringing an end
to years of tough and painful despair. . . . The weapons are love and
creativity—wild new clothes, fashions, strange new music sounds.'
The new movement was slowly creating an Alternative Society
which was international, inter-racial and equisexual. New words
were introduced into the vocabulary, so that by 1972 the new
edition of *Chambers' Twentieth Century Dictionary* included defini-
tions of acid, Black Power, drop out, Flower People, freak, groovy,
head, hippy, psychedelic, trip, and turn on.

'I do believe', wrote Richard Neville in 1971,[18] 'an alternative
society is emerging in the West, based on an alternative morality'.
Ranged against the new society was the 'greyworld: the world of
Straights, of the boxed-in mind, the boxed-in soul, society, glitter,
and false values, factories and smog, the businessworld, bureaucrats,
uncivil servants, repressions, wars, silent screams and suicides'.[19]
The real division which was emerging was over the fundamental
morality of the present social order. Drugs were an important
element in the growth of the counter-culture, but they are not, and
never were, the dominant feature. The use of psychedelics indicates
where people are at, it does not put them there. But what has
happened can be described as a rejection by large numbers of the
young of the dominant myths of Western society. 'Because of their
historical location at the end of a myth, that is, at the end of a
cultural era, they perceive the rewards of the going social order as
unrewarding—as overripe'.[20] So the psychedelic generation represents the onset of a new historical phase, characterized by an apolitical attitude, by a rejection of conventional economic objectives,
and by a post-industrial life-style. Yet the movement is not for the
most part escapist in the sense that it is not concerned with society
at all: it simply rejects both the methods and the underlying values
of the old order which, it believes, is passing.

There were some representatives of the older generation who
welcomed the emerging Underground in Britain. Geoffrey Ashe,
for example, saw it as 'the voice of a new kind of revolution'.
'For many years I've longed to witness at least the beginning of a

free, creative, counter-society, self-generated from the depths in a spirit of love; a clean break, a fresh start. Until lately, hardly anyone else seemed to want it. You do.'[21] He believed that in the Underground we were seeing the beginning of a spiritual Great Leap Forward, and he hoped for the creation of a network by which 'senior citizens' (over 30s!) could be closely linked with developments. In the same year, the American criminologist Lewis Yablonsky described the hippy society in the United States:[22]

> Hippie culture is a para-society in the sense that it exists primarily beneath the surface of American society. It is not clearly either a sociological subculture or a contraculture. Yet in certain respects it is both. A sociological subculture loosely translated comprises remnants of the larger society organised in a microcosmic fashion. A contraculture is one generally opposed to the larger society. In the pure hippie world, neither of these conditions is true. Hippie society attempts to be tuned in to a resonant unit, a deeper reality, or a cosmic consciousness of Man that is the pure framework for all societies.

The intellectual influences which have dominated the thinking of the counter-culture have not, for the most part, themselves been youthful. It has been claimed that 'the counterculture is in fact the creation of middle-aged adults who project it into the young, because, like Professor Reich, they believe the young are the new messianic people who will bring salvation to the world'.[23] One writer has referred to four new 'gospels'—Laing's *The Divided Self*, Levi-Strauss's *The Savage Mind*, Konrad Lorenz's *On Aggression*, and McLuhan's *Understanding Media*[24]—the uncritical acceptance of which has resulted in a general onslaught on reason.[25] Laing, it is claimed, questions the world's sanity rather than our own. Levi-Strauss believes in other people's gods, not our own. Lorenz offers a gloomy vision of a murderous instinct, while McLuhan shows us a world run by machines which change us. But there are other sources of inspiration, including those who took part in the Dialectics of Liberation Congress: David Cooper, Gregory Bateson, Jules Henry, John Gerassi, Paul Sweezy, Paul Goodman, Lucien Goldmann, Stokeley Carmichael, Herbert Marcuse. In addition to these, Frantz Fanon, Che Guevara, Allen Ginsberg, Timothy Leary, and William Burroughs cannot be ignored. Roszak's study, in fact, in spite of its title, is really an account of some of these

intellectual influences upon the Underground complex of thought
and action, and he includes, as well as those mentioned above,
such writers as Norman Mailer, the Cohn-Bendits, Norman Brown
and Alan Watts.

Ronald Laing is without doubt one of the giants of the counter-
culture and of the New Left. Through his books *The Divided Self*,
The Self and Others, and particularly *The Politics of Experience
and the Bird of Paradise*, a new model of schizophrenia has become
fashionable. In Laing's view, schizophrenia is merely a label
placed upon certain individuals by the agents of the dominant
culture and its power structure. What is seen and defined as mental
illness should properly be seen as the expression of an alienated
social order. Although recently Laing has come under heavy attack
from a number of quarters,[26] there is no doubt that his thinking
has influenced the search of many young people. From being a
psychiatrist with a new approach to schizophrenia, Laing has come
to be seen as a prophet with a new vision of consciousness. In relation
to psychiatric history, Laing represents the climax of one line of
thought about the psychoses, an approach which starts from the
view that schizophrenia is a result of family disturbances, and that
the 'mad' talk has in fact a sense about it which has to be discovered.
Schizophrenic behaviour in reality is a strategy invented by the
individual which enables him to survive in an unliveable situation.[27]
To understand his behaviour one has to study not simply the individual but the social system.[28] But there has been another approach
rejected by Laing and by increasing numbers of the youth anti-
psychiatry movements, which has seen schizophrenia and other
'illnesses' in metabolic-genetic terms. The search to establish a
chemical basis for psychosis goes back many years: in the 1950s,
for example, Osmond and Smythies suggested that a metabolic
disorder led to the production of a chemical substance in abnormally
large quantities in the body of a schizophrenic. In 1962 Friedhof
and Van Winkle in New York found an unusual substance in the
urine of a number of schizophrenics, generally known as the 'pink
spot', and suggested that the substance was chemically related to
mescaline. Laing's position turns such an approach on its head, and
in so doing places a major question-mark over conventional Western
assumptions. For he turns attention away from the physical and
biochemical changes to the inner experience.

Laing's importance clearly does not rest simply on the fact that he offered a new approach to the interpretation of psychosis. His questioning of the labelling processes and the stereotypes used in psychiatry have very serious implications for social and political action. 'There is no such "condition" as schizophrenia', writes Laing, 'but the label is a social fact and the social fact a *political event*.'[29] Thus the authority of the psychiatrist and of the medical-social machine which he represents is eroded. Mental illness assumes a political colour. The patient becomes a victim of social control, psychiatry the technique of such control. Negotiation with the patient is called, in the control jargon, psychotherapy, pacifying the patient is achieved by tranquillizers, while ever more humane and effective means of destruction—electric shocks and psycho-surgery —are being developed. It is all an 'amazing political operation'.

> Many patients in their innocence continue to flock for help to psychiatrists who honestly feel that they are giving people what they ask for: relief from suffering. This is but one example of the diametric irrationality of much of our social scene. The *exact* opposite is achieved to what is intended. Doctors in all ages have made fortunes by killing their patients by means of their cures. The difference in psychiatry is that it is the death of the soul.[30]

Laing attacked 'institutionalized organised violence', and his attack was taken up by many within the counter-culture as a prophetic insight into the relationship between the search for political liberation and that for psychic liberation.

In the development of Laing's thought one can see two movements, one towards political commitment, one towards the exploration of transcendental experience. In this he symbolizes the development of the Underground itself. The political orientation was clear in his 1965 preface to *The Divided Self*: 'The statesmen of the world who boast and threaten that they have Doomsday weapons are far more dangerous, and far more estranged from "reality" than many of the people on whom the label "psychotic" is affixed.'[31] But in 1970 Laing withdrew this preface, and seems to have rejected the role of political activist. Since then it has been the mystical path which has attracted him, and it is this aspect which dominates *The Politics of Experience and the Bird of Paradise*, in which he talks of exploring 'the origin or source of our experience' and of the experience of God. In this book too he sees the role of physicians and priests in terms of guiding men from this world to another world.[32] Now his critique of our society becomes openly and aggressively theological. 'The outer divorced from any illumination from the inner is in a state of darkness. We are in an age of darkness.'[33] He speaks of this age as one of famine of the Spirit and of the words of the Lord, and of a rebirth in which the ego serves the Divine.[34] As his mystical involvement increased, leading him to a Buddhist monastery in Ceylon, his popularity with the radical Left declined. Peter Sedgwick compared him to a 1930s Leftist who went to a Catholic monastery in Franco's Spain during the Civil War, and judged his withdrawal a betrayal.[35]

In the case of Herbert Marcuse, it is classical Marxists who see him as a betrayer of the cause, while the Underground has hailed him as a prophet. Like Laing, Marcuse has been concerned with liberation in a wide context, with psycho-sexual as well as social and political freedom, with 'liberation involving the mind and the body, liberation involving entire human existence'.[36] Liberation involves organic, instinctual, biological changes at the same time as political changes. Marcuse calls for the emergence of a form of reality which is the work and medium of a new sensibility in man, for a view of 'society as a work of art'. He sees sensitivity and sensibility, creative imagination and play as forces of transformation. In his paper of 1967 at the Dialectics of Liberation Congress, Marcuse spoke of the hippies as a 'serious phenomenon' which indicated 'the appearance of new instinctual needs and values', the unity of sexual, moral and political rebellion, the rejection of Puritan values, and the refusal to play the political game. He developed these ideas in *An Essay on Liberation*, published in 1969, in which he claimed that the hippy culture represented a potential agent of change. Earlier, in *One-Dimensional Man* he had drawn attention to the 'Make Love, Not War' buttons worn in anti-Vietnam war protests, and had seen behind this a conjunction of erotic and political dimensions. In his concern for sexual liberation as well as his insistence on political change, Marcuse has become one of the central figures in the new youth culture. Marxist writers, however, have viewed him with mistrust, and have criticized his hippy Marxism as an infantile disease.[37]

THE UNDERGROUND PRESS

One of the most powerful instruments in the shaping of new life-styles has been the 'Underground Press'. In 1969, one of the founders of *Oz* warned, 'Right round the Global Village, these tribal message sticks have become fire-brands; incendiaries of newsprint that have fired the foundations of the current structure and will presently raze it to the ground'.[38] Like the conventional media, the alternative papers provide materials for creating and maintaining a culture. As a large-scale social movement, the Underground Press owes its origins to the West Coast psychedelic culture, to the Free Speech movement at Berkeley, and to the events which followed them. *Berkeley Barb* is still today the best known of all Underground papers, and, like its British imitators, it focussed originally for the most part around psychedelic drugs and sexual liberation. 'Getting high' and 'getting laid' became the two major areas of confrontation, and symbolize the life-style of the new culture. American papers were frequently being charged with obscenity, and printers were warned off handling them. It was at this stage that the Underground began to be more politically conscious, but it was in France and Germany, not America, that students first set about political activity. However, the activity of the Underground Press made the 1968 Democratic Convention more sensational than it would otherwise have been. Since then, Underground papers have spread from colleges to schools all over the United States. In 1969 the *New York Herald Tribune* reported:[39] 'Underground newspapers which have spread from the colleges to the high schools and junior high schools are considered an important part of the protest movement. Three months ago, government officials estimated that there were 500 such papers being published in secondary schools.' From 1967 there has been an effective international liaison through the Underground Press Syndicate (UPS), set up by John Wilcock, who also founded three important papers, *Village Voice*, *East Village Other* and *Other Scenes*.

The early Underground papers were relatively dull in layout, but they were transformed by the spread of LSD. Papers then tended to utilize kaleidoscopes of colour, extraordinary designs and combinations, and in fact tried to become a 'visual trip'. *Oz*, for instance, was *experienced* rather than read! The *San Francisco Oracle* was the pioneer of this psychedelic format, and its issues of 1967–8 initiated a revolution in newsprint, with very violent and shattering uses of colour, of 'sculptured' type, and of three-dimensional pages. If cannabis was important as a symbol of unity within the counter-culture, LSD was far more important as a basis for the development of the Underground media.[40] The 'love-ins' and the 'be-ins', indeed the whole background of young California after the 1966 explosion, formed the context for the Underground Press. By 1970 there were probably around two thousand Underground papers throughout the world. Among the best known were *Avatar*, *Berkeley Barb*, *IT*, *Distant Drummer*, *Other Scenes*, *The Rag*, *Seed*, *Rat* and *Oz*. It was estimated that over a million Americans were reading Underground papers each week, while a European estimate was two hundred thousand. Editors were talking of expanding the medium of print. 'Why does a paper have to be in columns?' asked the editor of *The Word* in New Orleans. 'Must it be one colour? Why not scent it? Or print it on rubber? Or make it edible?'[41]

From the start there was a strong political element in many of the American papers. *The Ungarbled Word* in New Orleans, with a circulation of fifteen thousand in 1968, was attacking segregation and local corruption. But the two most successful and most outrageous papers on the West Coast, *Berkeley Barb* and *Los Angeles Free Press*, devoted a great deal of their space to ads, to cartoons, to articles on drugs and sex, and to local news. The original American paper was *Village Voice*, founded in 1955 in New York. John Wilcock, who worked for the *Voice* in its early years, started *East Village Other* in 1965, and *Other Scenes* came later. One of the aims of Wilcock's Underground Press Syndicate was 'to warn the Civilized World of its impending collapse and to consciously lay the foundations of the 21st Century'. Richard Neville too sees disruption as a central function of the Underground Press. 'Their editorial policies . . . seek an overthrow of society as we know it.'[42] But the actual approach differs very markedly from one paper to another. The Dutch Underground paper *Provo*, published in Amsterdam in 1965, proclaimed that it opposed capitalism, communism, fascism, bureaucracy, militarism, snobbism, professionalism, dogmatism, and authoritarianism. *Suck*, the original sex protest paper, was produced first in 1969 as an alternative to 'the kind of mind which could create obscenity laws'. In the main Underground papers, favourite themes have been drugs, pop music, Vietnam, Black Power and new political movements, police brutality, student protests, cinemas and theatre, and the search for new ideology and new life-styles.[43]

By the time of the first English Underground Press Convention at Manchester in June 1970, the principal papers here were *IT*,

Oz, Rolling Stone, Friends (later *Frendz*), and *Black Dwarf*. Later *Ink* appeared but did not survive. *IT* was originally *International Times*, and the first issue appeared in the autumn of 1966. Early in 1967, *Oz* appeared under Richard Neville's guidance. Prior to this, *Private Eye*, very much a pre-Underground journal but one which subsequently acquired a wide following with Underground Press clientele, had started in the early '60s. *Peace News*, the long-established pacifist paper, also acquired a readership which overlapped considerably with the Underground, and it acted as some sort of a bridge between the old and new Leftist groups. But the British Underground Press has differed from the American, as indeed the whole political and social structure is different in the two countries. Roger Lewis has pointed out that 'an alternative life-style in England does not entail any serious commitment'.[44] Only in Northern Ireland, for the most part, are people killed for their beliefs, and the daily pressures which exist in American society do not generally occur in Britain. Nevertheless, a genuine and influential Underground Press does exist here, and the number of journals of minority opinion is constantly increasing. Until recently, *Frendz* has probably been the most successful and valuable of the national papers. Its pages would include articles on politics, strikes, law enforcement, pollution and children's rights, as well as rock music and the internal concerns of the Alternative Society. At the time of writing, both *Oz* and *Frendz* have collapsed, and it is not yet clear if either will rise again.

Small Underground papers from the provinces appear and disappear frequently. Examples during 1972 included *Cope* from Belfast, *RAP* from Rochdale, *Pigeon* from the schools of Slough, *Fang* from Beverley, and *Playgue* from Barnsley. Others are constantly appearing. Cambridge seems to have produced more alternative papers in recent years than almost any other city outside London: papers such as *Cambridge Voice*, *GoodNews* and *The Other Britain*. Out of the Manchester scene in 1971 came *Manchester Free Press*, which, as well as publicizing information and welfare services, has campaigned for better housing and for tenants' rights, while *Mole Express*, also from Manchester, described itself as a 'liberated news-magazine and a vehicle for agitation and revolution, not an underground druggie sheet'. In Brighton, the Harvester Press has started to reprint radical/alternative papers on microfilm, and it has been suggested that the Underground Press Syndicate should take over such microfilming themselves. From Bottisham in

Cambridgeshire, Whole Earth Tools, an independent publishing house, has produced directories on communes, ceremonies and community radio. In addition, alternative papers have appeared on the political and religious wings and among sexual liberation movements. Thus *Workers' Press* from the Socialist Labour League and *Socialist Worker* from the International Socialists present a Marxist/Trotskyist view of the world, while newer anarchist papers such as *Black Flag* have joined the older ones like *Freedom* and *Anarchy*. Religious papers have included *Catonsville Roadrunner* and *Gandalf's Garden*, while women's movements have produced *Shrew* and *Socialist Woman*, and the gay scene has *Come Together*, *Gay News* and others.

ALTERNATIVE WELFARE

Another integral part of the counter-culture has been the setting up of switchboards and free advice services. Many of those in America are simply called switchboards, while others are connected to 'free clinics' and 'free churches'—Berkeley Free Church, Los Angeles Free Clinic, Haight-Ashbury Free Clinic, and so on. There are also a very large number of 'drop-in' centres, many of them attached to churches, and these may also operate telephone services. One of the oldest switchboards, the San Francisco Switchboard, deals not only with emergencies but also with requests for other facilities and agencies, jobs, housing problems, transport, buying and selling, messages, donations to other bodies, and a vast range of services. A 'Survival Resource List', issued in 1970 in San Francisco, gave information about suicide prevention, senior citizens' facilities, draft, post-prison problems, child care and maternity, homosexual groups, medical-psychiatric aids, urban aid, night-time crises, street car and coach routes, housing, legal and social welfare problems, meals and food, youth, coffee houses, drugs and alcoholism, family services, and art and education. All this information, mainly consisting of addresses and phone numbers, was compressed, along with a city map, into an eight-page folder. In Britain too the Underground Press is a major source of information about welfare facilities and other resource points. Release, which began in 1967 as a group involved with helping young people with drug arrests, soon became the main welfare agency for the British Underground. It operated originally from a small flat in Notting Hill Gate, and offered a 24-hour emergency phone service. In 1968, the first year in which statistics were collected, 603 cases were recorded, of which 61 per cent involved cannabis. By 1970 the total had risen to 3,846, and some 74 new cases were being dealt with each week. By this time too, Release was not merely dealing with drugs offences but with abortion and contraception, medical and psychiatric problems, immigration and passport, landlord and tenant, divorce and runaway children, and crisis accommodation.[45] The young people in the Underground became very welfare-conscious, but the new groups which were beginning to emerge were used and trusted more than the well-established 'straight' social work bodies.

At the same time as Release began, BIT Information Service was becoming not only the central information point for the London area but also the prototype for other centres elsewhere. Through its occasional journal *Bitman* and its newsletters, BIT circulates material about activities and facilities throughout Britain. There has been a good deal of overlap, as well as some rivalry, between Release and BIT. BIT grew out of *International Times*, and its initials stand for Binary Information Transfer, the smallest unit of information which can be fed into a computer. By 1971 BIT was receiving two hundred phone calls and ten or twelve personal visits each day. About a quarter of calls are for accommodation, and another quarter for jobs. But BIT has also acted as a distribution centre for information about the state of the Underground culture in Britain as a whole. Through *Bitman* and other literature, a constant supply of names and addresses of BIT-like facilities is disseminated far and wide. From the same address, the European office of the Underground Press Syndicate produces *Magic Ink Express*, a duplicated newsletter. In 1972 BIT was also broadcasting Alternative London News on BBC Radio London, though their newsletter predicted that 'BBC are bound to try to suppress it sooner or later', and by the time this appears, it may well have died. BIT itself has run into serious financial difficulties. In an attempt to aid similar projects and avoid yet more bankruptcies, the Alternative Society Ideas Pool was set up in 1973. The idea behind this is that before money is given to any new project, the following questions might be asked about it:

1. Is the scheme likely to be put into action and will the money be used to do this?

2. Will it help change or revolutionize British society in some way?

3. Will it help people fight their oppressions?

4. Will it help people expand their consciousness?

5. Will it help people communicate with one another?

6. Will it help people to improve their environment?

7. Will it help build up Alternative Society structures anywhere in Britain?

8. Is something like it already happening, or does it represent a new and inspired direction?

These questions certainly give some indication of the values and philosophy of the Alternative Society in Britain.

Since BIT's foundation, a very large number of welfare, legal and advisory groups on the BIT model have appeared. Advise, the first welfare and legal service for black communities, was set up in 1970, and aimed to provide a 24-hour service, including a free legal service for blacks in London, education of black people about their rights, creation of pressure groups on local and central government, and investigation of social and domestic conditions. From East London came EAST, based in East Ham, while White Light, offering legal and social advice, crash-pads, and help with jobs, opened in North London. In West London, the Gentle Ghost provided transport and help over repairs among other services. Nightline and Nutshell grew up in Birmingham, Search in Blackpool, BIT by BIT in Brighton, Response in Canterbury, Mother Grumble in Durham, Nexus in Glasgow, Beautiful Stranger in Rochdale, and so on. The handbook *Alternative London* had been preceded by a less ambitious booklet *Project London Free* which aimed to be a guide to alternative facilities. Later came information sections in the Underground papers as well as journals such as *Movement*, which appeared in January 1973, a politically-directed information source-paper. The dissemination of sheer information is now a large-scale operation in the counter-culture. BIT itself has 'consistently resented the Londonization of the Alternative Press',[46] and has encouraged the growth of papers and centres throughout the country.

Often it is bookshops and restaurants which form the centres for information. In London, Better Books in Charing Cross Road and

Indica Bookshop in Southampton Row played important roles in the early days of the Underground. The Freedom (anarchist) Bookshop, which has moved from Fulham to Whitechapel, had long served the anarchist movement, and now draws a wider audience, while Agitprop, formerly in Bethnal Green, Rising Free which succeeded it, and Centerprise in Hackney have strong political involvement. Watkins's shop in Cecil Court (off Charing Cross Road) has for many years been a major source for books on mysticism and the occult, but is now increasingly used by young people in search of spirituality. In Cambridge, the Cokaygne Bookshop stocks 'apocalyptic and millennial literature' as well as alternative papers from the United States and Britain. Also in Cambridge the Arjuna Restaurant is a cooperative vegetarian venture, the workers living in a commune outside the city where organic farming methods are used. In Liverpool, a 125-year-old Congregational church in Great George's was taken over as a 'community playground for the contemporary arts . . . working towards a quiet revolution'. Great George's has a working nucleus of about 25 artists, and has Third World and Underground films, poetry readings, puppet theatres, carnivals, workshops, work with heroin addicts and with old-age pensioners. In Manchester a complex range of groups and agencies has sprung up—newspapers such as *Mole Express* and *Manchester Free Press*, a BIT-type agency, MAGIC, a radical printing press, Moss Side Press, as well as active groups for gypsy rights, black unity, women's liberation, and others.[47] Elsewhere too the disenchanted young have moved towards experiments in community action and the building up of neighbourhood community projects.[48]

A good example of the kind of community project which has grown up was the creation in 1972 in Edinburgh of ELF (Edinburgh Liberation Front), set up to establish a true counter-culture in Edinburgh. Its manifesto began:

Your culture is everything you have—the way you live, the way you work, the way you act towards other people. It is everything you learn while you are growing and you are growing all the time. What is important, then, is for you to decide if your culture is what you want it to be.

Hate, waste, violence, loneliness, boredom, greed—this is the culture of modern Britain: the counter-culture must be characterized by love, meaningful systems of production, mutual aid, enjoyment, an interest in other people. The counter culture must stress

> people—not property
> —not things
> —not politics
> —not psychiatry
> —not Gross National Product

> life—not death
> —not violence
> —not pollution
> —nothing else

Life is all there is.

ELF stressed the uniqueness of each person and his need to develop freely, the need for job satisfaction, proper homes, for a new culture, and for an end to the destruction of the earth. 'We must have a revolution which will be a festival in which the dangerous madness of the old death culture will be cured by the laughter of the new.' With this in view ELF supported squatting movements, cooperative shops, art and theatre, and community action.[49]

NEW LIBERATION MOVEMENTS

At the heart of the Underground's concern for liberation has been the growth of campaigns for the rights of minorities. The three areas of struggle which have attracted most attention have been those for homosexuals' and women's liberation, and for justice for black people. In the United States, the 'gay power' movement, represented at the political level by the Gay Liberation Front, developed earlier than in Britain. Papers such as *Lavender Vision*, *Come Out*, *The Free Particle*, *Gay Power*, *The Effeminist* and *Gay Sunshine* have put the gay case in a very forthright way. In Britain the Albany Trust had grown out of the Homosexual Law Reform Society and had developed from being a largely reformist and educational group into one which by 1967 was more and more involved with casework and counselling. Later new organizations, such as Access and Reach, grew up to develop the counselling side, but the militant wing of the gay movement did not become apparent until the establishment of the Gay Liberation Front.

The first public demonstration by homosexuals in Britain took place on 25 November 1970 as a result of the conviction of a young man at Highbury Fields in London for 'gross indecency'. One hundred and fifty supporters of 'gay power' met at Highbury and read out a list of demands, a list which represents an important stage in the history of action by sexual minorities. The demands were:

1. That all discrimination against gay people, male and female, by the law, by employers, and by society at large, should end.

2. That all people who feel attracted to a member of their own sex be taught that such feelings are perfectly normal.

3. That sex education in schools stop being exclusively hetero-sexual.

4. That psychiatrists stop treating homosexuality as though it were a problem or sickness, thereby giving gay people sense-less guilt complexes.

5. That gay people be as legally free to contact other gay people, through newspaper ads, on the streets, and by any other means they may want, as are heterosexuals, and that police harassment should cease right now.

6. That employers should no longer be allowed to discriminate against anyone on account of their sexual preferences.

7. That the age of consent for gay males be reduced to the same as for straights.

8. That gay people be free to hold hands and kiss in public as are heterosexuals.

From its beginnings Gay Lib has grown at a rapid rate, and now publishes its own paper *Come Together*. It has women's groups, youth groups, and a street theatre. The women's group, which was formed in 1972, complained of 'sexism' within the movement, and began to work with Women's Lib 'to provide for all sisters a viable alternative to the exploitative "straight" gay ghetto scene into which we have been pushed by society'.[50]

Gay Lib has spread in a couple of years from London into the provinces. Edinburgh, South London, Durham and Birmingham were among the early branches. Warwick University started a branch in 1972, and Bath and Bristol merged in the same year. By 1973 there were over forty branches throughout the country, though London has remained the focal point of militant activity. At the beginning of the Autumn Term 1970, Gay Lib in London attacked the offices of *Sennet*, the London University newspaper, in protest against its 'sexist' attitude. It has continued to criticize the hetero-sexual bias of sex education material. Thus Camden Gay Lib attacked Dr Martin Cole's widely publicized film *Growing Up* on the grounds that it was a 'sexist film' which portrayed a 'most reactionary characterization of male and female roles' and reinforced false ideas about homosexuals.[51] Psychiatrists too have come under heavy fire, and at the end of 1970 a Counter-Psychiatry group developed in Gay Lib with the object of countering the false assump-tions made about homosexuality by psychiatrists. The purpose of psychiatric treatment of gay people, it has been claimed by members of this group, is 'to reinforce and normalize male-competitive capitalist power by making dissent look sick'.

> What demands explanation is not homosexuality but the fact that while GLF holds dances, dishes out *Come Together* and Manifestos, and campaigns for the sexual liberation of everybody, psychiatrists in the same town can continue to talk to their students and colleagues—and be believed—of perversions, neuroses, impulse disorders, character defects, socially damaging behaviour and the need for self-control, as if homosexuality is something perpetuated by maniacs somewhere else.[52]

Increasingly the movement for Gay Liberation has become insep-arable from the wider political struggles for the Underground, and part of a revolutionary movement.

This is true also of the feminist struggle. In 1969 a conference of the Underground Press Syndicate at Ann Arbor, Michigan, agreed on the following policies:[53]

1. That male supremacy and chauvinism be eliminated from the contents of the Underground papers. For example, papers should stop accepting commercial advertising that uses women's bodies to sell records and other products, and advertisements for sex, since the use of sex as a commodity specially oppresses women in this country. Also women's

bodies should not be exploited in the papers for the purposes of increasing circulation.

2. That papers make a particular effort to publish material on women's oppression and liberation with the entire contents of the paper.

3. That women have a full role in all the functions of the staffs of Underground papers.

In spite of this, a great deal of anti-female and pornographic material continues to circulate in the Underground press (though whether it is as bad as that in the Press as a whole is open to question). The *Playboy* mentality, in which women are playmates, bunny girls, toys, is too deeply rooted. Women are sex objects, their naked bodies are prized as sources of masturbatory fantasy as well as for their commercial value. It is against this exploitation of woman, not only by the media but throughout the social and political structures, that Women's Lib has directed its weapons.

The Women's Liberation movement has provided an attack on pornography and the obscene which is far more effective, and probably far more balanced in its perspective, than that of the Festival of Light. It has more far-reaching consequences, and is therefore feared far more than the Festival of Light's critique which fails to go beyond its narrow concept of the pornographic to the basis of oppression and injustice in society. Thus Women's Lib condemns the highly respectable *Playboy* culture for its stereotype and its commercializing of the body, and its substitution of fetishism for true appreciation.[54] Stickers announcing 'THIS EXPLOITS WOMEN' have appeared on the commercial hoardings. Miss World and similar contests have been condemned. What lies behind these attacks is more than a rejection of the passive role of women. It is a fundamental attack on the degrading of sexuality so that it becomes mere mechanics, or, in Germaine Greer's phrase, 'masturbation in the vagina'. In *The Female Eunuch*, Germaine Greer attacks 'the desexualization of the whole body, the substitution of genitality for sexuality'.[55] 'The permissive society has done much to neutralize sexual drives by containing them. Sex for many has become a sorry business, a mechanical release involving neither discovery nor triumph, stressing human isolation more dishearteningly than ever before.'[56] To view the sexual liberation movements as mere pretext for licence, as do many Christians, is totally to misunderstand the nature of their protest.

Women's Lib is concerned with more than emancipation. It is concerned with socialist revolution.[57] It rejects the limitations imposed by marriage and conventional family patterns. It opposes male-dominated politics, and is therefore only interested in 'demands' (such as free contraception) as short-term measures. One cannot 'demand' a revolutionary society from the state! The consciousness that radical feminism is moving towards some sort of libertarian viewpoint has meant that traditional Marxist analyses of exploitation have been found inadequate, and so, while the movement is certainly socialist-orientated, what is emerging is something quite different from the pattern of the old Left.

The liberation movements which have grown up within the counter-culture have tended to view sexism and racism as inseparable elements within an unjust society. So alongside the gay and female movements there has developed the struggle for Black Power. In the United States, the Black Power movement began as a search for identity, for black consciousness. Black people, argued Stokeley Carmichael, needed to redefine themselves, to create new and positive images.[58] So more and more black Americans began to call each other 'soul brother' and to relate their history to that of Africa. They began to develop a new sense of community which could resist the racism of American society and reject the values of middle-class America. They called for black consolidation. They saw themselves as part of a new force, the Third World: 'we see our struggle as closely related to liberation struggles around the world', said Carmichael in 1967.[59] The Black Power movement has had a strong appeal to young black students in the university campuses of America, and in 1967 the appearance of *Black Panther* was 'a turning point in the history of the black movement and also of the Underground press'.[60] *Black Panther* became a 'Black Community News Service', and by 1970 it had a circulation of 125,000.

Closely linked with Black Power was the growth of the Black Muslim movement.[61] In their philosophy, the black men were seen as descended from the 'original man' and therefore were seen as the hope of the world. The glorifying of blackness went hand in hand with the belief in the 'white devil' and in the demonic character of whiteness. But the Black Muslims' influence has not been at all

comparable to that of Black Power as developed by Malcolm X and
Stokeley Carmichael, even though the two movements were related.
Black Power has emphasized pride in being black, the African roots
of black Americans, and the need for self-determination. Black men
must develop a mythology, a history, a social and political organization, a culture and an ethos.[62] In Britain, it was only after Stokeley
Carmichael's visit to the Dialectics of Liberation Congress of 1967
that Black Power began to get a foothold. Obi Egbuna has written
that in 1966 the nearest to a Black Power body in Britain was
Michael Abdul Malik's Racial Adjustment Action Society (RAAS)
which was more a Black Muslim group.[63] There was in fact little
understanding, and considerable suspicion, of the Black Power
philosophy, which was viewed as 'violent' and 'black racist'. However, a few days after Carmichael had spoken at the Round House,
the Universal Coloured People's Association, meeting in Notting
Hill, adopted the Black Power ideology. Not long after, the Black
Panther Party was established in Britain with its monthly journal
Black Power Speaks.

Today in London there are a large number of black groups,
mainly in West and North London: the Black Workers' League
in Notting Hill, the Black Panthers, Advise, Black Liberation Front,
Black Workers' Co-ordinating Committee, Black Unity and Freedom
Party, Black People's Progressive Party, and so on. There are
newspapers such as *Black Liberator*, *Black Outcry*, *Black Voice*
and *Grass Roots*. The white Underground has come increasingly
to see the oppression of black people as a facet of the same unjust
society against which its own ammunition is directed. And as
Marcuse has inspired the student protest movements, so the writings
of Frantz Fanon have provided a theology for black revolution.[64]
In Fanon's thought, rooted in the bitter experience of the Algerian
revolution, the violence of the oppressed becomes the means of
salvation. Violence liberates, purifies and heals. Martin Luther King
called Fanon's *The Wretched of the Earth* the Bible of the Black
Power followers who had lost faith in the philosophy and method
of non-violence.[65] Certainly Fanon offers more than a political
strategy: he is concerned with the need to 'shake off the heavy
darkness in which we were plunged' and with the proclamation
that 'the new day . . . is already at hand'.[66] He urges his readers to
'try to create the whole man'. 'It is a question of the Third World
starting a new history of Man . . . we must turn over a new leaf,

we must work out new concepts and try to set afoot a new man.'[67]
It is this spirit which fires not only Black Power militants but many
others, black and white, within the counter-culture.

NEW COMMUNITY

From its beginnings the Underground has emphasized the idea of
community, and the quest for alternative life-styles has been a
fundamental feature of its growth. The movement into communes
has been the particular facet of this quest which has attracted most
publicity, although individual communes have mostly escaped the
notice of the media. The idea of the commune goes back beyond
the hippy culture. Joseph Ledger had set up a vegetarian society,
Ahimsa,[68] and a journal *Ahimsa Progress* appeared in 1964, followed
in 1965 by *Ahimsa Communities*, the organ of the breakaway Vegan
Communities of Tony Kelly. In August 1966 the Sarvodaya
Communities Newsletter appeared. Meanwhile, in November
1965, the Selene Community, the first actual commune, was formed;
however, not until August 1968 did the Commune Movement,
with its journal *Communes*, evolve from Selene. A little earlier, in
1967, the British Diggers had emerged under the leadership of Sid
Rawle, and soon there were a number of Digger groups, the Hyde
Park Diggers being the largest one, with an inner group, the Tribe
of the Sun. Later the London Street Commune, a beat solidarity
group centred on Piccadilly Circus, made national news through
occupying various premises in Central London.[69] Other Digger
groups appeared—the Hapt Diggers in 1967, the Coventry Diggers
in 1968—but the main group has now moved to an island off the
west coast of Ireland.

   The Commune Movement in Britain is strong and growing, as is
the literature on making communes.[70] The aim of the movement
has been expressed as a wish 'to create a federal society of communities wherein everyone shall be free to do whatever he wishes
provided only that he does not transgress the freedom of another'.
Many communes in their revulsion from technology have moved in
a rural direction. Some have a religious basis, while others are more
'therapeutic' in orientation, and many are inspired by social and
political action. The Kingsway Community grew out of Christian
ideals, and its members have mainly been addicts of various drugs.
The Blackheath Commune too was Christian-based but more politically involved. The Findhorn Trust in Moray, Scotland, certainly

the largest commune in Britain, has existed since 1962 and has a spiritual orientation, 'towards the Western occult tradition', though individuals in it may be drawn towards Christian, Buddhist or Vedantic Hindu ways of thinking.[71]

The appearance of the commune movement, it has been suggested, is one answer to the common accusation that the counter-culture has emphasized liberation, expansion of consciousness and aesthetics, but neglected the creation of new institutions.[72] Their 'revolutionary' potential lies in their example, in their refusal to wait for a future revolution.[73] But there are certainly some problematic areas. It has been argued that the average life of a religious community is fifty years but that of a secular one, five years, and this has been attributed to the systems of discipline and control in the religious groups.[74] In the secular communes in particular, the question of sexual relationships has been a thorny area, as indeed it was in the nineteenth-century Oneida Community, a Christian group which practised 'complex marriage'. Some of the religious, as well as the secular, communes are exploring ideas of 'group marriage', but the majority of them appear to follow the 'extended family' idea. Rejection of the nuclear family is almost universal: it is seen as leading to isolation and separateness, rather than to outgoing love and care.[75] Yet sexual exploitation remains, as do difficulties about privacy and property.

In the United States, the movement into communes has been most marked in the post-hippy development of California. As a general rule, the communes there are strongly opposed to publicity. They know only too well that the course of the psychedelic movement in America was largely determined by the public image of the hippy, an image created by the media. So the communes avoid drawing attention to themselves. They know that if they do so, Middle America will declare war on them, and large numbers of 'straight' young people will attempt to climb on to the commune bandwaggon. However, the media did discover them and declared 1969 'the year of the commune'.[76] In fact, the type of commune which began to increase most rapidly in both urban and rural areas was the 'crash-pad' type. Unlike other kinds of commune, the crash-pad type has been devoid of any real goals, discipline or philosophy, and the health and drugs problems are more than normally severe. They are the most unstable type of commune and the most dangerous.[77] Throughout the commune movement as a whole, the

non
drug
communes

incidence of drug use is extremely low, and, indeed, the communes
in California are among the most successful non-drug treatment
modalities. One of the leading authorities on the communes in
North California has suggested that the total consumption of psycho-
active chemicals in the communes is substantially less than the
average American norm.[78]

In addition to the communes, there are now a large number of
alternative styles of community. In the United States, the Synanon
movement was an early growth out of, and response to, the drug
scene. Synanon was founded in 1958 as an educational process,
a 'counter-epidemic force' within an increasingly disordered society.
The Synanon structure is like a large family, with strict disciplines
and an emphasis on group work, including the 'Synanon game' which
has been called a verbal street fight, and on the re-creation of
community.[79] Out of Synanon grew Phoenix, a therapeutic community using encounter group and confrontation methods in the
cure of narcotic addiction. In Britain, the Philadelphia Association
developed from the work on schizophrenia by Laing, Cooper and
Esterson; similarly, Kingsley Hall, an experimental community
for schizophrenics, grew up in East London in 1965. In Nottingham,
the Craft Centre in St Ann's district became well known to a wide
audience through an ITV film *A Completely Different Way of Life*.
By 1973 we read that 'the life within the centre now revolves around
the spiritual'.[80] A different but very important element in the alternative community movement has been the growth of Non-Violent
Action Groups such as that in Manchester (MANVAG), groups
which have derived inspiration and support from the Quaker and
non-violent direct action traditions.

The experiments in cooperative living have been many and varied.
The Free Universe Cooperative, created in 1971 in Brighton, was
concerned with achieving cut prices for food and organizing food
distribution. Each Saturday members of the cooperative would pay
a sum of money with their orders for the following week. During
the week a group of volunteers collated the orders, bought the food
from a fruit and vegetable market or 'cash and carry' store, and later
separated it into individual orders. Prices were calculated to match
wholesale prices as closely as possible. Similar ideas have been used
in Nirvana Market in Nottingham, and in St George's Hill and
CMPP Food Cooperatives in North London.

In 1972 in London a group called Community Music was set

up as an attempt to introduce the cooperative idea into pop music. The group stated its underlying beliefs as follows:

(1) that societies based on materialistic values destroy man's/woman's sensitivity, creativity and individual uniqueness.

(2) that most societies today whether they be capitalistic/state capitalistic or socialistic are to varying degrees materialistic/exploitative in nature.

(3) that revolution is unfortunately not the answer to a change in 'human values'.

(4) that our only hope in changing our societies is to set up structures that will in theory and practice create values and relationships that are based on mutual respect, compassion and love.[81]

This statement is an important and impressive example of the kind of values and beliefs which are helping to shape the search for an alternative society and which are motivating projects of various kinds.

The search for alternative forms of community has included alternative schools. There has been a revival of interest in those schools which already exist as alternatives—Froebel School in Roehampton, the Rudolf Steiner schools, St Christopher School in Letchworth, the Krishnamurti School near Alresford—but there have also been new developments, including the setting up of 'free schools'. In the United States, the New Nation Seed Fund was set up to support free schools. In Britain, the Scotland Road Free School was opened in Liverpool in 1971 as a school which would be totally involved in its environment and would be 'in the vanguard of social change in the area'. The idea of a free school is to cause the state system to fragment into smaller, all-age, personalized, democratic and locally controlled community schools. In 1970 an offshoot of the Californian Malcolm X Montessori School opened in Notting Hill, and a free school was opened in Islington in London in 1972.

As well as these kinds of experiments, we ought to include the spread of encounter groups, sensitivity or T-groups, and other forms of group work which emphasize closeness and physical intimacy. The T-group training phenomenon began in a small way in America in the 1940s and is now a major industry. It is based on the belief that human relationships can be improved by assembling groups of people who will talk freely about their relationships with each other. The T-group (training group) was first used in the context of training programmes, but in the 1960s there was a deepening of interest in personal growth and fulfilment rather than simple improvement in relationship skills. So out of T-groups grew encounter groups which emphasized non-verbal communication—touching, gestures, mimes, and so on. The encounter group aim is to enable the individual to experience his true self, to affirm his identity, to 'do his own thing'. So popular have these groups become that ready-made encounter group tapes are now available as well as a large number of books and therapeutic games.[82]

Finally, a factor of tremendous importance in the whole area of alternative communities has been the search for alternatives to the conventional systems of psychiatry and penology. Thus People Not Psychiatry (PNP) is not an organization but simply 'a scattered commune of friends', the idea being to encourage reliance on human contact and friendship rather than on psychiatric medicine. In the field of penal policy, Radical Alternatives to Prison (RAP) has attacked the prison system and recommended alternatives.[83]

A WHOLE EARTH

A growth in the counter-culture which has run parallel to some extent with trends throughout society has been the concern about the environment, and it is this which has been one of the strongest forces driving the young back towards political involvement. The ecological concern of the Underground is one which it shares with many 'straight' thinkers. An entire issue of *The Ecologist* early in 1972 attracted wide publicity and heated argument.[84] It argued that the resources of the planet were being squandered by a minority of its population, and that the commitment to 'growth' as the overriding goal had now placed the future of civilization in peril. Also in 1972 came the study by Professor Dennis Meadows and his colleagues, *Limits to Growth*, which presented a computer model of the world, designed by the Massachusetts Institute of Technology. On this model, the world system was judged to be faced with imminent collapse through excess pollution, exhaustion of mineral resources, or population growth.

The prophets of environmental doom are concerned with more than pollution of air and water, or with the accumulation of solid waste. They draw attention to the need to reduce population growth,

to divert resources and technology from wasteful use in rich countries to the needs of the Third World, to limit the expansion of
armaments, and so forth. But the central concern of ecology has
been with the dangers resulting from interference with the functioning of natural biological systems. Man, by his interference with
natural communities, is diminishing the capacity of the environment
for control of pests, for cycling of essential plant nutrients such as
nitrogen, phosphorus, and sulphur. This interference is moreover
occurring at a time when population growth is resulting in a rise in
material consumption, and therefore in more demands for the very
services which are being disrupted. Thus there is a good deal of
evidence that sewage and fertilizers are eliminating numbers of
ocean fish and making fresh waters less able to assimilate waste.
Concentrations of DDT in food have helped to reduce the population of certain fish-eating birds. In addition, there is a wide range
of chemical substances, such as the chlorinated hydrocarbon pesti-
cides, to which human beings are increasingly exposed. At present
over nine hundred species of wild life are in danger of extinction.
There is concern too about the effects of high concentration of lead
in the environment on hyperactivity, and therefore indirectly on
social violence. Although the ecologists have been criticized as
'false prophets of calamity',[85] there is no doubt that they have stirred
up a strong and growing sense of care about the earth and about
the distribution of resources and wealth within it.

Ecology as a theme hit the Underground Press in 1970 as 'a
magic new word, all about survival techniques and wilderness and
building communes and all that kind of stuff'.[86] Since then there
has been literature about alternative technologies, and on the use of
edible wild plants for food, thus avoiding the synthetic food system
to some degree.[87] New journals have appeared such as *Seed*, the
Journal of Organic Living.[88] The writers of *Seed* believe that 'correct
eating not only nourishes the body but actually helps raise the
consciousness level'. Conditioned eating of synthetics, on the other
hand, ties men closer to the machines which already dominate so
much of human life. Individuals have run their own private campaigns: thus one man has been issuing recipes for home-made soap
as an alternative to synthetic detergents. One finds throughout the
whole ecological movement among the young a strong sense of the
need for small-scale action as well as large-scale international change.
So counter-culture ecology is as much concerned with the building

and use of compost heaps as with theorizing about the world as a whole. It is involved with local demonstrations such as those by the Wimbledon Ecology Group in local supermarkets in 1972. There has been concern about such questions as artificial lighting or the dangers of neuro-toxins. Some writers, among them Michael Allaby of the Soil Association, have seen the ecological struggle as part of a wider movement for the reintegration of urban and rural and for the revival of the old crafts.[89] Other writers have stressed the links between ecology and mysticism, and have claimed that 'growing ecological awareness is almost sure to reinstate Mother Earth worship and the cultivation of symbolic protective entities such as friendly demons, dakinis and fairies'.[90]

The Friends of the Earth, which came into being in 1970, has provided a focal point of pressure on issues ranging from plastic packaging to the protection of wild life. Its director is a geologist, and most of its staff are postgraduates. During 1972 it was operating an 'Endangered Species Campaign', attacking the imports of whale products, and of tiger and leopard skins. Its campaign against non-returnable bottles helped to produce a Government inquiry on packaging. In 1972 a Friends of the Earth bookshop and coffee house opened in Islington, and this has provided a valuable centre for literature, posters, and so on. In 1972 also Friends of the Earth issued a *Whale Campaign Manual* as a guide to action 'for the millions of people who feel strongly about the over-exploitation of whales' and as a paper for Government consideration.

In many ways the ecological movement has brought together the mystical and political elements in the counter-culture. Running parallel with ecology in the strict sense has been the growth of 'pure food' and 'organic living' interests. London now contains grain shops, macrobiotic restaurants, and whole food centres with names like Ceres, Wheat, Pasture, Manna, and Cyrano. *The Organic Food Finder and Directory*[91] lists retailers and producers throughout Britain, as well as health food shops. Other more politically-orientated campaigners have viewed the ecological struggle as merely one aspect of the struggle against capitalism.

TOWARDS A POLITICAL UNDERGROUND

It should be clear from previous chapters that if one can speak of a mystical fringe of the Underground, one can also speak of a political fringe, and that both trends have intensified in recent years. There is no doubt that the thinking of the New Left groups and other young Leftist movements of the early 1960s helped to prepare the way for later youth radical developments. But they have been left far behind, although there is a lot of continuity with pre-Underground, Marxist and anarchist groups. Today's political perspectives on the youth counter-culture are peddled in a bewildering number of small magazines and newspapers which are extremely critical of some of the other trends which we have described. Thus *King Mob* was complaining around 1969:[92]

> It is no good pretending that the class war is over while you set up your commune in the woods, scour the markets for free food, smoke pot in the newly liberated cellars of your occupied zones. The working class is still there and there it remains until the class revolution liberates it and gives it control of the material environment. As long as it remains, the rebel youth, the hippies, the long-haired squatters are mere parasites, dependent on the slave labour of the working class to fabricate the commodities which these charming rabble rousers of the streets may steal or smash, use as gifts or toys.

Another English paper *Sub 70* wrote in 1971:[93]

> The pigs have got it all wrong: instead of busting people for shit, they should haul in all known revolutionaries and compel them to understand and undergo a course of shit and acid. There would be no better way of emasculation of the left and turning us all into hippy consumer slaves who present no credible alternative to the System because they have been integrated and absorbed by the capitalists.

There was a certain degree of hostility towards the drug culture and the hippies from the radical Left in Britain as early as the 1967 'summer of love'. Even before that summer, *Peace News* printed a front-page article by a Berkeley artist, 'The case against the drug culture'.[94] To him the whole LSD/marijuana world was escapism, 'the latest opium of the people in a more literal and potentially more dangerous sense than anything envisaged by Karl Marx'.

> It seems to me damnably unjust for some people to be flying around on psychedelic trips, while other people are down below,

stuck in dehumanizing kinds of employment, stuck in dehumanizing cities, being killed in wars. What is needed is not more
people blasted out of their minds. There are more than enough
people out of their minds already. What is needed is more people
in their minds, in their right minds. It is not really liberating,
not really humanizing, to have people hallucinating that everything
is beautiful. Everything is not beautiful.[95]

Peace News itself was equally concerned about the freak-out philosophy, and saw it as a loss of faith in the value of the psyche unaided
by drugs. Nor was the paper very impressed with the hippy use of
the concept of love: love called for *action* in the world, not vague
inner feelings. 'Dropping out' was equally suspect, and showed a
contemptuous and negative lack of faith in ordinary human beings
and 'a puerile evasion of the real problems which face us today'.[96]

Certainly one of the most fierce attacks on drug use within the
counter-culture came from Eldridge Cleaver of the Black Panther
Party.[97] Cleaver was contemptuous of Timothy Leary's assumed
role of 'a sort of secular God around which the universe is constructed, around which the revolutionary movement inside of the
United States revolves'. Freedom to Leary, claims Cleaver, simply
means 'getting high'. In contrast to this, the revolution needs sober
people with clear heads. The use of drugs, therefore, is a 'counter-
revolutionary activity'. Certainly the drug culture has played a
progressive role in the United States by attacking the values of
capitalist society, but that epoch is now past. As for Leary, he is a
dead god.

But to all those who look to Dr. Leary for inspiration or even
leadership, we want to say that your god is dead because his
mind has been blown by acid. And we say that if you think that
by tuning in, turning on and dropping out, you're improving the
situation, that you're changing society, it's very clear that you're
doing nothing except destroying your own brain, and strengthening the hands of our enemy. Because I think that in this day and
time when the enemy no longer needs our labour power, when the
enemy has machines to replace men, that they would very much
like to have everybody walking around with their mind blown
away by acid, so that they could continue to run their game down
on a mass of robots.[98]

The monster of American imperialism will not be destroyed by 'the whole silly psychedelic drug culture quasi-political movement' of Jerry Rubins and Abbie Hoffmans, but only by 'sober, stone cold revolutionaries, motivated by revolutionary love'. The drug culture, Cleaver argues, is part and parcel of the death culture.

In Britain, the conventional Leftist movements have been largely baffled by the counter-culture, suspicious of Women's Lib, indifferent to ecology, and naive over Black Power. The Communist Party is very much in decline among the young, and carries no weight with the Underground. Committed to 'the parliamentary road to socialism', the Party is not respected by the New Left. Its paper *Morning Star* probably sells less today than when it was the *Daily Worker*. The Trotskyist groups, however, are an important element in the political wing of the Underground. They include the Socialist Labour League who publish *Workers' Press*, the International Marxist Group, popularized by *Red Mole* (now *Red Star*) and by Tariq Ali, and International Socialism, whose journal of the same name is perhaps the best source for weighty, theoretical Marxist analysis. The anarchist and syndicalist groups continue to exercise some influence, but they have not had a very marked effect on the new youth movements. A more important growth which has drawn support from the counter-culture has been the Claimants' Unions, the first of which was formed in 1968. There are now over a hundred such groups throughout Britain: their aim is to press for the right to an adequate income for all people without means test, for a free welfare state with no secrets and the right to full information, and no distinction between deserving and undeserving.

It seems clear then that the counter-culture is now sharply divided into the mystical-orientated and the political and revolutionary wings. These two trends are moving further apart, although between them is a vast and confused area where ecology, macrobiotics, herbalism and the non-violent action tradition are found in an uneasy relationship. Dave Widgery, a prominent Underground journalist writing in 1972, emphasized that even in the early days of the movement 'the search was as much inward for revelation as outwards into politics. The colliding move towards both mysticism and socialism was an obsessional theme of the early Underground and was clearly juxtaposed in the 1967 Dialectics of Liberation Conference'.[99] Since then, there has been a strong shift of sections of the Underground press towards a more revolutionary stance. But is it *really* revolutionary? Is MacIntyre correct in saying that 'the sensibility of bohemia effectively cuts it off from the vast mass of mankind on whom the bohemians are in economic fact parasitic'?[100] Or are the Underground and the working classes moving closer together in a common struggle? It is on the answer to this question that the political future of the Underground depends.

7
Jesus Revolution

TURNING ON TO JESUS

In June 1971, *Time* published its famous article on the Jesus Revolution.[1] Jesus was at large again, it announced. In 1966 John Lennon had claimed that The Beatles were more popular than Jesus, but now The Beatles were shattered, and George Harrison was singing 'My Sweet Lord'. There was a resurgence of Christian belief, but the new Jesus scene was in marked contrast to most recent American theology. 'The Jesus revolution rejects not only the material values of conventional America but the prevailing wisdom of American theology. . . . The Jesus revolution, in short, is one that denies the virtues of the Secular City and heaps scorn on the message that God was ever dead.'[2] The *Time* article was merely the public revelation of a movement which had been gaining ground for some time, and has now become known internationally as the 'Jesus Movement'. Edward Plowman, the movement's principal historian, has seen 1967 as 'the year of the vanguard of today's swarming underground Church'.[3] It was in that year that storefront coffee houses were springing up in American cities, and ex-drug users were speaking of better 'highs' on Jesus. It was in 1967 too that Arthur Blessitt, the 'Minister of Sunset Strip', preached at a love-in in Los Angeles. By 1969 the *Hollywood Free Paper* and *Right On!* had appeared, and a Christian Underground press was born. Soon Jesus People were a familiar sight throughout the United States.

So the Jesus Revolution hit America. Slogans such as 'Turn on to Jesus' and 'Smile, God loves you' became known to millions through the medium of 'Jesus Stickers'. Coffee bars like The Way Word in Greenwich Village, The Catacombs in Seattle, and I Am in Spokane began to appear. 'Jesus Rock' music began to be popular, as did the 'One Way' sign—a clenched fist with one finger pointing upwards.

Some Jesus people would answer the telephone with 'Jesus loves you'. Many others wore Jesus shirts announcing 'Jesus is my Lord' and even Jesus wristwatches. The Jesus cheer—'Give me a J, give me an E' and so on—caught on too. At Fifth Avenue Presbyterian Church in New York in 1971, a child was baptized 'in the Name of the Father, the Holy Ghost and Jesus Christ Superstar'. Songs like 'Amazing Grace', 'Put Your Hand in the Hand' and 'My Sweet Lord' reached the charts. Well-known singers and musicians— Johnny Cash, Eric Clapton, Paul Stookey (of Peter, Paul and Mary), Jeremy Spencer (of Fleetwood Mac)—allied themselves with the Jesus people. Pat Boone, star of the 1950s pop scene, started to baptize in his swimming pool. In the summer of 1970, a young Baptist student working in Berkeley, California, noted that 'Jesus Freaks, or Jesus People, are found in growing numbers in Berkeley' and that many of them were formerly street drug users.[4]

In Britain it was almost certainly the arrival of Arthur Blessitt, a thirty-year-old Baptist minister from Los Angeles, in the summer of 1971 which brought the Jesus movement to the notice of the public. Blessitt had become famous for his work in Sunset Strip, Los Angeles, and for his use of the language of the drug experience in proclaiming the Gospel. His centre, His Place, in Los Angeles became a kind of church-cum-night club, and his 'toilet services', where former drug users flushed their pills down the lavatory, attracted a good deal of publicity. Blessitt also started to distribute gospel tracts outside the pornographic bookshops and even invaded the shops and inserted tracts between the pages of magazines. It was largely due to him that the Jesus cheer spread among many young Christians, and it was from him that the Jesus stickers arose. His arrival in Britain, however, coincided with, and profoundly affected, the growth of the Festival of Light, initially an anti-pornography movement. Arthur Blessitt became the high spot of the Festival's rally in Trafalgar Square in September 1971 at which a number of people made decisions for Christ or came forward for counselling. It has been argued that Blessitt and the Jesus people have radically changed the emphasis of the Festival in an evangelistic direction.[5] Certainly his arrival initiated a British-style Jesus movement which, while it has been more conventional and 'establishment' than its American counterpart, has exercised a strong influence, particularly within the evangelical wing of the institutional churches.

Jesus was becoming popular at about the same time for other

reasons. The coming of *Jesus Christ Superstar* and *Godspell* are often seen as part of the Jesus movement, though many Jesus people would be strongly critical of both of them. When *Jesus Christ Superstar*, opened in London in 1972, Jesus people demonstrated outside the theatre with slogans 'This is not *our* Jesus'.[6] In fact Andrew Lloyd-Webber and Tim Rice could not have been inspired by the post-hippy Jesus scene, for the origins of their work antedate these developments. Nor is their Jesus either the Son of God or a revolutionary but a Superstar. Neither show is based on the belief that Jesus is God and Lord, and so Jesus people who believe in the revelation of the Scriptures are unlikely to be very impressed by them. What they have done, however, is to restore the subject matter of Christianity to the popular discussions of young and old. Their contribution to the Jesus movement is therefore indirect but it is a real one. The influence of the *Godspell* songs has been considerable. But it would be absolutely wrong to see the Jesus movement as a vague and non-theological devotion to a human Jesus. Nothing could be further from the truth. In general, the doctrinal picture presented by the Jesus people is conservative, Biblically-based, evangelical and charismatic.

A good picture of the beliefs of typical Jesus people may be obtained from Ruben Ortega's collection of tapes of interviews in California.[7] What emerges from this study is a strong sense of mission—one young man described the purpose of the Jesus movement to be 'to get as many people right with God before they go to hell'—and a literal belief in Scripture and in dogma. Those interviewed had no sympathy with vagueness or with the view that all religions were equal. Only in Christ was salvation to be found. Of all those interviewed, 85–95 per cent were associated with Pentecostalism, and there was a firm belief in the gifts of the Holy Spirit, with most people (but not all) having spoken in tongues. There was a general opposition to pre-marital sex, although some disagreed, and there was a good deal of division over contraception. There was disagreement also over whether Christians should 'drop out' although the lack of interest in political activism was striking. Some saw the Civil Rights movement as a spiritual movement, while one young person believed that 'civil rights, like Women's Lib, comes from sin'.[8] Attitudes to women and to Women's Lib were fairly uniform: women were to be subservient, weaker vessels, and Women's Lib was described as 'sin', 'a manifestation of Satan', and 'a tragic

F

thing'.[9] There was division over rock music, even Christian rock, but uniform hostility to drugs and to homosexuality. Belief in Satan and in demons was universal, as was belief in prophecy and in the return of Christ.

Such beliefs are not very different from those of many evangelical Christians of an older type. What is different is the background of many of the American young people who have come through the drug and occult scenes, so that within the movement there is a strong emphasis on deliverance from these alien forces. Larry Norman's song 'Forget your hexagram'[10] tells young people to 'stop looking at the stars . . . don't mess with gypsies . . . and don't you listen to the dead'. Groups like Symphony of Souls, a community of about a dozen young Americans, came to Jesus after periods of LSD, occult sciences and colour therapy.[11] It is worth looking in more detail at some of the characteristics of the life-style which they now share.

First, the Jesus people believe in the return of Christ to judge the world. They may proclaim that the end of the world is imminent, that 'Jesus is coming soon', and that his millenial reign will be established on earth. Some will see pollution prophesied in Isaiah. 'We just love to see smog, because it's a sign of the pestilence which will cover the face of the earth before the Second Coming', said one young American disciple. The return of Christ is at hand, and people mention dates between two and forty years hence. The Jesus movement itself is seen as anticipating the return of Christ, and the movement will last until he comes. The most widely quoted text in this connection is from Joel 2.28–9 as cited in Acts 2.17 ff: 'And in the last days it shall be, God declares, that I will pour out my Spirit upon all flesh, and your sons and daughters shall prophesy, and your young men shall see visions . . .'.

In the charismatic and prophetic Jesus movement, these young Christians see the signs of the last days. But there are other signs too which they see foretold in Scripture. The European Economic Community is often seen as the last great, and Satan-controlled, dictatorship.[12] The increase of wars and of nuclear weapons (the fire of 2 Peter 3.10) and the spread of such rebellious pseudo-theologies as the 'death of God' and 'religionless Christianity' are all regarded as fulfilments of Bible prophecy. Clay Ford admits that he too feels the return of Christ soon is 'a likely possibility'.[13] But before Christ returns, the Gospel must be preached to all nations.

Secondly, the Jesus people have an ambivalent relationship to the political establishment and to political struggle, and also to the counter-culture. One will therefore find some Jesus people describing the mainstream society as 'controlled by the prince of this world' and advocating a drop-out life-style. This may lead to a support for non-violent resistance movements, for civil rights, and so on, but it may have the exact opposite effect. Among those interviewed by Ortega, there was a good deal of resistance to the draft although there were some who pointed out that God had told them to obey the Government. Attitudes to civil rights were confused, and most people took the view that there would only be true freedom when everybody accepted Christ. The non-political stance of the majority of Jesus people has made them highly suspect in the counter-culture. They are seen as phoney revolutionaries, offering the language of revolution but in fact siding with the status quo. Although Clay Ford believed that Jesus people were a source of hope for the Berkeley situation, he admitted that 'many of them do tend to ignore the responsibilities of the Christian faith in this world such as social involvement and dependability'.[14] He believed that Jesus people needed to realize the ecological, social and political implications of the faith. Certainly the political activism of the Underground finds little support among Jesus people. 'Anti-war and anti-establishment posters, which cover the walls of the hippie communes, are missing in the Jesus houses,' says Palms.[15] This is not entirely correct, but it is generally so. On the other hand, at times it is Jesus people who accuse the Underground of supporting injustice and exploitation, as in the famous conflict between *Right On!* and *Berkeley Barb* over Women's Lib. *Right On!* announced:

Among the powerful local enemies of women's liberation are the industries which exploit woman as a sex symbol and hold her up as simply an object for gratification of the selfish lust of males. . . . Establishments such as the topless-bottomless bars, dirty book stores, and sexually-oriented newspapers like the *Barb* and the *Free Press* are doing the cause of women's liberation immeasurable harm. . . . They spread pictures of women's bodies all over their pages in order to attract sales from sexually frustrated, chauvinistic males. We must take steps to let all the people know that anyone who publishes, sells or buys a paper like the

Barb is proving that he is against women's liberation and approves the degrading and abusing of women.[16]

Thirdly, Jesus people have an ambivalent relationship to old-style, evangelical Christianity. At two points conflict is most obvious: first, that of external dress and length and style of hair. For many evangelicals, the external trappings of the drop-out culture are evil in themselves, and so when a 'hippy' is converted the visible sign of his conversion is that he cuts his hair, dons a sports jacket and flannels, and is assimilated not only into a form of Christianity but also into bourgeois culture. One widely circulated fundamentalist magazine recently went to great lengths to repudiate 'the Jesus trip', pointing out that Jesus had short hair, did not break the laws of the land, was not anti-establishment, and was a 'family man'.[17] The second point of disagreement is that of rejection of the values of the dominant culture. Much evangelical Christianity has been solidly behind the accumulation of wealth, private enterprise and support of the capitalist spirit, and it has suspected left-wing movements and forces of protest. The history of American fundamentalist revivalism has not, for the most part, been marked by radical political views. But the Jesus people may reject the capitalist system for its Mammon worship, and their drop-out life may be seen as subversive of 'Christian civilization'. On the other hand, many of those within the Jesus movement are as reactionary and politically right-wing as their revivalist predecessors were. There is a conflict here within the Jesus culture itself, which comprises revolutionary, right-wing and 'non-political' viewpoints as well as 'hip' and 'straight'.

In Britain, the situation is rather different from that in the United States. More Jesus people have been absorbed into, or have emanated from, traditional evangelical groups. The Jesus Liberation Front, for example, based in Hemel Hempstead, is well within the tradition of fundamentalist evangelism. The tracts and booklets which it issues would delight the heart of all old-fashioned Gospel Christians. For example, their *Little Green Book* is very similar to the famous tract 'Four Things God Wants You To Know', while their tract 'The Permanent Revolution', in spite of its Trotsky-inspired title, is pure evangelical Gospel within. Membership of the JLF is free to all who have been 'born of the Spirit'. The group operates a 'Jesus Bus', collects and circulates tracts, books, posters and cassettes, and seems to work well with the established churches. Another important arm of the Jesus movement within the churches is *Buzz*, the colourful magazine of Musical Gospel Outreach. Stickers and Jesus badges are produced by such groups as New Life Centre, the Festival of Light, and various local Christian bookshops, as well as the groups mentioned above. Most of this activity is entirely acceptable to the evangelical churches, although there may be discomfort among more conservative elements. The groups which do cause anxiety, however, are those such as the Children of God, whose view of the mainstream churches is more hostile, and in 1972 the division became very marked when the Evangelical Alliance brought together a sizeable number of critics and disillusioned ex-members of this group.[18]

In Britain in 1971 the Children of God had been called 'the spearhead . . . of the Jesus Revolution'.[19] They established themselves in an empty factory in Bromley where a life of strict discipline was lived, involving periods of meditation, Bible classes, fellowship, singing, witness teams, instructions, and so on. Soon their well-produced newspaper *Truth* and their magazine *New Nation News* were being sold in the streets. The layout of *Truth* is identical with that of Underground newspapers, but the content is very different, with Biblical cartoons and articles about the 'new nation of love': 'In this world of human confusion, the Children of God live together in the love and harmony that the Lord of Heaven ordained men to live by, and this contradicts the lifestyles of the social orders of the world.'[20] The Children make sweeping claims. In a letter sent to various people in June 1972 they wrote:[21]

In the past ten months it has amazed us to see how much the Lord has done in Europe. He has given us 30 training centres in the key cities of Europe which are being operated by over 400 full-time voluntary workers from each of these countries. Each of these training centres has a regular daily schedule of Bible classes, practical training and personal witnessing. They have been personally witnessing to 33,907 people and have received decisions each month throughout the winter. The state of the world is now desperate and we believe that this is going to be our last chance to win thousands of the modern day youth to Christ and rescue them from the lap of drugs, Eastern religions, violent revolutionary movements and atheistic communism.

They went on to claim that at the Lincoln and Bickershaw pop festivals they acquired 32 new full-time workers, 2,900 decisions and witnessed to about 15,500.

The origins of the Children of God go back to a group founded in the early 1960s called the Texas Soul Clinic, set up by one Fred Jordan. After the collapse of the clinic, David (Moses) Berg and Arnold (Joshua) Dietrich founded the Children, and Fred Jordan has remained as a leader of the movement, though without apparently changing his name or abandoning his possessions. The Children of God present a radical rejection of 'the world' and adopt a prophetic and judgmental stance towards it. They believe in death to self and in leaving all to follow Jesus. Property is given up, and a new Biblical name is taken. Scripture is memorized and chanted, and the discipline in the communes is quite rigid.

Most writers on the Children appear to be critical of them, but their criticisms are very varied. Edward Plowman feels that they confront the world on Old Testament lines rather than on the basis of Christian love.[22] Micheal Jacob comments that 'to the Children, unity means obedience to the elders who have total control over all aspects of life' and cites a Scottish minister's view that they are 'more like a dictatorship than a religious group'.[23] Others have complained of the lack of evangelical teaching. Thus the Cambridge Inter-Collegiate Christian Union after meeting the Children of God said:[24] 'Love for Jesus is conversion. The Cross hardly figures at all, and the death of Christ is seen as an example of his love rather than an atonement.' Francis Schaeffer, whose centre at L'Abri in Switzerland has been a source of Christian help to many young seekers, accuses the Children of a regression to a legalism which is foreign to the Gospel.[25] The most vocal criticism has come from Mr John Hunt, Conservative Member of Parliament for Bromley, where the commune is situated. In his view it is a very dubious brand of Christianity which turned impressionable and often unstable young people against their parents or against society.[26] Questions continue to be raised about 'Moses' (David Berg), the mysterious leader about whom little seems to be known, but whose 'Mo letters' get odder and more eccentric. However, it is important, in evaluating these sort of criticisms of the Children, to ask whether some of them are not grounds for attacking Christianity itself. Those who are simply concerned to defend stable families and stable societies would find a lot to disturb them in the New Testament.

The criticisms of the Children and of other Jesus groups which have come from fellow Christians need to be looked at more seriously. There has been rejoicing as well as anxiety from within the churches. More than one writer has claimed that there is a strong Gnostic tendency among the Jesus people. 'The movement is rootless, naive and radically gnostic' claims one American writer.[27] Others have referred to the 'great danger from pride, a sectarian spirit and theological confusion' and have claimed that there is 'mounting evidence . . . that many of these people have fallen headlong into these traps'.[28] The former Editor of *Crusade*, David Winter, has expressed worries about the Jesus chants which he regards as too similar to Eastern mantras.[29] And so on.

From what has been said it should be clear that there is no single 'Jesus movement'. As Micheal Jacob has said, this 'is an imprecise phrase, covering a wide spectrum of people and organisations and incorporating many viewpoints'.[30] Arthur Blessitt, on his first visit to Britain in 1971, laid down five marks of the Jesus Revolution.[31] First, joy and happiness in worship. Second, a real commitment to Jesus Christ, to the historic and living Christ, and to the Word of God. Thirdly, a tremendous compassionate and humanitarian attitude towards our fellow men. Fourthly, a great zeal in telling others about Jesus Christ. Fifthly, a spirit of victory. Blessitt himself has become identified too with the use of drug slang in the service of the Gospel, and around this has developed a major controversy within the evangelical world.

Drug use as such is certainly rejected throughout most, if not all, sections of the Jesus movement. One girl brought her Methedrine and 'flushed it down the jar in the Name of the Father, the Son and the Holy Ghost'. While there is little support for the view which is occasionally expressed[32] that the apparent decline in heroin addiction in Britain was linked with the Jesus movement, it is certainly true that for many former users of psychedelic drugs and of cannabis, the 'Jesus trip' is the last of a series of 'experiences'. Should one therefore use such terms as 'the Jesus trip', 'turn on to Jesus', 'rush with Jesus', and 'get high on the Lord'? Leading the opposition to such language from within the Jesus scene has been David Wilkerson, a Pentecostal minister whose book *The Cross and the Switchblade* has made him famous all over the Christian world. David Wilkerson represents a very important element within the Jesus movement, and his writings have affected the course not only of the evangelical work among addicts but also of the charismatic revival in all the churches.

THE SQUARE JESUS SCENE

The Cross and the Switchblade first appeared in 1962, and it was largely as a result of the book that discussion of the 'baptism of the Holy Spirit' became related to 'the Holy Spirit's role in helping a boy rid himself of an addiction to narcotics'.[33] David Wilkerson did not claim any 'magical cure for dope addiction', but he did say that the Holy Spirit was 'a power which captures a boy more strongly than narcotics'.[34] Out of Wilkerson's work came Teen Challenge which soon developed into the main operation of charismatic Christianity towards drug users. Teen Challenge is characterized by a burning zeal for saving souls and a strong sense of spiritual power. Its position can be judged from its magazines and pamphlets. 'Crime, delinquency, drug addiction, sex, hate and fear are spreading around the world like a cancer', claimed one pamphlet. 'At the very brink of eternity', it continued, 'the music is getting louder, the curses stronger, the dances faster, the joking and laughter dirtier and cheaper, the loving more vile, the smoking and drinking heavier'.[35] The movement is as opposed to cannabis and tobacco as it is to heroin and LSD. 'You must quit smoking!' the same pamphlet warned. 'No addict can be permanently cured until he is off cigarettes for good. . . . Fufural is a toxin in tobacco that will drive you back to your needle . . . I dare anyone in the world to prove to me an addict is really cured if he is still smoking.'[36] Again, marijuana is called 'the most dangerous drug used today'.[37] In an open letter to a homosexual we are told, 'I have met only a few homosexuals who really wanted out of the life . . . you weren't born homosexual; you became one by choice! . . . Before you could "discover" you were homosexual, you had to reject your childhood teaching, kill your conscience, neglect and refuse Bible warnings, and flirt and play with a dirty mind and evil imagination.'[38]

This then is a group with very definite views and positions about the Christian way, which speaks with certainty and conviction, if not always with a strict regard for accuracy or the conclusions of research. David Wilkerson has gained a large number of followers in the Christian world, and it is fair to say that most of the Christian groups working with drug abusers in Britain were, directly or indirectly, inspired by his ministry and writing. Nevertheless there was some anxiety in the evangelical world after the publication of *The Cross and the Switchblade*, and in 1965 an article in *The Evangelical Magazine* expressed concern that 'an impression of imbalance is given at times in that the power of the Holy Spirit appears to be set against the power of drugs—without the centrality of the message of the Cross'.[39] On the whole, however, David Wilkerson has remained a popular and very acceptable figure in evangelical circles.

His position is very different from that of the 'Jesus Freaks', the Children of God or Arthur Blessitt, although he would certainly align himself with what he sees as the true Jesus movement, and his small pocket book is widely used by Jesus people.[40] He is, however, very critical of certain trends within the movement, although his position has not by any means remained static, as can be seen by comparing his *Purple Violet Squish* (1969) with *Get Your Hands Off My Throat* (1971). In the former volume, he describes and criticizes various groups: hippies, yippies, 'God is groovy' people, and so on. He is not impressed by hippies: 'a hippie is one who removes himself from physical and intellectual reality . . . believes only in himself'.[41] Father Philip Berrigan's action in pouring blood over military files in Baltimore is described as 'only one bizarre action of the unique yippie movement', a movement which is 'frequently sponsored by misguided liberals with noble sentiments'.[42] But some of Wilkerson's strongest words were reserved for David Berg, now known as 'Moses', one of the founders of the Children of God, who at that time was running the Light Club in Los Angeles. Berg had described Jesus as 'no namby-pamby cat' but one who 'really socks it to you with some really heavy stuff', who takes you 'on that ultimate eternal trip'. 'Man, he's the cool one. Being one of his hep cats is being where it's at. His program is really groovy but it's tough.'[43] For Wilkerson such language is anathema. 'You cannot win rebels by being like them. Put away your childish talk. God is not "groovy" or "hep" and Christ is not a "cool cat" . . . Take off your love beards and grow up.'[44]

Against the world of freaks and cats, Wilkerson places that of the 'squares'. Who are they?

A square is actually a goodnick who is scorned because he is not hip on new fads and persists in being unworldly, unsophisticated, unenlightened and refuses to bop. He doesn't dig far-out music and refuses to develop rock and roll fever. Squares do not demonstrate nor do they question every cultural, ethical, political and religious value of the day. Squares are conventional and conforming. They don't burn their draft cards and even wear service uniforms with pride. Squares are wheels who make the world go round. Before we go any further, let me confess that I'm a square.[45]

This is probably David Wilkerson's position still, though his recent writings show a changed attitude. 'God has been shaking me up recently', he wrote in 1971.[46] Now the tone is more tolerant, and the criticism is directed more towards the impatient establishment which labels the young rebels 'communists'. No longer does David Wilkerson ridicule hippies or long hair. Indeed, a whole chapter on 'Hair' reads like a recantation.[47] Wilkerson is still a square, but he is not the square he was.

At the same time he remains unhappy with a good deal of the Jesus movement, including its drug jargon about being 'spaced out on Jesus'. Often, he claims, these pseudo-Jesus people merely add Jesus to their lives of drugs and free love: 'Here were a group of young people who claimed to be Jesus people, an army of Jesus revolutionaries, who had not been to the Cross. They know nothing of being sanctified, of holy living, of separation from the world and old habits and immoral friends, Jesus was a bigger, better trip in a series of trips and experiences.'[48] He complains of young people who carry guitars and Bibles and sing 'Jesus songs', but who are still bound and full of self, still tied to the old life-style, 'a growing number of deceivers, walking after their own flesh, who promise liberty while they themselves are in bondage'.[49] Nor is he happy with some forms of Jesus ministry.

> In our desperate effort to relate to the spaced-out youth of our generation, we have innocently fallen into the subtle trap set by the enemy. Young people who have been 'tripping out' on drugs seek a substitute high. They seek another state of euphoria. They want to 'go up' on Jesus. But we must be careful to tell these young people the whole story—about tribulation, suffering, persecution, rejection by the crowd, separation and valley experiences. . . . I no longer use terms such as 'high' or 'trip' to relate any Christian experience. It has to be so much more— a total surrender—a death! Many today are so high on Jesus that

they can't settle down. But my Bible says every man is a phony unless he is securely grounded.[50]

So Wilkerson is highly critical of some key facets of current Jesus trends, but he still remains committed to the real Jesus revolution and considers himself part of it.

The refusal to use drug jargon about the Gospel is shared by a British evangelist, Frank Wilson, well known for his after-care of heroin addicts at the Life for the World centre in Gloucestershire. Frank Wilson has been influenced a good deal by David Wilkerson. In a recent newsletter from his centre he wrote:[51]

The last three years have been years of popularity of a certain kind of 'Jesus style' Christianity. Slogans like 'Turn on to Jesus' and 'Stay high on love' have become familiar to thousands of Christians. The one-time 'old-fashioned' evangelical has come out of his cocoon and fitted into this new 'Jesus revolution'. Strange as it may sound, when the people for whose benefit this new 'pop' image has been created, the drug user and young rebel, find Christ for themselves, they reject this association of ideas between the spiritual experience and drugs as being undesirable and dangerous. In our centre over the past five years there has grown a deepening love for the old-fashioned Gospel, the Scriptures and the things of the Holy Spirit of God. From the days of very unprofessional Gospel Rock groups and folk singers to the recent slogan-shouting banner-waving Jesus-style Christians, the work of evangelising young drop-outs and junkies has gone on quietly in the simple power of the Holy Spirit who is revealing the Christ of the Scriptures to young people and satisfying them.

This viewpoint is by no means uncommon. The use of drug jargon about the Gospel is increasingly suspect among young people, and there is an awareness of the danger of seeking for better and better 'highs' from religion. When Marx called religion the opiate of the people, he witnessed to the way in which religion often exhibits drug-like effects. Progress in the life of faith must involve less concern with experiences as such, and more concern with transformation of life and character.

THE NEW PENTECOSTALISM

In order to understand and attempt to evaluate the Jesus movements among young people it is necessary to examine a number of related developments within the Christian world. The most important of these is the charismatic revival in the non-Pentecostal churches. This revival is fundamentally theological, centring on the belief that there is a 'baptism of the Holy Spirit' which is different from baptism in water and from regeneration. The Holy Spirit is held to be with the believer and to have been the agent of his regeneration, but through the 'baptism' he becomes an inner presence and power. Thus in Pentecostal thought there are at least two 'religious crisis experiences', baptism and the baptism of the Spirit.[52] The outward sign of the latter is usually speaking in tongues. In the study of Jesus people cited above by Ortega, it was found that over 85 per cent of Jesus people were strongly influenced by the Pentecostal movement.[53]

The resurgence of Pentecostal experience in the non-Pentecostal churches first came to the surface in St Mark's Church, Van Nuys, near Los Angeles, in 1960. Its Rector, Dennis Bennett, on Passion Sunday of that year, told the congregation that he had been filled with the Holy Spirit and had spoken with tongues, and as a result one of the curates had publicly resigned, taken off his vestments and left the church. In fact the Van Nuys incident simply brought to the surface a movement which had been growing for some time. This was not a schismatic movement. Dennis Bennett insisted that 'no one needs to leave the Episcopal Church in order to have the fullness of the Spirit'.[54] Although he himself was forced to resign from Van Nuys, he subsequently became Vicar of St Luke's Church, Seattle. Soon afterwards the movement was spreading rapidly in the Episcopal Church.

The revival was perhaps even more marked among Roman Catholics in the United States.[55] Very largely as a result of the publication of *The Cross and the Switchblade*, the 'tongues' movement took root at Duquesne University and then spread to Notre Dame and Ann Arbor. The effect of Pentecostal experience on Roman Catholics has not generally been to force them out of the church but rather to deepen their devotion. Thus Plowman describes the way in which the Church of the Blessed Sacrament in Seattle has integrated Pentecostalism into its regular liturgical life. However, the future of Catholic Pentecostalism is uncertain. Certainly most Pentecostals would be unhappy with Catholic sacramental teaching. Hollenweger in his massive study of Pentecostalism merely notes that 'it is very hard to say how a Pentecostal revival within the Roman

Catholic Church will influence the relationship between denominational Pentecostalism and Catholicism or between these two groups and the ecumenical movement. The silence on this theme in the Pentecostal periodicals at any rate shows that this revival cannot be interpreted in the usual categories.'[56] One Roman Catholic writer, Emmanuel Sullivan, suggests that the Pentecostal movement may be one of the significant signs of progress towards visible unity.[57]

Those Christians who have received the 'gift of tongues' tend to describe the effect in various ways, but the common denominator seems to be that it has intensified the sense of the presence of God, of the immediate relevance of the Bible, and of the power of praise.[58] They see it as a manifestation of the Holy Spirit (Acts 2.4; 10.46; 19.6; 1 Cor. 12.10), but they concede that it can be used wrongly—without love (1 Cor. 13.1), out of turn (14.27), or at the wrong time (14.28). Yet even when there is abuse, as at Corinth, the gift ought still to be used (14.5) but in a disciplined way (14.5; 13; 28). Tongues are seen primarily not as a means of communication but as a sign of God's presence and power. The speaker is rarely understood though in a group manifestation he will be 'interpreted', this activity also being seen as a gift of the Spirit. The speaker in fact will not understand his own words: his 'mind is unfruitful' (1 Cor. 14.14) but his spirit is in a state of prayer. Many would claim that the initial in-filling of the soul with the Holy Spirit in the New Testament was normally accompanied by some objective manifestation such as tongues. The speaking in tongues therefore is an illustration of the fact that one has received the Spirit.

So the gift of tongues is seen as 'a spiritual breakthrough' which brings 'an awareness of having entered a vast new spiritual realm'.[59] The believer is now able to use the gift as part of his devotional life, and his prayer is enriched as the Spirit gives words to utter (Romans 8.26 is often used in support of this). It thus becomes possible to express praise and adoration beyond the confines of one's native language. Others stress its importance as an empowering of the church and of individual believers for evangelism. Michael Harper calls it 'power for the Body of Christ'.[60]

Is the gift and the movement of tongues a form of ecstasy? Such a claim is often made but does not appear to be substantiated.[61] Curiously, in the Bible the person who speaks in tongues is never referred to as being transformed in this way, although those who *hear* him are sometimes described as 'ecstatic' or 'amazed' (Acts 2.7; 10.45).[62] The phenomena of shaking, trembling, dancing, and so on are, of course, frequently associated with a certain type of Pentecostal manifestation, and such manifestations may be confused with both intoxication (Acts 2.13) and insanity (1 Cor. 14.23), but there seems little basis for the view that tongue-speaking is always uncontrolled by the mind. On the contrary, it often occurs in calm, quiet moments, and it has been claimed by one writer that 'trance' and 'highly aroused states' are almost unknown.[63] Many people receive and use the gift of tongues in a very quiet, gentle and matter of fact way, and it may well be that this is the most common form of the experience.[64]

However, the charismatic revival has not been without its critics within evangelical Christianity. Numerous books have appeared which criticize the Pentecostal theological position.[65] F. D. Bruner attacks the movement for its doctrine of the 'baptism of the Holy Spirit' and for its high emphasis on speaking in tongues. In the New Testament, he argues, baptism and the Holy Spirit are inseparably united: baptism itself *is* the baptism of the Holy Spirit.[66] He dismisses Acts 8 and 10, where the two appear to be separate, as exceptional cases which only confirm the norm.[67] The idea that there is a 'second experience' is, in Bruner's view, precisely the error which is attacked in Galatians—that of looking beyond the Gospel to some fuller blessing, in effect a new kind of legalism. Speaking in tongues can become a new form of salvation by works, and can be a purely selfish gift.[68] Other writers stress the same points: James Dunn has questioned the New Testament basis for believing in a special baptism in the Holy Spirit which is separate from the process of conversion and initiation.[69] Stibbs and Packer have argued that there is no Biblical warrant for desiring a revival of 'special manifestations' of the Spirit, and no evidence that they are more than temporary phenomena,[70] while Kurt Koch has warned of the serious danger of 'false tongues'.[71]

Yet in spite of its critics, Pentecostal Christianity has become a strong force, and it has provided a major link between the Jesus movement and some sections of the institutional churches. In Britain, in addition to the Jesus scene and the mainstream charismatic movement, there is another important Pentecostal growth, that among West Indians. The two main West Indian Pentecostal groups are the New Testament Church of God and the Church of

God of Prophecy.[72] The New Testament Church of God is the oldest of the immigrant sects in Britain, and it has grown at an amazing rate in recent years in areas of West Indian settlement. This group, however, is entirely black, and it is not clear to what extent the movement will link up with the already existing white groups. But it is another indication of the vigorous growth of Pentecostalism, which has produced the now strong mass movement of charismatic Christianity on the fringe of the institutional churches.

LIGHT VERSUS DARKNESS

However, it would be quite mistaken to see the Jesus and charismatic movements as being predominantly outside the church institutions. Indeed, in Britain, it is probably true to say that, with the exception of the Children of God, the Jesus people are drawn mainly from within the established churches. Some would claim that the British Jesus movements are not indigenous growths from the youth culture at all, but have been manufactured by the churches as ways of communicating with youth. There is some foundation for this view. The 'Jesus media' in Britain are, as was shown above, mainly associated with church organizations and church members—Musical Gospel Outreach, Fountain Trust, New Life Centre, Gateway Outreach, Festival of Light. Of these, the Festival of Light is the group which has attracted most publicity. Formed in 1971, the Festival was aimed both at attacking 'moral pollution' in the mass media, and at proclaiming the Christian Gospel as the answer. Most people associated the Festival exclusively with the first aim, and it has been viewed by its critics as a repressive movement against pornography and freedom of expression. But as it has developed, it is the second aim which has come more and more into the forefront of the Festival's activity. It has been argued that there is a conflict between the two aims, and that 'it is far from clear how long inherent differences in goals and methods can be obscured'.

> Enthusiasts and puritans have proved uneasy bedfellows before and, as in the past, there is the danger for the Festival of Light that, in the process of institutionalization it will alienate the charismatically motivated youthful wing who have so far provided its dynamic quality. As they turn to more immediately experiential modes of witness, they may take with them any current emphasis on humanitarianism and democratic pluralism, and leave behind

the coercive reformism and unalleviated moral indignation of a status-declining middle class.[73]

Many people would regard such a split as both inevitable and desirable.

The Festival of Light was the result of the return to England in 1970 of a missionary, Peter Hill. Appalled by the amount of erotic material in books, films, and so on, he spent a period in prayer, and had a vision of thousands of young people marching for righteousness. Hill gathered together a number of individual sponsors, including Lord Longford, Malcolm Muggeridge and Mary Whitehouse, and obtained support from a large number of evangelical Christians. So in September 1971 came Operation Beacon when over two hundred beacons were lit throughout Britain to symbolize the attack on the forces of darkness. A rally in Trafalgar Square gathered many thousands, and Malcolm Muggeridge called for a 'continuing process of moral and spiritual regeneration'. There were rallies and marches throughout Britain, and these later gave way to Festivals for Jesus.

In its first publicity folder the Festival of Light declared:[74] 'The organizers of the Festival believe that there are God-given standards for us to go by in the '70s, and that there are millions in Britain who want these standards defined and applied.'

But, as Micheal Jacob has said, 'to the youth culture the Festival was like a red rag to a bull'.[75] Its timing was either ideal or disastrous, depending on one's point of view. It came immediately after the *Oz* trial and the furore surrounding *The Little Red School Book*. It was widely seen within the counter-culture as the identification of Christians with the repressive and reactionary forces of the establishment. And they were probably correct in this view. *Time Out* commented about the inaugural meeting: 'The aim of the organizers was to fight "Moral Pollution", which in other words means a religious minority trying once more to dictate society's more wayward sexual habits.'[76] If the Festival had wished to increase these fears, they could hardly have done better than to include Lord Longford, Malcolm Muggeridge and Mary Whitehouse among their widely publicized supporters! All three were anathema to the counter-culture, and the publication later of *The Longford Report* on pornography merely reinforced the hostility of many young people. The fact that the Festival also included Bishop Trevor

Huddleston, a widely respected figure on the Left, was not enough to undo the damage. Rightly or wrongly, in the minds of many young people, the movement was seen as reactionary. The Underground press compared its blazing torches to those of Hitler's Festival of Resurrection. It was pointed out that the three 'purest' countries were Nazi Germany, South Africa and Greece, and there was a good deal of talk of Nuremberg and of a new religious fascism.

Micheal Jacob is guilty of exaggeration when he says that 'the fight of the year' was that of 'the Festival of Light versus the Festival of Life',[77] but there is no doubt that the Underground considered the movement a threat. The Festival organizers would probably not be over-concerned at hostility from such a quarter, and would accept it as a necessary element in their stand for righteousness. Indeed, the propaganda of the Festival has tended to paint a picture of a clear-cut conflict between good and evil, a crusade for righteousness resisted only by the perverse.[78]

The propaganda of the Festival is filled with warnings of 'a complete breakdown of society', of 'an active assault on the minds and morals of the nation'. The enemies of society are those who advocate a 'New Order', defined by the Festival as 'a society free from any kind of self-discipline and restraint'. Children's minds are said to be 'twisted and polluted by a constant diet of violence and perversion from their elders'.[79] The 1972 programme of the Festival referred to 'the moral pollution which is poisoning and degrading the nation', but by this time there was more concern with proclaiming 'the certainty of true freedom through Jesus Christ', and with 'taking Jesus to the people'.[80] The Festival literature itself is not very good on discipline when it comes to generalizations. Terms like 'moral pollution' and 'the contraceptive society' are thrown about uncritically. Statistics are quoted and experts cited in an unintelligent way. Serious thinking seems to be entirely absent.[81] There is an hysterical attack on 'permissiveness' which condemns in blanket fashion a whole complex of attitudes and behaviour patterns within society without any attempt at calm analysis or honest assessment. In public discussion, exponents of this line are often their own worst enemies, though, alas, they are often taken to be representative of Christianity too.

The Festival of Light was in fact greeted with approval by many Christians and by most of those within the charismatic movement who gave to it such descriptions as, 'a master stroke of the Divine

genius'.[82] No doubt to many people it did look like this. But en-
thusiasm is not a good substitute for intellectual accuracy, and many
Christians seemed to have swallowed the Festival's generalizations
without much thought. For our purposes, however, the Festival's
significance is twofold. First, it had the negative effect of increasing
the alienation of many young people from Christianity, because it
confirmed their belief, held already in a general way, that Christians
were on the side of the mainstream culture and against the forces of
change. Whether the impression was correct or not is beside the
point. But it is difficult to see how, on the basis of its literature,
anyone could have interpreted the movement in any way other than
as a massive defence operation for a middle-class, stable, Christian
society. Thus one local Festival for Jesus in 1972 announced:[83]

> These are days tense with the impending explosion of anarchy
> and terror. The hand of greed has lighted the fuse. We hear the
> cracking sound of frustration throughout these isles, we all wait
> for the strong steps of authoritative leadership to quench the
> flame and save our country from explosion. This is the time for
> spiritual power, authority with Christian character.
>   For now a most dangerous enemy seeks to destroy from within.
> It seeks to destroy moral values and by so doing destroy the family
> structure upon which this country is built. We know that Jesus
> Christ is the answer.

So Jesus is invoked by the frightened establishment, threatened by
change and afraid for its stability and security. This Jesus is a
quencher of explosions, a pacifier, cement for stable social orders.
It is hardly the Jesus of the Gospels who came to cast fire on the
earth, to bring not peace but a sword, and to set households, families
and nations in confusion (Matt. 10.34 ff; Luke 12.49 ff). There is
no hint in this kind of writing that God himself might possibly be
involved in the disturbance and the anarchy. For God is on the side
of law and order.
   It is hardly surprising then that many young people mistrust the
Festival and view it as a rearguard action by the old order. But, as
we saw above, since its early days the Festival has moved away from
its initial concern with pornography and erotica to a wider involvement with evangelism and testimony. One of the Festival's publications of 1972 was the *Living Jesus-Style Manual*, aimed to meet
the need for a clearer understanding of Christian morality. In fact,

what is offered is a series of Biblical texts throughout most of the booklet, while statistics and quotations from other writers are used to support particular positions. Again, one finds the highly selective view of morality, with a good deal of emphasis on sex and personal behaviour, and little or nothing about social ethics, war, the distribution of wealth, racism, and such issues. 'Dangers of a permissive society go unchallenged, unpublicised, or hidden behind pseudo-intellectual nonsense.'[84] The 'pseudo-intellectuals', presumably, are those who deviate from the position of the Festival of Light. But what is noticeable about the present trend in the movement is its quite unmistakable drift towards evangelical Christianity with a strong Pentecostal flavour.

In Britain, therefore, the 'Jesus scene' is more 'square' on the whole than in the United States. It is more allied with the institutional churches and more under the control of well-established bodies. Jesus people tend to be solidly behind law and order, to be 'non-political' (and, therefore, usually tend towards the Right), and to be opposed to most of the movements for political liberation. Will this situation last? Or will a more spontaneous Jesus movement develop from within the youth culture? Has the Festival of Light queered the pitch for such a growth? These are difficult questions to answer at present, but one thing is certain. Unless a form of the Christian movement does appear which embodies some of the striving for liberation and for justice which fires young radicals outside the church, the gulf between Christian and non-Christian youth will become wider. Christians will move further and further to the Right, and the Christian prophetic tradition will disappear. The Jesus movement could end in disillusion and despair.

Yet while the prophets seem to be few, and while Jesus people continue to promote a fundamentalist Gospel, Jesus remains a popular figure in many sections of the spiritual counter-culture. But it is the 'universal guru Jesus' rather than the Jesus of the crusaders. Thus Alan Watts, writing in the *Los Angeles Free Press* on 'Was Jesus a Freak?' says:[85]

It is obvious to any informed student of the history and psychology of religion that Jesus was one of many who had an intense experience of cosmic consciousness—of the vivid realisation that oneself is a manifestation of the eternal energy of the universe, the basic 'I am'. . . .

But to identify Jesus the man as the one-and-only historical incarnation of a Divinity considered as the royal, imperial and militant Jehovah is only to reinforce the pestiferous arrogance of 'white' Christianity—with all the cruel self-righteousness of its missionary zeal. . . .

Christianity has universality or catholicity only in recognising that Jesus is one particular instance and expression of a wisdom which was also, if differently, realised in the Buddha, in Lao-Tzu and in such modern avatars as Ramana Maharshi, Ramakrishna, and perhaps Aurobindo and Inayat Khan.

To Watts the Jesus people 'are following the old non-gospel of the freaky Jesus', and his criticism would find much support among those who are suspicious of spiritual exclusiveness. Yet Watts preserves spiritual inclusiveness at the cost of reducing Christianity to one among many traditions. Jesus remains popular, but it is not the Jesus of the Bible or the Creeds, it is not our Jesus. Is there any hope then for a Christ-centred radicalism?

THE LIBERATED ZONE

In the United States there has been a growing movement of Christian protest which is totally different from the Jesus movement. It is generally referred to as the Underground Church, a confusing term for the same reason that the term 'Underground' itself is confusing. In addition, Edward Plowman's book on the Jesus people was originally called *The Underground Church*, a phrase which has been used to describe a number of youth Christian movements which have little in common with each other. Some would therefore prefer the terms 'liberated Church' or 'New Left Church'. Basically this is a type of Christianity which is concerned with political liberation, and which sees the good news of the Kingdom of God as the basis for a deep political commitment. It is a movement which has been very much influenced by radical theology, and which expresses its position in new liturgical forms. Unlike the Jesus movements, its theology tends towards a 'Catholic' position, with a strong eucharistic and sacramental sense. Its politics are socialist, and it owes its growth as a movement very largely to the Vietnam War and to the Civil Rights struggle. Its main area of divergence from the Christian Left-wing movements of the past is that it is firmly set within the counter-culture, and has absorbed much of the

Underground philosophy and life. Like the Jesus movements, the Underground Church consists for the most part of young people.

The best known of the Underground 'youth churches' is undoubtedly the Free Church of Berkeley. Berkeley has long been a mecca for young people, and the Free Church, situated near Telegraph Avenue, is now one of the major facilities serving the young on the west coast. A newspaper in 1969 claimed that the Free Church was probably the best known address among the thousands of young people in Berkeley.[86] Since its foundation it was oriented towards runaways, the isolated and the casualty. Up to ninety a night would sleep on the premises, and a good deal of the early work was concerned with finding 'crash pads', with provision of food, and with counselling on a range of issues from draft resistance to bad LSD trips. Dick York, the young Episcopalian priest who has been the principal architect of the Free Church, was initially involved in 1967 in an experimental 'street ministry' sponsored by various denominations in the Berkeley area. After Dick York's flamboyant ordination in 1968, the church developed its own styles of liturgy and celebration. Christian festivals with rock bands, prayers and incense attracted large numbers of 'street people'. The slogan of the Free Church is 'the Liberated Zone', and over the entrance was a sign which announced, 'Turn on to the Liberated Zone. The Free Church loves you'. Around this concept a community formed which began to create its own philosophy and 'alternative life-style'. Dick York saw the church primarily as a pocket of resistance. 'I think the church was supposed to be a counter-community to the state, not based on violence, coercion, manipulation or exploitation. The church should resist the state where it is repressive and offer the alternative by its own life-style.'[87] So the Free Church remains strongly politically conscious, deeply committed to the peace and liberation movement. It offers counsel to conscientious objectors and draft resisters, and it played a central role in the occupation of 'People's Park' in Berkeley.

So from being 'an experimental and ecumenical service ministry to hippies and other transient youth in the South Campus area of Berkeley, California (Telegraph Avenue)', the Free Church's nature changed significantly. Dick York has described the change thus:[88]

For two years the Free Church has served the people: with finding crash pads, helping drug freak-outs, aiding psychiatric and

medical emergencies, helping develop a Free Clinic, counselling
runaways and running a switchboard. But a new thing happened
that we were not expecting. The community of Free Church
volunteers began demanding a Church: experimental liturgy,
baptism, rap groups on the radical Jesus. The sponsoring
Churches responded in several ways: some were excited, others
said in horror, 'That isn't what we intended you to do at all!'
They could see themselves cooperating in an ecumenical patern-
alistic service ministry but many were threatened by the prospect
of a radical youth church.

Nevertheless what has emerged is a radical youth church and it has
formed the model for other growths elsewhere. More and more too,
the liberated churches in the Bay Area were looking to the underlying causes of youth alienation. Lyle Grosjean, Director of the
Ecumenical Ministry of Haight-Ashbury, warned in 1969 that 'the
uptight maintenance of control over the young, and ministries
among the young will result in crucifixion in which we will participate
followed by resurrection in which we will not'.[89]
   As the Free Church grew, it acquired the accoutrements of more
structured organizations. It began to publish a monthly letter
called *The Subversive Church*. The clergy had office hours, and the
telephone switchboard offered, among other facilities, a Free
Church Demonstration Information Service. For a period in 1969
there was no place of worship. This was due to the fact that the
Free Church held a memorial service for Ho Chi Minh, as a result
of which Trinity Methodist Church refused to allow use of their
building. The Free Church continued to cause trouble to the
authorities. Towards the end of 1969 Dick York and some Free
Church colleagues demonstrated at the National Council of Churches
Convention in Detroit, holding an exorcism and carrying coffins.
Dick York poured red paint over the main speakers' table in protest
at the Council's refusal to accept a draft card from a young man
resisting induction and asking for their help. 'The blood of the
Vietnamese and the American soldiers is dripping from the minutes
of this Convention', he announced.
   Elsewhere in the United States radical Christians have been
aligning themselves with the counter-culture, but bringing to it a
Christian prophetic voice. The basic features of these movements
are three. First, a rediscovery of the protest tradition of Jesus and

the prophets and a vision of the Kingdom of God on earth. Secondly, a commitment to the Underground and its life-styles, although there will be dissent and criticism at various points. Thirdly, an identification with the non-violent movement, a rejection of the 'American way of life' and a support for Civil Rights and movements for justice. A directory issued from Berkeley lists free Christian communities throughout the United States, and a covering note suggested that to qualify for inclusion a church should be 'ecumenical, and involved in peace, liberation, and/or ecology'.[90] A number of volumes and papers have developed the theological position of the liberated churches,[91] and a *Free Church Collective Handbook*, issued from Berkeley, gives advice on setting up collectives, or house churches.

The best summary of the general outlook of the Free Church is contained in a statement issued by its staff on 5 November 1969 and known as the 'November Fifth Statement'.[92] It would probably find general acceptance among many Underground churches and its tone and theological position clearly show the contrast with the Jesus movements:

The Free Church of Berkeley is a community within the revolutionary Movement which relates to the radical tradition of Jesus, the Prophets, and the Church of Liberation.

'I will make for them a covenant on that day with the wild animals, with the birds of the air, and with the creeping things of the earth.' (Hosea 2.18) We recognize the Spirit of God at work in the movement of our brothers and sisters for the restoration and preservation of the ecological balance of our planet. We believe that uncontrolled production and consumption constitute violence against ecological law and order. We admit our complicity individually and collectively, in the pollution of our environment by chemicals and radiation, in the exploitation of natural resources and wilderness, in the horror of overpopulation. Therefore we dedicate ourselves to working toward a life-style which holds a viable ecological order as a sacred and revolutionary priority.

'I will break bow, sword and battle out of the land, and allow them to sleep in safety.' (Hosea 2.18) 'I will make with them a covenant of peace . . . and they will know that I am the Power of history, when I break the bars of their yoke and liberate them from the hand of their oppressors.' (Ezekiel 34.25–7) We recognize the Spirit of God in the movement for peace and liberation throughout the world. We join in the struggle for the liberation of oppressed peoples (the poor, the Third World, racial minorities, women, and youth) from exploitation and racism at home and from imperialism abroad. We dedicate ourselves to serve the victims of force and oppression, avoiding the trap of the colonialist mission in perpetuating a corrupt system and recognizing that the highest form of service is organizing the oppressed for resistance. We will struggle for the establishment of social and political structures which are just, humane, and participatory. We will resist institutions of war, conscription, racism, imperialism and injustice, and shall attempt to offer an alternative through the life of joy and suffering in our voluntary community of brothers and sisters.

'I will marry you to myself for ever, marry you with integrity and justice, with tenderness and love.' (Hosea 2.19) We recognize the Spirit of God at work in the struggle of our time toward sexual intimacy, vocational creativity, psychic integrity, and inter-personal sensitivity. We resist those institutions of our society which dehumanize and destroy real interpersonal relations. We accept the imperative to develop attitudes and life-styles that are personally and communally liberating and non-exploitative. In celebration we will be freed to work toward the ecological and social revolutions.

This concern with 'celebration' quickly led to the creation of an Underground liturgical life. 'The church ought to do its thing', wrote a young Californian priest,[93] and the church's thing was liturgy. John Pairman Brown, Berkeley's resident liturgist and theologian, wrote:[94] 'The human race can only become the unity which in principle it is, if each solemnly takes off his old clothes, spattered with blood and dirt, and undertakes to go a new way. And the new way is to sit down and break bread together, each deferring to his neighbour. So the Church of Jesus is constituted by those two actions of washing and eating, with a form of words referring to his example.' So out of Berkeley came *The Covenant of Peace—A Liberation Prayer Book*, and in the liturgical forms the underlying theology of the church is most clearly and very powerfully expressed. This is a prayer book for all those Christian groups which are involved in the struggle for peace, justice and environmental renewal. 'Each item carries a clear witness against militarism, exploitation and pollution—in a word Sin'.[95] The volume includes a Calendar, Litanies and Liberation Prayers, forms for Baptism (Going Through the Waters), weddings, prison visiting, memorial of the dead, the Eucharist (the Freedom Meal), a Disarmed Forces Prayer Book, and Guerrilla Liturgies for particular occasions.

Berkeley's Calendar includes not only St Anthony of Egypt, St John of the Cross and the Cure d'Ars, but also Camus, Jan Palach, Gandhi, Camillo Torres, A. J. Muste, Buddha, Martin Luther King, and Karl Barth. Among the events which are commemorated liturgically are the bombing of Dresden, the murder of Malcolm X, the murders at Sharpeville, the Selma march, the Vietnamese victory at Dien Bien Phu, and the burning of draft files in Chicago. The litany for deliverance includes prayer that we may be delivered from napalm and fallout, poison, torture, conscription, crowding, eviction, propaganda and segregation. Among those invoked in the Litany of the Saints are Francis, Pope John, Dag Hammarskjöld, Teilhard de Chardin, Thoreau and Bonhoeffer. There are intercessions for black liberation, for defence against demonic powers, for economic justice, and for national liberation movements, while a collect for the President asks God to 'inspire him with distrust of his advisers'. There is an insistence in both the baptism and wedding rites on the need for population control, and this is one of the few liturgies which has written family planning into the promises. Throughout these services there is a very strong sense that the Christian community is a resistance movement, faced with evil forces embodied in the political structures of America.

Political conflict is also theological, and the Guerrilla Liturgies bring this out. Thus on Ash Wednesday the rite is an Act of Disaffiliation entitled Burn Out the Mark Of The Beast. It begins: 'Friends, in the knowledge that demonic forces have infiltrated the institutions of our society, we have gathered here to disaffiliate ourselves from the powers of darkness and to enlist in the army of life.' Again, in the rite of Decontamination, for use on Palm Sunday and at other times, there is an exorcism. 'In his name I declare this place *decontaminated* from the fallout of religion and pride and fear, and *reconsecrated* to hope and life and love. The demons returned to the nothingness from where they came. Earth! Water! Air! Fire! Witness our liberation.' In the Eucharistic liturgy too the emphasis

is on liberation, and on the new world order which the Freedom
Meal initiates. 'Bread means revolution'. The Free Church would
agree with the Christian Socialists of the nineteenth century, who
saw the Mass as the regular meeting of rebels against a Mammon-
worshipping world order.

YOUTH, THEOLOGY AND REVOLUTION

In order to understand the emergence of the Underground Church,
it is important to be familiar with the theological movements in-
fluencing radical Christians. One needs to see such writers as Harvey
Cox, Dietrich Bonhoeffer, Jurgen Moltmann and the German
'theology of hope' school, and the 'death of God' theologians as
essential elements in the background of thought which led to the
new radicalism. But it is the idea of the 'radical Jesus' which has
been the central idea in the liberated churches. An article in *The
Christian Century* in 1968[96] identified five strands in the new theological radicalism. First, the movement from a non-religious to a
historical basis, an abandonment of a man-centred view, and a sense
of hope for the future. Secondly, a new optimism based on 'Christo-
logical humanism', with a stress on discipleship to Jesus rather
than justification by faith. Thirdly, a new realism about society,
liberating men from corrupt institutions and setting up new counter-
communities. Fourthly, a new eschatological perspective, replacing
evolution by prophetic witness as the way things get done. Finally,
a new sectarianism based on the pluralism of 'Christian ghettoes'
where the more people there are doing their thing, the better. Such a
radicalism has reacted, as the 'death of God' school did, against a
God who was too abstract to be involved in human affairs. God is
now seen as active in historical crises, in revolutions and liberation
movements, and there is a strong sense of involvement in the world.

To some extent too the new radical youth churches connect
historically with a number of older, pre-Underground pockets of
rebellion within the Christian movement. One of these is the
Catholic Anarchist tradition, represented in America by the
Catholic Worker group in New York City's Bowery district.[97] Since
the 1930s the monthly *Catholic Worker* has propagated the 'Green
Revolution' and has refused to pay taxes, while in New York itself
the house of hospitality provides free food, clothes and short-term
accommodation. The ethos and work of this group inspired a
number of groups in Britain, including the Simon Community.

Peter Maurin, who founded the *Catholic Worker*, had a three-fold formula: cult (liturgy), culture (education and study), and cultivation (cooperative agriculture). His two stalwart colleagues, Dorothy Day and Ammon Hennacy, made the Catholic Worker movement a centre for non-violent civil disobedience, and in the 1960s it was a focal point for draft and tax resistance. Peter Maurin was steeped in the writings of Proudhon, Marx and Kropotkin, as well as Belloc, Chesterton, Christopher Dawson and Romano Guardini—and the Papal Encyclicals. For him, voluntary poverty was the beginning of social revolution. The alternative Christian society based on poverty and non-violence must be set up immediately within the shell of the old society.

In the years that preceded the growth of the Underground, this small group provided almost the only Christian link with the anarchist movement, and the *Catholic Worker* was probably the only Christian publication sold at Freedom Bookshop in London. Christian anarchists of the Catholic Worker type were meeting during the days of the Committee of 100, and there is still a Christian Anarchist group in London. The political theology of the Catholic Worker was simple. The present capitalist society was not in accord with justice and charity. In economics, its guiding principle was production for profit. In psychology, it saw man as a mere economic factor in production. In morals, it was based on class war. So the Catholic anarchists insisted on 'a complete rejection of the present social order and a non-violent revolution to establish an order more in accord with Christian values'. Only by direct action can this be accomplished, they said, not by conventional political methods:

> We believe in a withdrawal from the capitalist system so far as each one is able to do so. Toward this end we favour the establishment of a Distributist economy wherein those who have a vocation to the land will work on the farms surrounding the village, and those who have other vocations will work in the village itself. In this way we will have a decentralized economy which will dispense with the State as we know it and will be federationist in character as was society during certain periods that preceded the rise of national states.[98]

This is in essence a pre-capitalist critique of capitalism which seeks to return to an agrarian society. But in many ways, this and other

similar drop-out groups anticipated the Christian radical movements
of the present.

In Britain, there has been no exact equivalent to the Underground
Church. In 1968, however, a young radical group called CHURCH
attained notoriety by their demonstrations at, and criticisms of,
the Lambeth Conference. Though they included members of the
institutional churches, they were not impressed with the church's
witness to Christ. 'The Church (at least as we see it in England)
is characterized by having betrayed Jesus. Jesus himself was a
liberator, and his life seems to make sense as a possible human way
to freedom. . . . My interpretation is that Jesus was not a teacher but
a liberator. He was not a builder but a liberator. He was not a
hawker of tradition: he was a liberator.' The church, on the other
hand, had turned Jesus into doctrine and was concerned now with
handing on a tradition. Worse than this, the bishops were the
inseparable allies of the ruling establishment.

> If the bishops walk around in robes, attend the top civil and
> political functions (and have their photo in the newspapers
> swatting a wasp away from Princess Margaret: one day's news
> from Lambeth), have police protection, spend their time talking
> about who they will or will not allow to receive communion—
> are they men whom other people will treat seriously? No, the
> bishops are already seen to have opted out of the situation most
> people in England are in.[99]

David Hart, himself at the time an Anglican curate, was plagued
by the monster of the episcopate. The only question for a bishop,
he suggested, was: Shall I resign now, or later? The church was
'a totalitarian monster' and represented 'illegitimate authority'.[100]

In October 1969 members of CHURCH demonstrated at St
Paul's Cathedral against a service to mark the disbanding of the
Middlesex Regiment. They held a Eucharist on the steps which
was broken up by the police. After the event a group of young
Christians wrote to a radical Christian journal:[101]

> Last Saturday's affair showed the cathedral's present position
> in a dramatic form. When the great west door was opened, and
> the cathedral hierarchy stood to welcome the Lord Mayor and
> his party, these clerics looked down upon limousines and wooden
> crosses. Which group would the cathedral be *seen* to support?

... Whom does St Paul's show solidarity with? The forces which sweep away the Eucharist to make straight the way for marching feet? Or those foolish people with balloons and slogans who believe that the church is the sacrament of a new society, not the shrine of an unjust world.

In April 1969 the next stage of the movement began with the first issue of *The Catonsville Roadrunner*, described as a radical Christian monthly. The group who started it were basically the same group that made up CHURCH, and it is from this point that one sees the beginnings of a move towards a real Underground Church in Britain. From being a pale and rather naive imitation of Berkeley, very precious and introverted, *Roadrunner* has become one of the most significant organs of Christian protest, at a time when radical Christian journals are virtually extinct. It represents a tradition of youth Christianity which is totally at variance with the Jesus movements, but which represents an important direction, and may, in the long run, prove to be of more lasting value. *Roadrunner* was produced 'by and for the revolutionary Christian scene' and was described by its original editors as being 'about love, about Jesus, about liberation, about justice, for real'. Early articles were concerned with war and peace issues, reports on Spain, South America, on the Berkeley Free Church, and on South Africa. Later came issues on communes, drugs, sex and the Church Commissioners. At the beginning of 1972 *Roadrunner* moved from London to Manchester, its present base, and since then it has become an integral part of the radical scene in the north-west.

Roadrunner, and the radical Christian tradition which it represents, is often accused of being only nominally Christian. Micheal Jacob complains that it 'seems to have left Christianity behind'.[102] Clay Ford, in his account of Berkeley, made a similar complaint against the Free Church which, he felt, 'comes close to being a left wing political organization, ministering only to the physical needs of the street people'.[103] The danger of losing contact with spirituality is one which worries some *Roadrunner* followers, and this lay behind the Seeds of Liberation conference held at Huddersfield in January 1973. So Peter Jones wrote in *Roadrunner* just before the conference that radical Christians were in danger of losing their original spiritual roots, and Viv Broughton, one of the founders of CHURCH and of *Roadrunner*, was pointing out that 'there are spiritual dimensions

to political liberation just as there were spiritual dimensions to
political oppression'.[104] There has been an awareness of the need
for contemplation, and of Dan Berrigan's words, 'The time will
shortly be upon us, if it is not already here, when the pursuit of
contemplation becomes a strictly subversive activity'. The Berrigans
are among the heroes of the Underground Church along with Archbishop Helder Camara, Thomas Merton, and Dick York. But the
spirituality of the conventional churches is very suspect, and
Roadrunner is filled with cynicism and mockery towards conventional
religion.

Among the supporters of the new radical Christianity are many
who stand outside the institutional churches and who feel the urgent
need to build an alternative church, rejecting the claims of the
present church to be the Body of Christ.[105] But there are others,
like the Berrigans, Colin Morris and Paul Oestreicher, who appear
in the pages of *Roadrunner*, who stand within the institutions, but
would be associated with the general standpoint of the Underground
Church. The first issue of *Roadrunner* itself claimed that 'our first
task must be to resurrect the lifeless corpse of the church community'.[106] But the institutional churches themselves suffer severe
condemnation. *Roadrunner* would be solidly behind the sentiments
expressed by the Berrigans and their colleagues in a statement
issued before burning sixty draft-card files with home-made
napalm:

> We are Catholic Christians who take the Gospel of our Faith
> seriously. . . . We confront the Catholic Church, other Christian
> bodies, and the synagogues of America with their silence and
> cowardice in face of our country's crimes. We are convinced that
> the religious bureaucracy in this country is racist, is an accom-
> plice in war, and is hostile to the poor. In utter fidelity to our
> faith, we indict the religious leaders and their followers for their
> failure to serve our country and mankind.

So the new radical church stands as a protest against ecclesiastical
as well as political corruption.

The conflict between protest and celebration is present in the
Underground Church as in the Underground itself. 'Celebrate life'
is a commonly used slogan. The atmosphere of *Roadrunner* is very
different from that of the old-style protest movements of the
Christian Left with their heavy and intense supporters (although

Conrad Noel's Catholic Crusade was not unlike CHURCH in some respects). Geof Bevan in an early *Roadrunner* emphasized the element of celebration, dancing and laughter. 'Life is theatre. Doing your thing and getting away with it is good, revolutionary theatre. Letting yourself be arrested, going through all that illegitimate legal crap and voluntarily walking into the gaol is bad, masochistic theatre. It is the duty of the revolutionary to stay out of gaol. Never explain what you are doing. Then they will understand and understanding is the first step to control. Do the creative thing—burning —taking over—building alternatives—and maybe people will get it. If they don't, sod 'em, maybe they'll get it next time.'[107] For some, however, this is mere hippy evasion, unrealistic, pseudo-radicalism. But the celebration approach received a boost from Harvey Cox's portrayal of Christ as a harlequin and of the liturgy as wild fantasy. 'Comic hope is the mood of our embryonic religious sensibility today. . . . Its Christ is the painted jester whose foolishness is wiser than wisdom. Its church meets wherever men lift festive bowls to toast joys remembered or anticipated. Its liturgy is the exuberant enactment of fantasy before the eyes of a prosaic world.'[108] The radical youth church represents, on a small scale, a recovery of vision and of poetry, and its mood is characterized by the sense of celebration as much as by protest and resistance.

But protest and resistance are there also. John Pairman Brown brought this out strongly in his sermon at Dick York's ordination in 1969. 'Jesus is a child of the Galilean Resistance: he rejects its tactics and goals; but he sticks to the death by its cry against injustice. The "kingdom of God" was its name for the happening it wanted to see. Jesus adopts its name and its proletarian constituency: but he transforms both name and people. He says that the liberated zone they were hoping for wasn't future but present.'[109] On this view, Jesus makes more sense today that at any time in between. For now a more vicious imperialism lords it over man, and it is in a situation of organized violence that the Christian must walk knifeedge between violence and counter-violence. In Dick York's words, 'Jesus wasn't in the establishment non-violence bag' and 'the apostles were Vietcong', yet Jesus insisted that the Kingdom of God, the revolution, could not be achieved with human weapons. The Christian is therefore committed to revolution, but sees it as God's revolution.

The Jesus people and the radical Christians have one word in common: Revolution. But they differ fundamentally in their use of the idea, and the central disagreement is about eschatology. In general the Jesus movement is adventist and otherworldly. The radical church is concerned with the Kingdom of God as a present reality, in conflict with the powers and values of the present world order. It is this conflict, between two differing interpretations of Christianity, which will form the most important division between the Christians of the future.

8
Churchquake?

Why do they not look to Christianity? Again there are many reasons here. Perhaps the most important is that Christianity has through nearly 2,000 years of history condoned too much violence, blessed too many wars, and created too much hatred for it to preserve much credibility. Today the organized Churches seem in the main to be on the side of repression, of big business, and all the established values. The attempts of the Churches to relieve the poverty of the Third World seem pathetic when one remembers the strength of the powers whose vested interest lies in the preservation of this poverty. At a more personal level, most of the people in the Underground experienced Christianity as a negative system breeding guilt and fear, denying spontaneity in the name of a facile otherworldliness. The more modern style Christianity with its emphasis on human relationships, political involvement and social work, its greater permissiveness and its respect for human values, does not impress them any better because of its timidity with respect to spiritual values and the supernatural. The Christianity of the secular city has even less to offer them than that of the ecclesiastical city. In both these forms Christianity with its voluminous intellectualism and activist preoccupations seems too bound up with what they diagnose as the diseases of western culture.

They have a great respect for the figure of Jesus as portrayed in the Gospels. Unlike most modern exegetes, they take it for granted that he enjoyed a state of exceptional enlightenment and was sustained by a beatific union with the one he called God. They are sceptical of the exclusive claims of orthodox Christianity, and the intellectual arguments of the theologians leave them cold. Many are not unaware of the Christian mystical tradition. *The Cloud of Unknowing*, Dame Julian, Eckhart, even St John of the

G

Cross are found on their shelves along with Eastern classics. They are treated as witnesses to a universal mystical tradition. But it is not easy for them to find centres where they can learn these methods or masters willing to guide them.[1]

BAD CHURCH VIBRATIONS

I have quoted at length this passage by Father Paulinus Milner, a Dominican who has been an important presence within the Underground spiritual scene, because it expresses so well why the church is, on the whole, not acceptable to these new seekers. Father Milner isolates three general areas of the church's life which condemn it and neutralize its impact: its support for, and condoning of, war and violence, its general acceptance of the status quo and of established values, and its apparent lack of deep spirituality. In the first area, the Christian record on war is a bad one. The traditional doctrine of the 'just war' has been distorted until it has become meaningless. As Pairman Brown stresses, a just war is one fought by my side, an unjust war is one fought by the other side.[2] The established churches invariably support military violence when it is practised by the Government in power, or at least they remain silent. Non-violence, however, is recommended to the victim of oppression, whether in North America or in Southern Africa, but such recommendations, by those who are seen to represent wealth and security, carry little if any weight. Martin Luther King was hailed and praised after his death by many churchmen who, during his life, opposed all that he stood for. The exploited feel that the church's advice to them—'Be non-violent, resist not evil'—is insincere, is based on self-interest, and, historically, is seen to be hypocritical. It is easy to recommend non-violence to other people. And in practice, the established churches have tended to support repressive violence but oppose revolutionary violence. They recommend non-violence to the weak, while violence is practised by the powerful, with the church's blessing.

It is no longer possible, if it ever was, to hide this support for militarism by the established churches, from either the Third World or the younger generation at home. Westminster Abbey stands like a monument to modern war. The god Mars might well be a more suitable patron for many of our cathedrals with their flag-waving, militaristic performances. It is absurd to expect such places to make sense to the young rebels, or to speak to them of the poor man of

Galilee. Moreover, when the young hear accusations of 'moral pollution', 'permissiveness' and immorality coming from men who openly support war and injustice, they are more and more confirmed in their belief that Christians operate on the basis of a highly selective (and convenient) view of morality. Clergymen who parade about with service medals amidst weapons and regimental standards do incalculably more damage to Christianity, in the minds of these young people, than do those who hold 'liberal' views on sex. This is not to say that it is not possible to stand by one's principles in the fields of political *and* sexual morality. But the truth is that very few do so. Trevor Huddleston is a shining exception. In general, 'absolute moral standards' turn out to be about sex, not about war. The young see this as doublethink. For them 'Make Love, Not War' and 'Lay, Don't Slay' are popular slogans which express a preference. The church may denounce them as immoral, but its denunciation will cut no ice, for its hands are stained with blood.

So in the growth of a counter-culture, the Vietnam War has been a focal unifying factor. The evil of Vietnam has helped to expose other evils. It is ironical that, while many Americans bewailed the spread of heroin addiction at home, the very war which was producing violent opposition and helping to create a strong counter-culture, was also spreading the heroin epidemic, fed from within the reactionary regimes supported by the American Government itself. So one result of the war has been a massive increase in heroin addiction. Again, it became clear that black servicemen were being sent to Vietnam to fight for a freedom which they did not enjoy at home. At least, on the issue of the war, the Episcopal Church and other Christians have earned respect by their establishment of, and support for, draft counselling centres. But crucially the war has placed the biggest of all question marks against the essential goodness of American capitalism and imperialism. In the Second World War, Hitler dropped rather less than eighty thousand tons of bombs on Britain. But since 1965 the United States has dropped over seven million tons of bombs in Indo-China. What is this 'Christian civilization' which needs to be defended by such barbarism? Is it worth defending? Christianity, the religion of western imperialism, is seen as an oppressive force, the inseparable ally of aggression.

Secondly, the church is seen generally as part of the established order. In spite of individual reformers, its official record on social justice is not a good one. In the nineteenth century, the bishops either opposed, or failed to support, Roman Catholic emancipation, the removal of Jewish and nonconformist disabilities, abolition of hanging, extension of the franchise, educational reform, and the limiting of child labour, and, indeed, there was scarcely any issue of social justice from which they emerge with credit. 'The Church of England does not have a good record with regard to Labour questions', said the 1920 Lambeth Conference with characteristic understatement.[3] The church has been noticed clearly to side with wealth against poverty. It is identified with the unyoung, uncoloured and unpoor of Britain as well as of the world. In Britain, the Church of England is an upper and middle-class institution, associated with propping up conventional structures. As a recent writer has said, 'its ethos and outlook is that of an agrarian age' while 'the church leaders who have any real grasp of the way in which a technologically-dominated society functions and coheres can be counted on the fingers of one hand'.[4] In areas of violent social change, the church stands in many cases as a monument to the past. Devotion too reflects and perpetuates this situation: it is refined and proper, 'carefully insulated from the world in which coal is mined and lemon-meringue pie is made'. 'Betjeman is only too justly its poet; away from the horrors of concrete and the internal combustion engine, it kneels among the bad copies of Murillo and Raphael, or the high culture of asymmetric and angular stained glass decorations, and sighs because it must leave the quiet pew for the office or the kitchen sink.'[5]

I am not, of course, unaware that there is another side to the picture, that there are urban ministries of great power, and that many Anglicans are closely involved with contemporary issues. But the general picture remains depressing, and it is certainly the picture which many of the young see, and which keeps them far away from the church.

The evidence to support the view that the Church of England is a predominantly upper-class and middle-class institution is overwhelming and has often been presented, but the salient facts bear repetition. The very presence of the church in urban working-class areas was an afterthought of the Industrial Revolution. The population of Britain grew from five million in 1700 to six million in 1750, eleven million in 1800, twenty-one million in 1850, and thirty-seven million in 1900. Yet apart from fifty churches built in Queen Anne's reign, there was no church building until an Act of 1818. In 1843 the Church of England in Lancashire could only provide seats for 40.3 per cent of the county's population. Engels in 1844 noted that 'all the writers of the bourgeoisie are unanimous on this point that the workers are not religious and do not attend church'. The 1851 census bore this out strongly. The myth of the devout working-class was propagated by the Hammonds[6] but is now seen to be fallacious. Even Methodism probably only affected at most one-tenth of the population. The Roman Church alone gathered large numbers of working-class people, but they formed part of the *Irish*, not the English, working class. By the end of the nineteenth century the complaint that the parish system had broken down in the urban areas was a common one. 'The parochial system is no doubt a beautiful thing in theory and is of great value in small rural districts', said Lord Shaftesbury in 1855, 'but in the large towns it is a mere shadow of a name'. Booth in 1902 pointed out that the great section of the working class 'remains, as a whole, outside of all religious bodies'.[7]

The Paul Report of 1964, which also summarized the work of other researchers, exposed clearly the class nature of the Anglican ministry in England. Every diocesan bishop in office in 1960 had been to a public school, as had most bishops for a hundred years, almost all had been to Oxford or Cambridge, and about half had connections with the landed gentry or the peerage. Of 494 ordinands studied by Coxon and cited by Paul, 35 per cent were from public schools, 43 per cent from grammar schools, and only 22 per cent from secondary schools.[8] Some 67 per cent described themselves as middle class. In view of this, it is hardly surprising that the Church of England functions best in middle-class communities. Moreover, the pattern of distribution of clergy showed what Paul described as 'a haphazard distribution of men',[9] with 41·7 per cent of the clergy serving 11·2 per cent of the population, and 14·6 per cent of the clergy serving 34·7 per cent of the population.

It is in the poor urban areas that one sees the class nature of Anglicanism at its most painful. It is in the urban twilight zones, districts of deteriorating housing in those parts of cities which were middle-class residential districts in Victorian times, that one sees groups and races in conflict. Yet it is there that church communities often represent what Robert Moore has called 'a ritual re-establishment of the old order'.[10] Rex and Moore's study of Sparkbrook, Birmingham, painted a depressing picture of the churches as the upholders of a 'stable' society which was rapidly passing away, upholders of a dying culture.

So in society we see the church identified with conservatism rather than with change, with conformity rather than with revolt, identified, that is, with one segment of the population. 'The society of the status-ridden career, of the expense account, of the large bureaucratic corporations, tends to produce a majority of conformists, and a minority of eccentric anarchic rebels. The stereotype of the organization man has as its counterpart the stereotype of the Beat generation.'[11] In the conflict of the old and new orders, the church is solidly behind the old order. Clergymen may still proclaim that they are strangers and pilgrims, but it is obvious that they are established strangers and endowed pilgrims.

Thirdly, the church is seen as a non-spiritual or even an anti-spiritual force. So much of the ferment which has shaken the youth culture has left the church unaffected. As one young priest has commented, 'there has been almost a complete lack of dialogue between Christians and the exponents of secular mysticism'.[12] It is in fact significant that the mystical revival among young people has occurred at a time of spiritual confusion in the institutional churches. At exactly the time that liturgical reform was leading to simpler forms of worship and the casting out of unnecessary garments, the colourful psychedelic youth of 1967 began to wear chasuble-like vestments acquired in Portobello Road. Against the background of 'South Bank radicalism' and the Harvey Cox of *The Secular City*, the hippy mystics began to seek for a very different city. It has been said that the hippies discovered the transcendent at the point at which the new theologians lost it. But it was certainly true that for many years before the youth mystical scene exploded, mysticism had been under heavy fire in the Western Christian tradition. The social gospel of the early years of the century had seen the mystical quest as escapist pietism, while later Biblical theologians, influenced by Karl Barth, suspected the search for union with God as unbiblical, subversive of evangelical truth, and the ultimate attempt of fallen man to grasp at the Divine. It is not surprising that the church did not appear to be very favourable to mysticism. Moreover, in 1961 William Hamilton was writing of the remoteness and irrelevance of the God of conventional orthodoxy and claiming that 'it is a very short step, but a critical one, to move from the otherness of God to the absence of God'.[13] So the 'death of God' school became a force in American theology at exactly the same time as young people outside the church began to seek God by other means and other routes.

So for a number of reasons, the church in the West has been left behind in the current spiritual quest among the young. As one young person expressed it, the vibrations that come from the church are bad vibrations. Again, one needs to emphasize, there are exceptions, some of which have been mentioned in earlier chapters. But, taken as a whole, the church remains substantially unaffected by the movements which we have described. Yet it would be absurd to give the impression that nothing had happened within the institutional churches, and we need therefore to consider the kind of changes which have already happened during the period under discussion.

SIGNS OF HOPE

We can point to eight areas in particular where a considerable amount of activity has taken place, but much of it has been confined to the mainstream churches and has only spilled over in the direction of the counter-culture at a few points. In the first place, there is, and has been for some time, a growing dialogue between Christian spirituality and the East. Dom Bede Griffiths, in his well-known study *Christian Ashram*, which was subtitled 'Essays towards a Hindu-Christian dialogue',[14] opened up a whole field of Indian religious ideas in relation to Christianity. Thirty years earlier, Rudolf Otto had written a good deal about the classic types of Eastern and Western mystical experience.[15] More recently, the works of R. C. Zaehner,[16] Klaus Klostermaier,[17] Kenneth Cragg,[18] John V. Taylor,[19] J.-M. Dechanet,[20], Enomiya-Lassalle,[21] and Dom Aelred Graham[22] have presented major contributions to the dialogue of religions. From Rome since 1969 there have appeared a number of small works aimed at providing guidelines for such dialogue on a wider scale.[23]

The relationship of Zen to Christian spirituality has occupied the minds of a number of well-known writers including Thomas Merton,[24] Dom Aelred Graham and Father Enomiya-Lassalle. Graham suggested that 'the spirit of Zen may find a congenial dwelling place within Catholicism' and that 'Catholic spirituality . . . moves at the same profound level as the metaphysical tradition behind Zen Buddhism'.[25] Enomiya-Lassalle has argued that 'the Zen method can coexist with Christian meditation and even render the good service of disposing for prayer',[26] and he went on to explore the ways in which Zen meditation might be of help to the Christian ascetical tradition. Thomas Merton claimed that there were close similarities, but also contrasts, between Zen and Catholic mysticism. 'On the psychological level, there is an exact correspondence between the mystical night of St. John of the Cross and the emptiness of *sunyata*. The difference is theological: the night of St. John opens into a divine and personal freedom and is a gift of "grace". The void of Zen is the natural ground of Being—for which no theological explanation is either offered or desired.'[27]

Others have written articles favourable to Zen, one writer calling it 'a way of Christian prayer' and observing: 'One feels that St. John of the Cross or St. Teresa of Avila would have warmly approved; also the author of *The Cloud of Unknowing* and many others, including those who maintain the Hesychast tradition of prayer in the Orthodox Church . . .'[28] And there is much more to the same effect.[29]

Again, there has been a growing dialogue between Christians and Hindus, a dialogue which received new impetus as a result of Pope Paul VI's encyclical *Ecclesiam Suam* of 1964.[30] Dom Bede Griffiths has stressed the need for Christians and Hindus 'to meet in the interior depths of the soul'.[31] More recently we have become acquainted with the remarkable work on prayer by Abhishiktananda, a Benedictine living at the Saccidananda Ashram near Tiruchirupalli,[32] while in Britain Father William Slade has begun a pattern of contemplative prayer involving Yoga exercises at a small centre in Sussex. At the level of prayer, Christians have begun to draw upon and learn from the techniques of Hindu Yoga.

The second notable development has been the growth of interest among Christians in contemplative prayer, a movement not unrelated to the spread of Eastern religions, though itself having much wider growth. The writings of Thomas Merton have been of outstanding importance. His *Seeds of Contemplation*[33] appeared first in 1949 and became extremely popular. Later came a large number of books, including a study of the use of the Psalms in contemplation[34] and a book on contemplative prayer itself, published soon after Merton's death.[35] Writing in the preface to the latter book, Douglas Steere brings out the importance of Thomas Merton who was, he pointed out, 'not only open to the existentialist voices of our time but to the important but largely neglected contributions to monastic culture which come to us through the insights of fellow contemplatives among the Zen Buddhists, the Hindus and the Muslim Sufis'.[36] Merton too was held in great regard in the peace and non-violent movements, and through his writings many have come to understand more clearly the unity of contemplation and action. Other major influences in the popularizing of ideas about the life of prayer have included Teilhard de Chardin,[37] Archbishop Anthony Bloom[38] and Monica Furlong,[39] while more restricted audiences have found help from such writers as Dominic M. Hoffman,[40] Neville Ward,[41] Paul Hinnebusch,[42] Hans Urs Van Balthasar[43] and Pere Voillaume.[44]

Contact with the contemplative orders has also been a major resource point for the revival of prayer life. In the Anglican Church, communities such as the Sisters of the Love of God at Fairacres, Oxford, have exercised a profound influence. Through the writings of Mother Mary Clare and of their former warden, Gilbert Shaw, increasing numbers of Christians have been led to less rigid and more affective forms of prayer. Most of the material issued by the sisters is in pamphlet form and is very suited to intelligent young people, many of whom have found an immediate rapport with contemplatives.[45] Among other writers of popular pamphlets, Dr Martin Israel deserves a mention: a pathologist with a deep interest in the relationship between psychology and spirituality, his contributions on the spiritual life are extremely valuable.[46] In addition to such sources, there is the vast and increasing amount of material on the spiritual tradition of the Orthodox Churches. Largely through the writing and speaking of Archbishop Anthony Bloom, more people are now familiar with the Orthodox, and there are many within the Western churches who have gained considerably from use of the Jesus Prayer, from participating in the Orthodox Liturgy, and from the study of Orthodox spirituality.[47]

Thirdly, since the 1950s there has been an explosion within the American and British churches of the 'pastoral counselling' movement. The significance of this for spirituality is not only that it has focused attention on what are termed 'disorders' of the emotional and spiritual life, but also that it has emphasized the importance of relating psychological to spiritual wholeness. While it is true to say that the pastoral counselling movement has tended towards a 'problem-solving' approach to human life, it has undoubtedly led many Christians to a deeper awareness of the mechanisms of their inner worlds. Study of the frontiers of theology and psychology by such writers as C. G. Jung,[48] Victor White,[49] Michael Fordham[50] and, more recently, Frank Lake and his Clinical Theology school[51] has inevitably had effects on our understanding of prayer. Thus Lake says,[52] 'A dark night of the spirit in which "god" appears in all the most terrifying forms, such as could put the Christian off wanting to trust him at all, has to be traversed by those who are called to move out of a detached spirituality with schizoid undertones into a life of union with God as he meets and loves us through the touch and sensitivity which others can extend to us as soon as we stop distancing them.' Some priests, such as Father Christopher Bryant, have devoted a great deal of time to exploring the relationship between depth psychology and such areas as prayer, self-examination and repentance.[53] But by far the most significant aspect of the counselling revival has been that 'straight' Christians or Christian-orientated people have been brought into direct personal contact with individuals in crisis situations. The work of the Samaritans is the most striking example of this, but there are others. A recent writer in a homosexual journal has even complained of the excessive Christian influence on the Campaign for Homosexual Equality and has given this as his reason for not joining it![54] Yet it still remains true that this is an approach which is directed towards problems—their identification, avoidance or solution. A 'hang-up theology'[55] is not an adequate expression of Christian belief.

Fourthly, as explained earlier, the resurgence of Pentecostalism has been to a great extent within the non-Pentecostal churches of America, Europe and Britain. Today there are many Anglicans who speak of the 'gifts of the Spirit', of the 'baptism of the Spirit' and the gift of tongues, and churches are transformed by the Pentecostal movement into centres of burning faith and zeal. It is at this point that the movement within the institutional churches most clearly links up with movements outside it, for the charismatic and Jesus movements are inseparable. Pentecostalism affects, to some degree, the majority of Jesus people. But even prior to the Jesus movement, Pentecostalists were among the leading Christian figures in work with drug abusers.

Simon Tugwell in his important study points out that 'the beginning of contemplation is, in scholastic terms, the conscious coming into play of the gifts of the Spirit bestowed in principle at baptism, but only now beginning to exercise their proper role in actual life and experience'.[56] But there are many experiences of the Spirit, not one special privileged type, and it is very probable that the experience of contemplative prayer and the charismatic experience, characterized by speaking in tongues, are not so far removed as one might think. The gift of tongues is often the first introduction to praise, and so it becomes 'the moment of spiritual breakthrough, parallel to tears, or the prayer of quiet'.[57]

It is important, however, not to accept the new Pentecostalism uncritically. Though it does represent a search for a theology of living experience and a recovery of the lost unity of theology and prayer, it tends to be occupied with inward holiness and private redemption only, and 'has developed no theological instrument to deal with major human issues'.[58] The record of the older Pentecostalist groups on issues of social justice is poor.[59] 'Our big conferences have no pronouncements to make upon the burning issues of the day, such as war, race, sex, youth, atheism, want', complained a leading Pentecostalist in 1964.[60] Michael Harper, the leading spokesman of the new Pentecostal movement, has himself pointed to three major weaknesses: a tendency to denigrate the human mind and thought and to claim special revelation; a tendency to pietism; and an elitist trend. 'In South Africa the largest Pentecostal Churches support the government's policy of apartheid, and in North America the large Pentecostal Churches are not normally associated with causes like racial integration or poverty programmes.'[61] On the other hand, the new Pentecostal expansion in the Third World—in South America, Africa and Indonesia—may change this reactionary posture, and more even than in Britain, young people are being drawn to the Pentecostal churches there.

Fifthly, we should notice the liturgical revival, and the increased emphasis in both Roman and Anglican churches on corporate worship and celebration. The centrality of the Eucharistic rite has been stressed until today it is accepted, in theory at least, throughout most of the Anglican churches. There is a continuing search for new styles of liturgy, with experiments in language, modern music, house churches, and so on. Some of this new liturgical sense has attracted young people, the most spectacular example being the Taizé Community, where a whole cult has grown up with a strong sense of celebration and joy, expressed corporately in the Taizé Liturgy. As a result, many thousands of young people flock to

Taizé, and a Council of Youth is in preparation. The Taizé atmosphere is quite different from the Jesus movements. There is a strong
emphasis on the resurrection and the common life of a new community, and on the Christian presence as a sign of contradiction in a
society dominated by profit and individualism. The spirit of Taizé
is re-created in cell-groups in many areas of different countries, and
there is great insistence on the church and the Eucharist as focal
points of community. God, say the Taizé people, 'is preparing a
spring time of the church: a church devoid of means of power,
ready to share with all, a place of visible communion for all
humanity'.[62] But, while such a movement as this has had a powerful
international impact, the liturgical revival as a whole has mainly
affected those already within the churches.

Sixthly, we saw above that the Underground Church tradition,
as represented in Britain by *Roadrunner*, was not entirely outside
the boundaries of the institutional church, and that there was a
significant area of overlap at this point between the establishment
and the counter-culture. This should not be overstated, but one
cannot ignore such events as the Seeds of Liberation conference
which SCM organized in Huddersfield in 1973, or their recent
handbook *People's Church*. Many full-time priests of the Church
of England would identify themselves with the radical tradition of
Christian social action. But there is very little direction of this
feeling into political organization. The Christian socialist movement
is more or less extinct, and there is no authentic left-wing movement
of any significance in Britain which derives its inspiration from
Christian theology. The young Christian radicals have few reference
points, and, while many Christians are vaguely left-wing in their
outlook, there has been little serious theological work on the political
consequences of being a Christian.

Seventhly, we should mention the dialogue between Christians
and Marxists. This has certainly been an important development,
and a number of volumes of essays have been published.[63] Unfortunately, the debate has tended to be carried on at a high-powered
level, and local churches and local Marxist groups have largely been
unaffected by and even unaware of it. In addition, the dialogue
seems to have been restricted so far to leftish Christians and to the
mainstream members of the Communist Party of Great Britain.
But, as we have seen, the Communist Party enjoys little favour in
the counter-culture, and even Marxism itself is increasingly criti-

cized. Dialogue between Christians of various political shades, and
the complex range of revolutionary political groups in the Underground has scarcely begun.

Finally, it is very important to recognize that 'paperback theology'
has transformed the whole structure of the Christian propaganda
machine. No longer do views filter slowly through the ecclesiastical
tubes, but they are fired violently upon the unchurched public.
Honest to God, which appeared in 1963, was criticized in some
quarters not for what it actually said, but rather because it bypassed
what were naïvely believed to be the 'proper channels'. But such
protests belong to an age long past. Today there is a ready market
for serious theological writing, not least outside the church. No
longer can the pulpit be the sole, or even the most important,
method of delivering Christian truth. Theologians now speak
directly to the man in the street, and so theological knowledge is
widely disseminated, even if it circulates in a confused way.

These are all important changes which have affected the church,
but they have not brought the church into direct contact with what
has been happening among the young, with the possible exception
of the Pentecostal movement. The dialogue with Eastern religions
has not for the most part had any relation to the Eastern mystical
revival in the Underground. The spread of contemplative prayer
has not on the whole been related to the contemporary spiritual
quest among youth. The areas of pastoral counselling and liturgical
renewal are fairly inward-looking, and, allowing for the exceptions
previously mentioned, have not affected very large numbers of
young people outside the institutions. The Christian-Marxist
dialogue does not seem to connect with the Marxist movements of
the political Underground. So, although there are signs of hope and
of change, they tend to run alongside the counter-culture, and only
interact with it at a few points. They are important indications of
change *within* the church, and their importance for communities
outside it is indirect. So while it may be true that 'the prospect of a
New Reformation is clearly in sight',[64] it is not clear how such a
movement is going to affect the increasing numbers of people for
whom the affairs of the institutional churches are of little, if any,
interest.

THE MESSAGE FOR THE CHURCHES

How can the Christian communities in the West learn from, and

be of service to, the new spiritual revolt among youth? I would
identify five urgent needs which can be classified as follows. First,
the need to deepen the contemplative and mystical dimension in
Christian spirituality, and to recover a viable pattern of spiritual
direction. Secondly, the need to understand the spiritual motivation
behind much drug use, and to point to alternatives. Thirdly, the
need to learn from, and use, the accumulated spiritual experience
of the East, as well as to learn from, and use, the insights from the
counter-culture itself. Fourthly, the need to understand and cope
with the increasing problems of occultism. Finally, the need to
rediscover a revolutionary Christian social and political tradition.
In short, what I am arguing for is more theology, but it must be
relevant and applied theology, not the arid intellectualism which is
often passed off as theology. The recovery of such a living theology
is more important than changes in dress, furniture or language. For
the real crisis for the church today is a theological crisis.

First of all, I believe that it is absolutely vital that lines of communication and dialogue should be established between the Christian
spiritual tradition and the movements within the counter-culture.
But this presupposes that the Christian spiritual tradition is still
alive. I believe that it is, but there is certainly a great deal of
ignorance and confusion within the church. Many clergy have little
idea of, or acquaintance with, their own traditional disciplines of
prayer and contemplation. In many theological colleges, the practice
of prayer and fasting is at a low ebb. There is continuous criticism
of 'traditional spirituality', often by people who seem not to have
read the writers whom they attack. So it is at a time when young
people outside the church are busy rediscovering the traditional
writings of the East that many Christians are dismissing out of
hand the masters of the spiritual life in the Western church. So it is
that the clergy are often the last people to be consulted about the
spiritual quest. Ronald Laing has written:[65]

> How many priests have first hand awareness of such meta-egoic
> experiences which thousands of young people seem desperately
> to need? . . . How many people ever go to priests for guidance
> in these respects, for orientation? How many priests know about
> this even at second or third hand? How many regard it as relevant,
> even to their vocation to have this knowledge? How many
> theological colleges or seminaries discuss these issues?

Frank Lake has equally harsh words to say about some clergy.[66]

> The mishandling of spiritual transitional states has other results than the arrest of spiritual growth and maturation. The alien mental contents which are being ejected in the course of sanctification are, in the minds of untrained clergymen, labelled 'For psychiatrists only'. The whole significance of what is going on in this Christian person is missed. The Holy Spirit is moving in, and the clergyman is frantically engaged in trying to stop the dispossessed devils from being pushed out.

So from two psychiatrists comes the call to take priesthood seriously. The priest is seen by Laing as one who guides men into another world. 'Among physicians and priests there should be some who are guides, who can educt the person from this world and induct him to the other. To guide him in it: and to lead him back again.'[67]

We need to devote a good deal of attention then to the ideas of priesthood and the cure of souls. The priest is primarily a man of God, concerned with the vision of God, that is, with prayer. 'The sole aim of priesthood', wrote Marie de la Trinité, 'is the contemplation of the Divine.' I believe this to be true. Priesthood is an office which demands a profound spirituality. 'It is the office which inwardly, ritually and ascetically shares the dying and rising of Christ.'[68] We need, therefore, priests who are steeped in prayer, who have learned the deep things of the Spirit, who are at home in silence and darkness. We need, in short, priests who are contemplatives in the world. It is here that Thomas Merton's description of the role of the monk in the modern world can be applied to the priest and, indeed to all Christians.

> . . . this is an age that, by its very nature as a time of crisis, of revolution, of struggle, calls for the special searching and questioning which are the work of the monk in his meditation and prayer. . . . In reality the monk abandons the world only in order to listen more intently to the deepest and most neglected voices that proceed from its inner depths. . . . This is the creative and healing work of the monk, accomplished in silence, in nakedness of spirit, in emptiness, in humility. It is a participation in the saving death and resurrection of Christ.[69]

But are we in fact leading men to this high view of priesthood? There are signs of hope but there is still too much sloppy and undisciplined thinking about the pastoral ministry, which leaves the spirituality of the priest an open question. Clergy are often seen as leaders, counsellors, social workers, managers, but not as spiritual guides. Yet, if my account is at all correct, it is guidance in the spiritual quest which so many young people want, and it is because priests are seen as being incompetent at this level that they make so little impact. I believe that Martin Thornton is correct when he says:[70]

> One calls in a plumber because he understands plumbing, not because of his wide experience of life, and one is coached by a golf professional *because* he is *not* a weekend amateur. One is suspicious of a doctor who has read no medical book for twenty years and knows nothing of modern drugs, and I suspect that intelligent modern Christians are getting suspicious of clergy who are for ever engaged in something other than prayer, learning and suchlike professional occupations.

One of our greatest needs at present is for priests who are concerned primarily with the search for God.

I would therefore strongly endorse Thornton's view that 'spiritual direction is our greatest pastoral need today'.[71] If clergy are to be of any value to the large numbers of young people who are seeking personal illumination and who are considering the Christian path, they will need to be competent in spiritual disciplines. 'Priests of the future, it may be, will learn not only to preside at the Eucharist, but to lead the faithful in meditation, after the manner of an Eastern guru.'[72] This will involve serious training of the priest for such spiritual work, and mean efficient planning so that he is free to devote a great amount of time to it. Planning is not the enemy of spirituality but its necessary condition. It is only when there is proper organization of manpower, using any of the insights of current social and industrial theory which are applicable, that the priest can hope to be liberated from the complexity of activity and be able to see where his major emphasis needs to be laid.

If the priest is to be a useful spiritual guide, he needs to familiarize himself with the tradition in which he stands. I believe that much of the suspicion of 'traditional spirituality' is misplaced. What is termed 'traditional spirituality' is in fact a vast range of schools and traditions within the field of the life of the Spirit, and to generalize about them is unwise and dangerous. Of course we need to assess the value of particular ways of prayer or approaches, and there will be some which ought to be rejected. The tendency to disparage the material world, for example, has been a destructive influence on much Western spiritual writing, and the effect of the view, expressed by Thomas à Kempis, that union with God demands a withdrawal from human beings, can only be termed disastrous. At the same time, it is quite wrong to dismiss in a blanket manner the entire history of asceticism on the grounds that it is based on wrong ideas of God, or of the relation of God to the world, and so on. The spiritual writers of the past were not so naïve or ignorant as we often suppose, and their writings can teach us a great deal about questions which we wrongly suppose to be modern. 'Traditional spirituality is a system of far greater profundity, relevance and flexibility than many Protestant theologians are prepared to admit.'[73]

The failure to take note of the experience of the spiritual masters has recently been criticized by a number of writers. The Bishop of Willesden has rightly pointed out that the fashionable impatience with history has had the effect that we have been asked to travel down roads which have already been shown to be dead ends.[74] On the other hand, in the field of Christian spirituality, there have been attempts to recover some of the *methods* of prayer used by the masters but without the accompanying disciplines and relationship with God. Aelred Squire in a recent valuable study[75] has attempted to initiate a dialogue between the teachings of the old Christian fathers and those who, like Matthew Arnold, are

wandering between two worlds, one dead,
The other powerless to be born
With nowhere yet to rest my head.[76]

It is by a rediscovery of the Christian tradition of prayer and mysticism that we shall realize the richness and variety of this life and of those who are skilled guides within it. Nothing could be further from the truth than the view that 'traditional spirituality' is a dull and rigid system. It may well be, as Eric James has said,[77] that for many young clergy the traditional spiritual disciplines have gone dead, but this is as often the result of sheer unfamiliarity and ignorance as it is of the inadequacy of the methods themselves. For within the tradition there is an enormous diversity. The spirituality of the New Testament itself and of the early fathers[78] is a vast world of tremendous power and praise.[79] Among the fathers, such writings

as those of Gregory of Nyssa[80] or the Pseudo-Dionysius[81] are of
outstanding significance in the history of mysticism. The Middle
Ages contained a wide range of Christian spiritual teachers,[82]
including the Benedictine[83] and Cistercian monks,[84] the twelfth-
century school of St Victor,[85] the Franciscans and Dominicans. The
fourteenth-century flowering of mysticism produced such works as
The Cloud of Unknowing, Walter Hilton's *The Ladder of Perfection*,
Julian of Norwich's *Revelations of Divine Love*, and Thomas à
Kempis's *The Imitation of Christ*,[86] as well as the works of Eckhart,
Ruysbroeck and Richard Rolle.[87] The tradition of English spirtua-
lity, both before and after the Reformation, is in itself a vast treasure
house of guidance and wisdom.[88] In addition, there is the whole
field of the Eastern mystical writers in the Orthodox tradition, not to
mention the heritage from evangelical and Puritan sources. The
world which opens up is one of variety, richness, excitement and
progress.

Progress is in fact one of the key contributions of the spiritual
masters to our understanding. They saw that the life of prayer was
characterized by development and conflict. The 'holy warfare' was
a familiar idea. They spoke of *growth* in the inner life. In the
Carmelite tradition, as represented supremely in the writings of
St John of the Cross, there is a stress on the experience of darkness
in the life of faith.[89] St John is full of warnings against an unhealthy
interest in collecting 'good experiences'. For him, the crucial period
of spiritual growth and maturing is the 'dark night of the soul', the
crisis through which a man is led by the Spirit of God. St John's
teaching has a particular relevance for our time when 'it may be
confidently said that many many souls in this country at the present
day reach this stage' of the dark night and the beginnings of contemplation. But, the same author comments sadly: 'Because few
directors are able to recognize the state or have sufficient knowledge
of the principles involved at this point, only a very small proportion
of such souls is adequately directed'.[90] The writings of St John of
the Cross have additional relevance to the present concern with the
frontiers of theology and psychiatry.[91] Most of all, St John is
concerned to emphasize that the experience of darkness is a necessary
element in the knowledge of God. As Dom Hubert van Zeller says,
'in the journey of the spirit, the traveller moves fastest at night'.[92]

Above all, we need to learn from the tradition that the 'spiritual
life' is not a separate dimension, but is a description of the entire

life of a man in relation to God. The separation of 'theology' from 'spirituality' must be firmly rejected. *Theologia* is the science of God, it is the search for God. 'A theologian', wrote Evagrius of Pontica, 'is one whose prayer is true.'[93] Until the twelfth century, theology was not so much a way of knowing as a way of prayer. After St Thomas, theology began to lose its roots in prayer and contemplation. Today's young spiritual seekers will only be drawn by a theology which is firmly rooted in experience and in the vision of God, not one which merely gathers information about, or peripheral to, God. Here the Eastern fathers are quite explicit. 'It is a great thing to speak of God, but still better to purify oneself for God', wrote St Gregory Nazianzen.[94] St John Climacus emphasized that 'the climax of purity is the beginning of theology',[95] and that the goal of our search is to be transformed into the Divine nature. Theology is a process of renewal. 'It is an existential attitude which involves the whole man: there is no theology apart from experience; it is necessary to change, to become a new man. To know God one must draw near to him. No one who does not follow the path of union with God can be a theologian.'[96] The knowledge of God comes through a process of faith and prayers.[97]

If the church is to recover credibility with modern man, it needs to become more, not less, theological. The priest in each parish needs to see himself as a theologian, one who points to the mystery of God. 'Other disciplines will be judged primarily on the quality of their articulation; theology will be judged primarily on its ability to point to mystery. The only distinctive function theology can or need claim is that of being the guardian and spokesman of insight and mystery.'[98] The priest's primary function therefore is to point men to God, and in so doing he stands within a tradition of prayer and experience. In the current revival of magic and occultism, the resource points for literature are a relatively small number of bookshops and journals. Yet every parish in Britain has a priest who ought to be such a resource point for the Christian tradition of spirituality. If he is not there to be a spiritual guide, what is he there for?

Secondly, I believe that we need to recognize that behind a great deal of drug use there is a fundamentally spiritual motivation. To reject the route taken is not to reject the object of the quest. Instead of seeing all young drug users as disturbed, delinquent and decadent, we need to look beneath the surface and our labelling processes, and

ask, 'What is the desired aim and object of this individual's use of
this drug?' I have suggested that the use of drugs and the search
for God may be more closely linked than we have thought.

The use of drugs by religious people is of great antiquity. Hallucinogenic herbs and mushrooms have been used in the context of
religious worship, drugs have been taken as aids to meditation and
to relaxation. It was shown in earlier chapters that chemically
induced 'religious experiences' are no new phenomenon. What is
important from the standpoint of spirituality is whether the external
chemical agent helps or hinders the union of the soul with God.
There needs therefore to be continuous 'theological monitoring' of
the psychedelic claims, and this can only be done by theologians
who stand both within the drug culture and within their own spiritual tradition. It is a difficult role, but one with which theologians
are familiar in other areas.

If we have learned from the teachers of prayer, we should have
some guidelines for the evaluation of psychedelic drug use. Three
points seem to me to be important. First, there is in principle no
theological reason why certain psycho-active chemicals should not
play some role in spiritual development. On this, if on nothing else,
Alan Watts and Professor Zaehner are agreed![99] But the question
which needs to be asked is: are they likely to aid or hinder the soul's
openness to the operation of the grace of God? One American priest
has argued that 'the psychedelic experience can be a temporary
breaking down of the numerous blocks against transcendent reality
which the personal ego of man has erected'.[100] Allan Cohen, on the
other hand, claims that 'the adoption of psychedelics as a way or
method for attaining higher consciousness is a barrier to the goal
itself'.[101] Secondly, the spiritual writers are unanimous that the
use of *any* means of awakening consciousness or any ascetical
discipline is open to abuse. So St John of the Cross warns against
dependence on experiences or 'apprehensions', and claims that such
dependence creates 'a complete impediment to the attainment of
spirituality'.[102] Thirdly, the aim of Christian prayer is not expansion
of consciousness or enlightenment but the vision of God. Techniques and methods must be assessed in relation to this ultimate
goal. Moreover the Christian is more concerned with such virtues as
love, humility, peace and joy than with expansion, ego-transcendence
or cosmic consciousness. There is little evidence so far that
psychedelic drugs can be of more than marginal importance in the

awakening of love. Yet it is he who loves, who is born of God and shares God's nature (1 John 4.7; 3.9).

There is another facet of the use of drugs which needs to be mentioned. There is abundant evidence that the caring professions, including the priestly ministry, place those within them under conditions of severe emotional stress. It is in such conditions that drugs, particularly of the sedative-hypnotic type, are likely to be abused. Among the clergy the drug of choice is invariably alcohol, and there is sufficient evidence of severe dependence and of heavy drinking problems and alcoholism among bishops and clergy to give one cause for alarm. Pastoral care of drug abusers needs to be applied to those within the ministry, who are often the most neglected. But it is important to be sensitive to the possibility that one's own ministry may be jeopardized by abuse of alcohol. 'There but for the grace of God go I', is profoundly true. Drug abuse is an occupational hazard of human caring.

It is no accident that the young look to the East for guidelines. It is there, rather than in the Western Christian societies, that they believe they can see true spirituality. What can Christians learn from the Eastern traditions? There is so much. We can deepen our understanding of insight and consciousness, that is, of the necessary conditions of faith, from a study of Zen. We can learn a great deal from the Hindu texts about the discipline of body and mind— the necessary condition of the beginnings of prayer. We can learn from Eastern approaches to meditation and contemplation and from their teachings gain help for our own lives of prayer. Many have found that, through the practice of Yoga, the grace of Christ is able to flow more freely. Certainly this way is not for all Christians, but there are many who would agree with Déchanet that Indian methods of control over thought and over their psychic being can be of profit to us in the West in the search for inner peace. Déchanet has pointed to a number of specific areas—the use of breath-control in prayer, the use of silent meditation, for example. He offers a pattern for ascetical discipline, derived from Hindu Yoga, which can aid the growth of Christian prayer.[103] Similarly Abhishiktananda uses the Indian *namajapa*, or prayer of the name, and develops it in a Christian way.[104]

From the East too we can learn of the importance of the *guru*, the enlightened one, and of the need for care in choosing such a teacher.[105] We can learn a lot about the relationship of prayer and

action. 'Could Zen's function in the West be to heal the breach
between religion and daily life?' asks Dom Aelred Graham.[106] We
can learn how to increase our capacity for solitude and silence.

On the other hand, there is a great deal that we can learn from
the youth culture itself: the meaning of spontaneity and natural
celebration, the importance of music, rhythm and the use of the
body, the sense of 'togetherness' which is often more apparent at
pop festivals than in churches, and so on. It is easy to romanticize
the Underground. There is as much viciousness and phoneyness
there as anywhere else. Yet there is a real spiritual awareness in
many places which Christians ignore at their peril, and this is often
in part the result of the interest in the East.

A fourth area in which a great deal of serious theological work
needs to be done is the field of occult involvement and dabbling
with magical practices. Again, it is ironically at a time when many
Christians discount, rather than renounce, the Devil and his works,
and evil forces, that numbers of the young are discovering for
themselves the awful reality and power of evil. But here we need to
distinguish a number of elements in the revival of the occult. There
are cases of physical and psychological disturbances which may be
wrongly identified with evil spirits. There are cases of involvement
with such practices as ouija boards, seances and various spiritualistic
phenomena. There are incidences of poltergeists and haunted houses.
And there are the witchcraft and Satanist groups. None of these, in
themselves, constitute demonic *possession*, nor are they 'black magic'.
The marginal occult practices are statistically the most common,
while cases of actual possession are relatively rare.

If we look for orientation to the New Testament, there is no
doubt that demonology is an important element there. Every New
Testament writer makes some reference to demonic power or powers.
Nor are the demons a peripheral element. The conflict of Jesus
with the powers of evil is something absolutely central to the
Gospel message.[107] In this emphasis, the New Testament was
influenced by apocalyptic demonology with its strong sense of the
kingdom of evil.[108] In the Gospels, however, the stress is on Satan.
Jesus saw his ministry of casting out demons as one element in the
greater work of casting out Satan and destroying his kingdom.[109]
Indeed, throughout the New Testament, there is the belief in
Satanic power and in the activity of demonic forces, although there
is a distinction between disease and the demonic (in such passages

as Matt. 10.1; Mark 1.32, 34; 6.13). The powers afflict and distort not only individuals but political institutions.[110] Thus imperial Rome is seen as the dwelling place of demons and foul spirits (Rev. 18.2). But, says the New Testament, Christ has conquered such powers (Col. 2.15; Eph. 1.21), and his victory is shared by the church. Thus, while cases of actual possession are relatively uncommon in the New Testament, the activity of the powers (archai, exousiai) and the rulers of this age (kosmo-kratores) in afflicting and disturbing men is everywhere assumed. The Son of Man was manifested precisely in order to destroy the works of the devil (1 John 3.8) and by sharing human nature he destroyed the devil's power over men (Heb. 2.14).

In evaluating and interpreting the New Testament data, however, there are two common dangers. The first is Biblical fundamentalism. It is unfortunate that Michael Harper's book on demonology,[111] which is widely used by charismatic Christians, seems to depend on a pre-critical and more or less literalist view of the Bible, as do the works of Unger[112] and Koch[113] on which he relies. This does not mean that such works are of no value, but one cannot build a sound theology of evil on unsound foundations. There is a real danger that, confronted with an epidemic of alleged occultism, some Christians might regress to a fundamentalist approach because it appears to be effective. Yet, however tempting the fundamentalist view may be, one cannot evade the responsibility of serious theological work. Among Biblical fundamentalists, one common dangerous tendency is to attribute all forms of 'evil' to demons, including many phenomena which have a perfectly straightforward biochemical or psychological explanation, and many which are not evil at all. One can easily become obsessed with demons, and it may be argued that obsession with demonic activity is itself demonic! Certainly, many of those involved in the exorcism movement seem to go off the rails and become very unbalanced, both psychologically and theologically. A second danger in the belief in demons is that one runs close to a Gnostic view of the world in which the devil becomes an ultimate force of evil, equal to God who is the ultimate force of good.

Yet, it seems to me, we cannot abandon the truth which the New Testament demonology embodies: that there are non-human spiritual powers of evil. The conventional view that cases of 'possession' can all be explained in terms of physical or psychological disturbance does not seem to me to be adequate, and it is now questioned by some psychiatrists.[114] One French neurologist has called for cooperation between doctors and theologians in this area,[115] while others have pointed out the relationships between possession and other conditions. 'The possession syndrome may be associated with psychoses or neuroses, some with clouding of consciousness, some with epileptiform convulsions. Others with a more insidious onset may remain lucid and with full insight, able to discuss the possession, the passivity of feelings. There are abnormal somatic sensations, weakness, anxiety and depression.[116] Cases of physical and psychological illness too may easily be mistaken for demonic possession. Anaemia may be confused with possession, but vitamin B12 and iron tablets will suffice, rather than exorcism! States of vitamin deficiency and of drug use often cause confusion in identifying spiritual states. Schizophrenia, epilepsy, psychopathy, senile dementia and mental handicaps all need to be carefully distinguished.[117] Yet when such diagnoses have proved unsatisfactory, one should not rule out the possibility of possession or of 'occult subjection'.

Those who are involved with the occult need careful spiritual guidance. It might be added at this point that those Anglican bishops and clergy who are themselves involved with Freemasonry are not, in my view, suitable persons to be involved in this ministry. Freemasonry is 'very close to the occult traditions'[118] and so long as we tolerate involvement with this cult by Christians, we are in no position to condemn others for involvement with other forms of occult and pagan methods. It is important to see the care of those who have been involved in occultism as one facet of the total healing ministry of the church, liberating men from slavery and subjection. Sacramental confession is of immense value, and after-care is vital. The individual who has been released needs to be built up and nourished in the life of faith, and the priest will need to guide him in study of the Scriptures, in prayer and in the Christian life. Laying on of hands and anointing can be of value in the context of a continuing ministry, while exorcism will be used where there is clear evidence of non-human influences. Exorcism must never be seen as 'Christian magic'. Certainly the pagan exorcisms are an exercise of personal power, meeting magic with magic. Christian exorcism is the binding of evil powers by the triumph of Christ and is an exercise of the *exousia* of Christ over the powers. In exercising the ministry of exorcism in relation to individuals, very great caution is needed. Prayer, confession, laying on of hands with anointing, and communion will suffice in most cases, and only when there is strong evidence of demonic activity should one exorcise. It is the demon, not the human, who is exorcised. Nevertheless, this ministry is an important one, and it is probably largely because the church has failed to act against evil at the level of the spirit that so many have turned to pagan rituals for spiritual help and direction. As occult involvement increases, so the practice of the Christian warfare, involving contemplation, fasting and healing ministry, must increase also. The recovery of contemplative prayer and the recognition of the depths of the power of evil are closely linked.

Finally, no Christian presence will be adequate today which is not concerned with the transformation of the world. For too long we have distorted the Gospel into individualist pietism and ignored the hope for the renewal of the earth, for a new world in which righteousness dwells. Today it is non-Christians who are taking seriously the demands of justice and equality, the demands of the material universe itself, and the responsibility for creating a new order. The Christian social ethic seems to be in exile.

It has been shown that two trends in the counter-culture, that towards mystical enlightenment and that towards political radicalism have been moving further apart, and at least in this respect the Church of England is like the Underground! But the Christian social tradition claims that to hold together these two trends is an essential element in the Gospel. The revolution in the external world and in the inner world of man is one. Yet in practice a good deal of the Christian social hope has only entered the modern world through Marxism, the last and greatest of the Judaeo-Christian heresies. When Spengler called Christianity the grandmother of Bolshevism and Marx the last of the Schoolmen, he testified to the origins of Marxist thought in the Judaeo-Christian tradition, and other writers have also pointed to these origins. Marxism is 'the newest of the universal salvation religions',[119] it is 'a secularism and an atheism such as only a Christian culture can produce . . . the form under which the concepts of traditional Christianity have entered into the contemporary world'.[120] Today, however, a good deal of institutional Marxism has become rigid, and its prophetic and humanist elements have been lost.

Yet the Marxist hope has transformed large parts of the world, and it is only our insularity in Britain which prevents us from seeing revolution as the central facet of our age. Revolution is not a Biblical concept. But the New Testament speaks of *metanoia*, *dunamis* and *koinonia*—repentance, power and common life—and of the transforming of creation, of new heavens and a new earth. Revolution occurs when the new order meets the old. So much conventional Christianity has lost the sense of a new world, and reduced the Christian hope to mere individual salvation. But the young seekers outside the church are looking for a re-uniting of the inner quest with the outer. An earlier generation of rebels, the Catholic socialists of the early years of this century (who have many similarities with the present Underground Church) had a strong sense of the need to change the world. Conrad Noel, the 'red vicar' of Thaxted and founder of the Catholic Crusade, for instance, held 'the conviction that Our Lord preached the destruction of the world, or more properly the Age in which he lived, and the impending substitution upon this earth of another "world" or renovated order of things, a Divine Commonwealth or Age to Come'. He saw the church as 'the organ of that coming age, the nucleus of the univeral Kingdom wherein dwelleth righteousness, the midwife of a new world in the pangs of birth'.[121] It is this awareness which needs to be rediscovered. Its rediscovery, claimed the Anglican prophet Canon Percy Widdrington in the 1920s, would 'involve a Reformation in comparison with which the Reformation of the sixteenth century will seem a small thing'.[122]

The conflict between an otherworldly and a revolutionary view of the Christian Gospel is a basic feature of the contrast between the Jesus movement and the Underground Church. But the conflict runs throughout the entire Christian world, and it cuts across denominational barriers and divisions. It is the conflict between Billy Graham and Martin Luther King, between Enoch Powell and Trevor Huddleston. What is the Christian hope for this world, for society, for the environment, for politics? From the days of the Guild of St Matthew, the Catholic Crusade and the Christian Social Union, the Christian Left in Britain has declined, and all that has remained is a vaguely theological reformism.[123] Recently, however, there has been a revival of concern about theologies of revolution and conflict. Out of the resistance to Nazism came a number of theologians in Germany who owed a great deal to Karl Barth—men such as Dietrich Bonhoeffer, Martin Niemoller and Helmut

Gollwitzer. From Germany too have come the 'theologians of hope', Jurgen Moltmann, Johannes Metz and others, who have wrestled with the demands of political revolution.[124] In Britain, the writers on the Catholic Left have attempted to work out a sacramental and socialist theology.[125] So far, however, most of this theological thought has not been 'earthed'. To the common man, the Christian hope is set firmly in another world, in that country of which we sing 'soul by soul and silently her shining bounds increase'. In social and political terms, the church is behind the old order, for other-worldly theology in most cases produced this-worldly conformism.

A commitment to the Kingdom of God is vital for any Christian, but the Kingdom must be seen as beyond this present order and at many points incompatible with it. Conflict is an inevitable part of the Gospel. As Harvey Cox has written, 'there is no need to create a new revolutionary theology' because 'rightly understood the Bible itself is a revolutionary document'.[126] The problem for the contemporary church is that it has lost its understanding of the necessity of conflict, and it has narrowed and distorted its message of salvation. Moltmann writes:[127]

> If we take seriously this eschatological background in the prophets against which the proclamation of the Gospel by Christians takes place, then the goal of the Christian mission must also become plain. It aims at reconciliation with God (2 Cor. 5.18 ff), at forgiveness of sins, and abolition of godlessness. But salvation, δωτηρια must also be understood as shalom in the Old Testament sense. This does not mean merely salvation of the soul, individual rescue from the evil world, comfort for the troubled conscience, but also the realization of the eschatological *hope of justice*, the *humanizing* of men, the *socializing* of humanity, *peace* for all creation.

So a theology of the Kingdom must be *Biblical*. The Bible is the most dangerously subversive set of data which the church possesses. But it must also be *catholic*, integral, whole, and for all people—not precious, elitist, culturally confined, narrow, sectarian, cliquish. It must be aware of the need for total *renewal*. Nothing less than death and rebirth will satisfy the Gospel demand for transformation, for a new man. Finally, it will be *revolutionary*. The church, if it is true to the good news of the Kingdom of God, will be placed in a situation of conflict and of warfare against the principalities and powers, against the false values of the present world order. When the church is seen to stand for the new age and to suffer for its witness, young people may begin again to take it seriously. Or is it already too late? Only God knows the answer.

References

CHAPTER 1

1 Richard Neville, *Playpower* (1970), p. 14.
2 T. R. Fyvel, *The Insecure Offenders* (1963 ed), 18, 23.
3 Peter Worsley in *New Society* (22 July 1965), p. 11.
4 Fyvel, op. cit., p. 60.
5 Cf. the language used by the judge in sentencing Ronald Fletcher to three years' imprisonment and fourteen members of his 'gang' to varying degrees of imprisonment in 1962. 'This gang warfare has to be stamped out.' 'Turning 'em over in Finchley' (*Observer*, 15 July 1962).
6 Lewis Yablonsky, *The Violent Gang*. 1962.
7 D. M. Downes, *The Delinquent Solution* (1966), p. 117.
8 See Paul Barker and Alan Little, 'The Margate offenders: a survey' (*New Society*, 30 July 1964).
9 *Brighton Evening Argus*, 18 May 1964.
10 *Evening Standard*, London, 19 May 1964.
11 18 May 1964, cited in Charles Hamblett and Jane Deverson, *Generation X* (1964), p. 19.
12 Alec MacGuire (*New Society*, 18 May 1964), p. 5.
13 Cf. Jeremy Bugler, 'Puritans in boots' (*New Society*, 13 November 1969), p. 762: 'The style first appeared in 1967, either in the East End of London or the industrial north.'
14 Cf. Bugler, ibid: 'The conventionality of the skinheads, in urban working class society, is paramount. They endorse accepted values.' Bugler appears to be under the misapprehension that the term 'bill' (police) was of skinhead origin: it is in fact a long-established term used by ex-convicts and delinquent youth.
15 Bernard Davies, 'Non-swinging youth' (*New Society*, 3 July 1969), p. 8.
16 *Daily Mail*, 27–30 November 1967.
17 Albert Cohen, *Delinquent Boys: The Culture of the Gang* (1955), p. 13.
18 J. Milton Yinger, 'Contraculture and subculture' (*American Sociological Review*, 25.5, October 1960), pp. 625–35.
19 R. A. Cloward and L. E. Ohlin, *Delinquency and Opportunity: A Theory of*

Delinquent Gangs (1961), cited in Downes, op. cit., p. 13. See also Yablonsky's
The Violent Gang. 1962.

20 Downes, op. cit., pp. 134, 135.

21 Colin Fletcher, 'Beat and gangs on Merseyside' (*New Society*, 20 February
1964), pp. 11–14.

22 See David Downes, 'The gang myth' (*The Listener*, 19 April 1966), pp.
534–7.

23 Cf. Charlie Gillett, *The Sound of the City.* 1971.

24 Orlando Patterson, 'The dance invasion' (*New Society*, 15 September 1966),
p. 403.

25 Charles Reich, *The Greening of America* (1971), p. 183. Cf. also Theodore
Roszak, *The Making of a Counter Culture* (1969), p. 63.

26 Dan Morgan, 'Rocking the boat' (*The Guardian*, 4 November 1971). For an
earlier view of Prague see Paul Jones, 'Taking pop to Czechoslovakia'
(*Tribune*, 31 December 1965). *The Observer* on 14 September 1969 noted,
'The Blossom Toes were in the Czechoslovak Socialist Republic to preach
revolution. They preach it in their music, which is a strange hybrid of beat
and electric guitar Asian jazz. "I'm a peace-loving man—but haven't you
ever wanted to shout NO", they screamed, and the crowd whistles back its
approval.'

27 Cf. Andrew Weiner, 'Political rock', *New Society*, 27 January 1972, and
Mick Farren's letter in ibid., 10 February 1972. Farren argues that 'a
generation of white kids getting into their bodies for the first time in
centuries . . . is the major contribution of rock and roll as a force for change
in society.'

28 Cited in Richard Neville, op. cit., p. 84.

29 E. P. Thompson, 'The New Left' (*New Reasoner*, Summer 1959), pp.5, 3.

30 J. M. Cameron, 'Welfare capitalism: criticism and diagnosis' (*The Listener*,
15 September 1960), p. 407.

31 'Outside the whale', pp. 141–94, and 'Revolution', pp. 287–308.

32 Ibid., p. 308.

33 Ibid., p. 191.

34 Ibid., pp. 188, 189–190.

35 Cited in David Boulton, ed., *Voices from the Crowd* (1964), p. 59.

36 Labour Party, *Annual Conference Report 1960*, p. 25.

37 *New Advance*, February 1961. For a detailed account of the Labour youth
movements of this period, see Will Fancy and John Phillips, 'The Young
Socialists' (*International Socialism* 10 Autumn 1962), pp. 3–14.

38 *Daily Worker*, 8 August 1945.

39 *Labour Monthly*, April 1955.

40 *Marxism Today*, May 1959.

41 Arnold Kettle in *Marxism Today*, October 1960.

42 On the intellectual disillusionment with the Communist Party see Neal

Wood, *Communism and British Intellectuals* (1959), and Alasdair MacIntyre, 'Communism and British intellectuals' (*The Listener*, 7 January 1960).

43 E. P. Thompson, 'The New Left' (*New Reasoner*, Summer 1959), p. 9. The whole article, 1–17, is invaluable.

44 A. H. Hanson, cited in *New Reasoner* (Winter 1958–9), p. 90.

45 *The Times*, 16 April 1963.

46 Christopher Driver, *The Disarmers* (1964), pp. 59–60.

47 Ibid., p. 118.

48 Ralph Schoenman, 'Resistance in mass society' (*Peace News*, 25 August 1961).

49 This speech was reported in *Peace News* on 13 April 1970. *The Observer* on 16 April 1961 also reported Russell as saying on this occasion. 'We used to call Hitler wicked for killing off the Jews. but Kennedy and Macmillan are much more wicked than Hitler. . . . We cannot obey the murderers. They are wicked. They are the wickedest men in the story of man, and it is our duty to do what we can against them.'

50 Raymond Williams, ed., *The May Day Manifesto*, 1968.

51 Tariq Ali, *The Coming British Revolution* (1972), pp. 104, 105.

52 Michael Schofield, *The Sexual Behaviour of Young People*. 1965.

53 S. Cohen and A. Waton, *New Society*, 4 November 1971.

54 Richard Neville, op. cit., p. 74.

55 Ibid., p. 73.

56 See Germaine Greer, *The Female Eunuch*. 1970.

57 Anthony Storr in *Sunday Times*, 14 November 1971.

58 Cited in *Dublin Review* (Summer 1967), p. 87.

59 V. A. Demant, *An Introduction to Christian Sex Ethics*, 1963.

60 The most fantastic example of this is Thomas Wood, *Chastity not Outmoded* (S.P.C.K. 1965), p. 17.

61 *Church Times*, 11 January 1963.

62 See, for example, his *Time for Consent*, 1967.

63 John Clellon Holmes, cited in *Beat Poets*, selected by Gene Baro (1961), p. 5.

64 Ibid., Allen Ginsberg, 'The Reply', pp. 31–2.

65 Lawrence Lipton, *The Holy Barbarians* (1960), p. 135.

66 Ibid., p. 156.

67 Jack Kerouac, *On the Road* (1961), pp. 56, 40.

68 Ibid., p. 90.

69 Ibid., p. 213.

70 Jack Kerouac, *The Subterraneans* (1962), p. 5.

71 David McReynolds, 'Social rebels or juvenile delinquents?' (*Peace News*, 12 August 1960).

72 Geoffrey Ostergaard in *Freedom*, 27 August 1960.

73   Lawrence Lipton, op. cit., p. 126.

74   Ibid., pp. 146, 153.

CHAPTER 2

1   R. Cockett, *Drug Abuse and Personality in Young Offenders* (1971), p. 36.

2   G. B. Adams, 'Patients recieving barbiturates in an urban general practice' (*Journal of the College of General Practioners*, 12, 1966), p. 29.

3   Peter Parish (*Drugs and Society*, 7·1, April 1972), p. 12.

4   Ibid., pp. 13–14.

5   See my *A Practical Guide to the Drug Scene* (1973) for a fuller account.

6   On amphetamines see P. H. Connell, *Amphetamine Psychosis*, 1958, O. J. Kalant, *The Amphetamines: Toxicity and Addiction*, 1966, and my *A Practical Guide to the Drug Scene*, 1973, Chapter Two.

7   Council on Drugs: 'Abuse of the Amphetamines and Pharmacologically Related Substances' (*Journal of the American Medical Association*, 183, 2 February 1963), pp. 362–3.

8   Committee on Alcoholism and Addiction: Dependence on Amphetamines and other Stimulant Drugs. (*Journal of the American Medical Association*, 197, 19 September 1966), pp. 1023–7.

9   See David E. Smith ed., 'Speed Kills: A Review of Amphetamine Abuse' (*Journal of Psychedelic Drugs*, 2·2).

10   For a fuller account of the differences see my 'The natural history of two drug cultures' (*New Society*, 1 June 1972), pp. 464–6.

11   P. H. Connell, *Amphetamine Psychosis* (1958), p. 71.

12   *Drug Addiction*, Second Report of the Interdepartmental Committee (1965), para. 40.

13   William Burroughs, *Junkie* (1966), p. 12.

14   Richard Neville, *Playpower* (1970), p. 119.

15   P. T. d'Orban, 'Heroin dependence and delinquency in women—a study of heroin addicts in Holloway Prison' (*British Journal of Addiction*, 65.1, 1970), p. 76.

16   I. Pierce James, 'Delinquency and heroin addiction in Britain' (*British Journal of Criminology*, 9.2, 1969), p. 123.

17   Official Records of the Economic and Social Council, 22nd Session, Supplement 8 (E/2891), para. 133.

18   *Cannabis*, Report by the Advisory Committee on Drug Dependence (H.M.S.O., 1968), para. 36.

19   T. H. Bewley, *Bulletin on Narcotics*, 18.4, 1966.

20   Don Aitken, 'Cannabis', MS. St Anne's Soho, 1970.

21   Ian Hindmarch, *Drugs and Society*, 1·1 (October 1971), pp. 21, 24.

22   Ian Hindmarch, ibid., p. 21.

23   Michael Schofield, *The Strange Case of Pot* (1971), p. 74.

24   Op. cit., para. 39.

25 David E. Smith ed., *The New Social Drug* (1970), p. 5.

26 *The Marihuana Problem in the City of New York*, 1944. There is a shortened version of the report in David Solomon ed., *The Marijuana Papers* (1969), pp. 281–390.

27 Cited by Alfred R Lindesmith in Solomon, op. cit., pp. 23–4.

28 Erick Goode, 'How the American marijuana market works' (*New Society*, 11 June 1970), p. 992.

29 *Marijuana and Health*. 1971.

30 David E. Smith, op. cit., p. 5.

31 Cited in *Peace News* (13 May 1966), p. 3.

32 *Hapt*. 1968.

33 Richard Neville, op. cit., p. 114.

34 W. H. McGlothlin in Solomon, op cit., p. 456.

35 J. R. Reynolds, 'Therapeutic uses and toxic effects of cannabis indica (*The Lancet* 1, 1890), pp. 637–8.

36 H. Isbell et al., 'Effects of (–)Δ^9-Trans-Tetrahydro-Cannabinol in Man' (*Psychopharmacologia*, Berlin, 11, 1967), pp. 184–8. Δ^9 THC is sometimes referred to as Δ' THC. See note 44 below.

37 W. D. Paston, in *Drugs and Society*, 9.1 (June 1972), p. 17.

38 A. T. Weil and N. E. Zinberg, 'Clinical and psychological effects of Marijuana in Man' (*Science* 162, 13 December 1968), pp. 1234–42. This is reprinted in Smith, op. cit., pp. 11–34. There is a more popular version of the experiments in Solomon, op. cit., pp. 391–400.

39 *Cannabis*, Wootton Report, op. cit., para. 30. And also the excellent survey of the clinical literature on cannabis in Appendix 1 of the Report.

40 David E. Smith and Carter Mehl, 'An analysis of marijuana toxicity', in Smith, op. cit., pp. 63–77.

41 See, for example, Ahmed Benabud, 'Psycho-sociological aspects of the cannabis situation in Morocco' (*Bulletin of Narcotics*, 9.4, 1957), pp. 1–16; I. C. Chopra and R. N. Chopra, 'The use of the cannabis drugs in India' (ibid., 9.1, 1957) pp. 4–9; T. Asuni, 'Socio-psychiatric problems of cannabis in Nigeria' (ibid., 16.2, 1964), pp. 17–28.

42 *British Medical Journal*, 26 August 1967.

43 Elizabeth Tylden, 'Pot is Not so Mild' (reprinted from *University College Hospital Students Magazine*, August 1969).

44 H. Isbell et al., *Studies in Tetrahydrocannabinol* (1968), p. 4844. See note 36 above.

45 *Cannabis*, Wootton Report, Appendix 1, pp. 50–1.

46 Cited ibid.

47 Joel Fort, 'Pot: a rational approach' (reprinted from *Playboy*, October 1969).

48 Howard S. Becker, in Charles Hollander, ed., *Background Papers on Student Drug Involvement* (1967), p. 72.

49 *The Non-Medical Use of Drugs* (1970), pp. 118–19.

H

50 J. T. Ungerleider, D. D. Fisher, S. R. Goldsmith, M. Fuller and E. Forgy, 'A statistical survey of adverse reactions to LSD in Los Angeles county' (*American Journal of Psychiatry*, 125, 1968), pp. 352–7.

51 J. R. Unwin, 'Non-medical use of drugs with particular reference to youths' (*Canadian Medical Association Journal*, 101, 1969), pp. 72–88.

52 David E. Smith, 'Acute and chronic toxicity of marijuana' (*Journal of Psychedelic Drugs*, 2, 1968), pp. 37–47.

53 Smith in *The New Social Drug*, op. cit., p. 76.

54 Professor J. W. Fairbairn, *The Times*, 4 November 1971. See also the papers in Richard E. Horman and Allan M. Fox, eds. *Drug Awareness*. 1970.

55 Timothy Leary, *The Politics of Ecstasy* (1971), p. 283.

CHAPTER 3

1 Cited in *The Amphetamines and Lysergic Acid Diethylamide* (LSD), Report by the Advisory Committee on Drug Dependence (1970), para. 83.

2 R. A. Sandison, A. M. Spencer and J. D. A. Whitelaw, *Journal of Mental Science*, 100 (1954), p. 498.

3 Ibid. See also R. A. Sandison and J. D. A. Whitelaw, 'Further studies in the therapeutic value of lysergic acid diethylamide in mental illness' (*Journal of Mental Science*, 103, 1957), pp. 332ff; A. A. Kurland et al., 'The therapeutic potential of LSD in medicine', in R. C. DeBold and R. C. Leaf, ed., *LSD, Man and Society* (1969), pp. 20–35.

4 Humphrey Osmond, *Annals of the New York Academy of Science*, 66 (1957), p. 418.

5 Aldous Huxley, *Heaven and Hell* (1956), p. 63.

6 Havelock Ellis, 'Mescal, a new artificial Paradise', *Annual Report, Smithsonian Institution* (1897), pp. 537–48.

7 G. T. Stockings, 'A clinical study of the mescaline psychosis with special reference to the mechanism of the genesis of schizophrenic and other psychotic states' (*Journal of Mental Science*, 86, 1940), pp. 29–47.

8 See further on this Max Rinkel and Herman C. B. Denbar, *Chemical Concepts of Psychosis*, 1958, and Leo Hollister, *Chemical Psychosis: LSD and Related Drugs*. 1968.

9 See on the distinction between psychedelic and psychotic experience, M. Siegler, H. Osmond and H. Mann, 'Laing's models of madness' in R. Boyers and R. Orrill, *Laing and Anti-Psychiatry* (1972), pp. 99–122.

10 N. Malleson, *British Journal of Psychiatry*, 118 (1971), pp. 229–30.

11 *The Amphetamines and LSD*, op. cit., para. 107.

12 W. N. Pahnke and W. A. Richards, 'Implications of LSD and experimental myticism' (*Journal of Religion and Health*, 5, 1966), pp. 175–208.

13 R. G. Smart and K. Bateman, 'Unfavourable reactions to LSD' (*Canadian Medical Association Journal*, 97, 1967), pp. 1214–21. On the dangers of LSD see also Sidney Cohen, *Drugs of Hallucination*, 1965, and *The Beyond Within*, 1970; J. T. Ungerleider, ed. *The Problem and Prospects of LSD*, 1968.

14 Benjamin Paul Blood, *The Anaesthetic Revelation and the Gist of Philosophy*, 1874.

15 William James, *The Varieties of Religious Experience* (1902), p. 388.

16 Alasdair MacIntyre, *New Society*, 6 April 1967.

17 Theodore Roszak, *The Making of a Counter-Culture* (1970), p. 164.

18 Roszak, op. cit., pp. 165–6.

19 Allan Cohen interviewed in *IT*, 5–17 December 1969, p. 19.

20 Cited in Warren R. Young and Joseph R. Hixson, *LSD on Campus* (1966), p. 57.

21 Timothy Leary, Ralph Metzner and Richard Alpert, *The Psychedelic Experience* (1966), p. 11.

22 Timothy Leary, 'The religious experience: its production and interpretation' in G. M. Weil, Ralph Metzner and Timothy Leary, eds., *The Psychedelic Reader* (1965), pp. 191-2.

23 Ibid., p. 195.

24 Ibid., pp. 195–6.

25 R. C. Zaehner, *The Times*, 1 May 1971.

26 *The Politics of Ecstasy* (1971), p. 287.

27 *Psychedelic Prayers after the Tao Te Ching* (1966), Foreword. Cf. *The Politics of Ecstasy*, p. 103: 'Unless you have an experienced guide . . . it would be confusing.'

28 Ibid.

29 League for Spiritual Discovery. MS, 1966.

30 *Los Angeles Free Press*, reprinted in *IT*, 79 (8–21 May 1970), p. 20.

31 *East Village Other*, September 1969, cited in Richard Neville, *Playpower* (1970), p. 119.

32 *The Politics of Ecstasy*, p. 38.

33 Ibid., p. 48.

34 Ibid., p. 69.

35 Ibid., p. 113.

36 Ibid., p. 184.

37 Ibid., p. 212.

38 Ibid., p. 223.

39 Ibid., p. 242.

40 Cited in Richard Neville, op. cit., p. 29.

41 The word itself is derived from Haight Independence Proprietors.

42 Nicholas von Hoffman, *We are the People Our Parents Warned Us Against* (1968), pp. 38–9.

43 *All Saints Episcopal Church Rector's Notebook*, 20 January 1970.

44 Cited in David E. Smith, John Luce and Ernest A. Dernberg, 'Love needs care: Haight-Ashbury dies' (*New Society*, 16 July 1970), p. 98.

45 J. F. E. Shick, D. E. Smith and F. H. Meyers, 'Use of amphetamine in the Haight-Ashbury subculture' (*Journal of Psychedelic Drugs*, 2.2, 1969), p. 140.

46 Smith, Luce and Dernberg, op. cit., p. 99.

47 H. R. Brickman, 'The Psychedelic "hip" scene: return of the death instinct' (*American Journal of Psychiatry*, 125·6, 1968), pp. 766–72.

48 Herbert Marcuse, *One-Dimensional Man* (1966), p. 256. Cf. his chapter 'The New Sensibility' in *An Essay on Liberation* (1972 edn), pp. 31–54.

49 Allan Y. Cohen, 'LSD and the search for God', MS, St Anne's Soho, London, 1969.

50 Ibid.

51 Ibid.

52 'Blessings in shades of green' (*The Times*, 15 July 1967).

53 Monica Furlong, *Contemplating Now* (1971), p. 88.

54 Among the many works of Walter N. Pahnke see 'Implications of LSD and experimental mysticism' (*Journal of Religion and Health*, 5.3, 1966), pp. 175–208 (with W. A. Richards); 'Drugs and mysticism' (*International Journal of Parapsychology*, 8.2, 1966), pp. 295–320; 'The Psychedelic mystical experience in the human encounter with death' (*Harvard Theological Review*, 62.1, 1969), pp. 1–32. Pahnke's major (unpublished) work is a Harvard Ph. D. thesis 'Drugs and mysticism, an analysis of the relationship between psychedelic drugs and the mystical consciousness'.

55 R. E. Masters and J. Houston, *The Varieties of Psychedelic Experiences*, 1966.

56 In R. C. DeBold and R. C. Leaf, ed., *LSD, Man and Society* (1969), pp. 63–4.

57 William James, *The Varieties of Religious Experience* (1902), p. 388.

58 This is argued by Peter G. Moore 'A phenomenological comparison between the allegedly mystical experiences induced by drugs and those experiences conventionally entitled mystical' in Paul H. Ballard, ed., *Psychedelic Religion*. Occasional Paper, Collegiate Centre for Theology, University College, Cardiff.

59 Sidney Cohen, *The Beyond Within* (1970), p. 102.

60 Alan W. Watts, *The Joyous Cosmology* (1962), p. 17.

CHAPTER 4

1 Rudolf Steiner, *Mysticism and Modern Thought* (1928), etc.

2 Alan Watts, *The Joyous Cosmology* (1962), etc.

3 Gerald Heard in C. Isherwood, ed., *Vedanta for the Western World* (1952).

4 *Bhagavad-Gita*, 6, pp. 16–17.

5 Philip Kapleau, *The Three Pillars Of Zen* (1966), pp. 288–9.

6 Cited in R. C. Zaehner, *Drugs, Mysticism and Make-Believe* (1972), p. 99.

7 Ibid., p. 119.

8 *The Politics of Ecstasy*, pp. 112–13.

9 C. G. Jung, *Collected Works*, Volume 14 (1954), p. 262.
10 Roszak, op cit., p. 126.
11 Alan Watts, *This Is It* (1967) edn, cited Roszak, p. 136.
12 Cited in Alan Watts, *The Spirit of Zen* (1936), p. 50.
13 Ibid., p. 176.
14 Ibid., p. 121. See D. T. Suzuki, *The Training of the Zen Buddhist Monk*, 1934, on the Zen communities.
15 D. T. Suzuki, *Introduction to Zen Buddhism* (1934), p. 74.
16 Christmas Humphries, *Zen Buddhism* (1961), p. 42.
17 Ibid., p. 44.
18 Thomas Merton, *Mystics and Zen Masters* (1967), pp. 12–13. Merton's *The Zen Revival*. London, Buddhist Society, 1970 is probably the best short account.
19 Roszak, op. cit., p. 134.
20 Ninian Smart, *The Religious Experience of Mankind* (1971), p. 680.
21 H. M. Enomiya-Lassalle, S.J., *Zen-way to Enlightenment* (1967), p. 126.
22 R. C. Zaehner, *Concordant Discord* (1970), p. 294.
23 *The Platform Scripture*, Wing-tsit Chan (1963), p. 147. See Zaehner, p. 291.
24 See I. K. Taimni, *The Science of Yoga* (1967).
25 *Alternative London* (1971 edn), pp. 103–4.
26 From leaflets issued by the Society for Creative Intelligence.
27 Fred E. Dexter in *12th Annual Conference*, International Narcotic Enforcement Officers' Association (29 August–3 September 1971), p. 68.
28 F. M. Brown, W. S. Stewart and J. T. Blodgett, 'EEG Kappa rhythms during Transcendental Meditation and possible perceptual threshold changes following'. Paper at Kentucky Academy of Science, 13 November 1972, MS.
29 On the research work see Demetri Kanellakos, 'Report on some of the current scientific studies on Transcendental Meditation', MS, and R. K. Wallace, 'Physiological effects of Transcendental Meditation' (*Science*, 167, 27 March 1970), pp. 1751–4.
30 Op cit., p. 6.
31 Cited in John K. Garabedian and Orde Coombs, *Eastern Religions in the Electric Age* (1969), p. 144.
32 *The Guardian*, 17 February 1972.
33 Cited by John Windsor in *The Guardian*, 18 February 1972.
34 *Report of International Inter-Religious Congress on Meditation and Action* (1969), pp. 21–2.
35 *The Sufi Messenger Quarterly*, January 1971.
36 Ibid.
37 Robert Graves in introduction to Idries Shah, *The Sufis* (1964), p. ix.
38 Seyyed Hossein Nasr, *Sufi Essays* (1972), p. 12.

39 Examples are L. Massignon, *Essai sur les origines du lexique technique de la mystique musulmane*, 1954, and H. Corbin, *Creative Imagination in the Sufism of Ibn 'Arabî* (E. T. 1969).
40 F. Schuon, *Understanding Islam* (E.T. 1963); *Dimensions of Islam* (E.T. 1970).
41 T. Burckhardt, *An Introduction to Sufi Doctrine* (E.T. 1959).
42 Seyyed Hossein Nasr, op. cit., p. 169.
43 Cited in Garabedian and Coombs, op. cit., p. 62.
44 *Back to Godhead*, 29, p. 1.
45 Leaflet, 'What *is* God?'.
46 Leaflet, 'Krishna Consciousness: what we believe'.
47 Socrates in Plato's *Phaedo*, cited by Hayagriva Das Brahmachary in *Two Essays on Krishna Consciousness*.
48 Swami A. C. Bhaktivedanta, 'Sex Life and Spiritual Life' (*Back to Godhead*). Undated.
49 Ibid.
50 *Back to Godhead*, 24 (August 1969), p. 3.
51 'Psychedelic drugs and Krishna Consciousness', MS. This is a very useful paper, issued by the International Society for Krishna Consciousness, 61 Second Avenue, New York.
52 *Meher Baba, The Avatar of the 20th Century* (Cosmic Meher Centre, Navsari), p. 14.
53 Ibid., p. 15.
54 *An Introductory Sketch on the Life and Work of Avatar Meher Baba and his Expositions* (Calcutta, 1962), p. 57.
55 *John Bull*, 7 May 1932.
56 *An Introductory Sketch*, etc., op. cit. p. 9.
57 See *Life at its best*. Sufism Reoriented, San Francisco, 1957.
58 *An Introductory Sketch*, etc., op. cit., p. 16.
59 Ivy O. Duce, *Sufism* (Sufism Reoriented, San Francisco), p. 6.
60 *Gems from the Discourses of Meher Baba* (Circle Productions, N. Y., 1945), p. 41.
61 Ibid., p. 42.
62 *God in a Pill? Meher Baba on LSD and the High Roads* (Sufism Reoriented, San Francisco, 1966), p. 1.
63 Allan Y. Cohen, 'The Journey Beyond Trips' (*A.R.E. Journal*, 3.4, Virginia Beach, 1968), p. 31.
64 Ibid., p. 2.
65 Ibid., p. 3.
66 *Meher Baba's Universal Message* (Meher Spiritual Center, Inc., Myrtle Beach, South Carolina).
67 *The Times*, 14 November 1972.
68 On 'Man Alive' on BBC2 TV, 31 May 1972.

69 See leaflet *The Meaning of Life*.
70 *Frendz*, 33 (1972), 8.
71 *The Times*, 14 November 1972.
72 See the interview with Raja Ram (*Gandalf's Garden*, 6, 1969), pp. 9–10.

CHAPTER 5

1   Murray Bookchin, 'The new Enlightenment' (*PeaceNews*, 26 May 1972).
2   Timothy Leary, *The Politics of Ecstasy* (1971 edn), p. 212.
3   Ian Dallas in *IT*, 64 (12–25 September 1969), p. 22.
4   Lisa Bieberman, *P.I.C. Bulletin*, 21 (December 1968, Cambridge, Mass.).
5   Lisa Bieberman, *Phanerothyme* (Psychedelic Information Centre, Cambridge, Mass. 1968), p. 5.
6   Roszak, op. cit., p. 125.
7   John C. Lilly, *The Centre of the Cyclone: An Autobiography of Inner Space* (1937), p. 16.
8   R. D. Laing, *The Politics of Experience and The Bird of Paradise* (1971), pp. 114–15.
9   Ibid., p. 119.
10 Charles Reich, *The Greening of America* (1971), p. 258.
11 *Frendz*, 33 (1972), p. 8.
12 I. M. Lewis, *Ecstatic Religion* (1971), p. 20.
13 Andrew M. Greeley, 'The new American religion' (*Concilium* 9.7, November 1971), p. 111.
14 *Other Scenes*, 204 West 10th Street, New York 10014.
15 *Bitman*, 3 (1971), p. 11.
16 *East Village Other*, 1–15 November 1967.
17 Roszak, op. cit., p. 140.
18 David E. Smith, 'What it is like to run a clinic in Haight-Ashbury' (reprinted from *The Osteopathic Physician*, January 1970), p. 6.
19 David E. Smith, 'LSD and the psychedelic syndrome' (*Clinical Toxicology*, 2.1, March 1969), p. 71.
20 From a talk given at St Anne's House, Soho, London, on 9 June 1970.
21 *Gandalf's Garden*, 3 (1968), cover.
22 Ibid., 6 (1969), p. 20.
23 Ibid., 3 (1968), p. 4.
24 Ibid., p. 12.
25 *Inner Garden Newsletter* 3, Midsummer 1971.
26 *Time*, 19 June 1972, p. 38. For more accounts see Nat Freedland, *The Occult Explosion*, 1972, a valuable study on which I have drawn for a good deal of the factual information.
27 Ibid.

28 See Jonathan Eisen, ed., *Altamont: Death of Innocence in the Woodstock Nation*. 1970. Cf. Nick Cohn, *Rock from the Beginning*, 1969.

29 Freedland, op. cit., p. 15.

30 Kurt Koch, *Occult Bondage and Deliverance* (1970), p. 46.

31 Ibid., p. 52.

32 C. G. Jung and W. Pauli, *The Interpretation of Nature and the Psyche*. 1955, p. 49. See Jung's essay 'Synchronicity: an acausal connecting principle', pp. 3–146.

33 *Occult Gazette*, March 1970.

34 Billy Graham, *The Jesus Generation* (1971), p. 161.

35 Roger Lewis, *Outlaws of America* (1972), p. 55.

36 Freedland, op. cit., p. 151.

37 Margaret Murray, *The Witch Cult in Western Europe*. 1921.

38 Freedland, op. cit., p. 160. Alex Sanders (whose story is told in *King of the Witches*) claims to have recruited 1,623 witches and organized them into 107 covens.

39 *Bitman*, 3 (1971), p. 104.

40 Cf. Geoffrey Ashe, ed., *The Quest for Arthur's Britain*, 1971.

41 Jon Pepper, 'The hippie vale of Avalon' (*The Guardian*, 20 December 1969).

42 Cited, ibid.

43 John Michell, *City of Revelation* (1972), p. 134.

44 Ibid., p. 55.

45 Nicholas Saunders, *Alternative London* (1971), pp. 100–21.

46 Peter Marin and Allan Y. Cohen, *Understanding Drug Use* (1971), p. 69.

47 Aleister Crowley, *Magick in Theory and Practice*, 1929.

48 Kenneth Grant, *The Magical Revival* (1972), p. 20.

49 Grant, op. cit.

50 Ibid., p. 210.

51 Ibid., pp. 5ff.

52 Christmas Humphreys, *The Field of Theosophy* (Theosophical Publishing House, 1966), p. 10, says that originally 'the main purpose was the study of spiritualistic phenomena'.

53 See H. P. Blavatsky, *The Secret Doctrine*, 1888, and *The Key to Theosophy*, 1889.

54 J. I. Wedgwood, *The Place of Ceremonies in the Spiritual Life* (London, St Alban Press, 1927), p. 7.

55 On Ward and others see Peter F. Anson, *Bishops at Large*, 1963, and Ward's own books such as *The Psychic Powers of Christ*, 1936.

56 On Palatine in relation to the present scene see Freedland, op. cit., pp. 103ff.

57 *A Call to Arms* (The Sovereign Imperium of the Mysteries), p. 27.

58 Ibid., p. 7.

59 Ibid., pp. 25–6.

60 *Illuminism. Who and What are the Illuminati?* by Richard, Duc de Palatine, 33 90 96 R + C IX G.D.

61 See Kenneth Grant, op. cit., pp. 5ff.

62 *A Call to Arms*, p. 20.

63 *The Brotherhood of the Illuminati*, p.1.

64 *The Brotherhood of the Illuminati, Introductory Monograph*.

65 C. D. Boltwood, *Spiritual Cataclysmic Movements in the Heavens and on the Earth-Planet*.

66 From a leaflet. Crow is the author of *A History of Magic, Witchcraft and Occultism* (1968).

67 Aniela Jaffe, ed., *Memories, Dreams and Reflections of C. G. Jung* (tr. Richard and Clara Winston, 1963), p. 196.

68 C. G. Jung, *Modern Man in Search of a Soul* (1933), p. 238.

69 See C. G. Jung, *Psychology and Religion: West and East*. Tr. R. F. C. Hull, 1958. On Jung's views on Gnosticism see Victor White, O.P., *God and the Unconscious* (1964), pp. 203–27.

70 Origen, *Contra Celsum* 1.32.

71 Cf. R. M. Grant, 'Early Alexandrian Christianity' (*Church History* 40.2, 1971), pp. 133–44 on Pythagoras's influence on the Gnostics. J. Kennedy, *Journal of the Royal Asiatic Society* (1902), pp. 377–415, argues that Basilides's system was a 'Buddhist Gnosticism'.

72 Gospel of Truth, cited in *The Jung Codex* (1955), p. 53.

73 R. M. Grant, *Gnosticism and Early Christianity* (1966), pp. 8–9.

CHAPTER 6

1 F. R. Leavis, *Lectures in America* (1969), p. 51.

2 D. H. Lawrence, cited in Colin Clarke, *River of Dissolution* (1969), p. xiv.

3 Franz Kafka, *The Castle*, 1926, and *The Trial*, 1925.

4 Colin Wilson, *The Outsider* (1967 edn), pp. 27ff.

5 I have relied on an unpublished paper by Caroline Coon, 'The hippy and the psychedelic scene' given at St Anne's House, Soho, on 4 March 1969.

6 *Frendz*, 30, 23 June 1972.

7 Milton Gordon, 'The concept of the subculture and its application' (*Social Forces*, 26, October 1947), p. 40.

8 J. M. Yinger, 'Contraculture and subculture' (*American Sociological Review* 25, October 1960), p. 627.

9 Theodore Roszak, *The Making of a Counter Culture* (1970 edn), pp. xi–xii.

10 Ibid., p. 64.

11 David Cooper, ed., *The Dialectics of Liberation* (1968), p. 9.

12 Roszak, op. cit., p. 64.

13 *Gandalf's Garden*, 6 (1969), p. 11.

14 Ibid., p. 29.

15 Richard Neville, *Playpower* (1970), p. 14.
16 Cf. Jeff Nuttall, *Bomb Culture* (1970), pp. 160ff.
17 The text of this article is printed in full in Nuttall, op. cit., pp. 204-6.
18 *The Guardian*, 27 September 1971.
19 *Gandalf's Garden*, 6 (1969), p. 11.
20 Mark Messer, 'Running out of era: some nonpharmacological notes on the psychedelic revolution' in David E. Smith, ed., *The New Social Drug* (1970), p. 161.
21 Geoffrey Ashe, 'Letter from an Over 30' (*IT* 38, 23 August–5 September 1968), p. 15.
22 Lewis Yablonsky, *The Hippie Trip* (1968), p. 24.
23 Andrew M. Greeley, 'The new American religion' (*Concilium* 9.7, November 1971), p. 115.
24 R. D. Laing, *The Divided Self*, 1960; Claude Lévi-Strauss, *The Savage Mind*, 1962; Konrad Lorenz, *On Aggression*, 1963; Marshall McLuhan, *Understanding Media*, 1964.
25 Michael Wood, 'The four gospels'(*New Society*, 18 December 1969), pp. 972-5.
26 See Robert Boyers and Robert Orrill, eds., *Laing and Anti-Psychiatry*. 1972. Cf. Peter Sedgwick, 'Laing's claims'(*New Society*, 15 January 1970), pp. 103-4.
27 R. D. Laing, *The Politics of Experience and the Bird of Paradise*. 1971 edn.
28 R. D. Laing, *Intervention in Social Situations*, 1969. See also R. D. Laing and A. Esterson, *Sanity and Madness in the Family I. Families of Schizophrenics*, 1964.
29 *The Politics of Experience*, p. 100.
30 R. D. Laing in *The Dialectics of Liberation* (1971 edn), p. 19.
31 Cited by Peter Sedgwick in Boyers and Orrill, op, cit., p. 35.
32 *The Politics of Experience*, p. 114.
33 Ibid., p. 116.
34 Ibid., pp. 118, 119.
35 Sedgwick in Boyers and Orrill, op. cit., p. 46.
36 Herbert Marcuse in *The Dialectics of Liberation*, p. 175.
37 See further on Marcuse, Paul A. Robinson, *The Sexual Radicals*, 1970, and Alasdair MacIntyre, *Marcuse*, 1970, as well as Marcuse's own books *Eros and Civilisation*, 1962, *One-Dimensional Man*, 1966, and *An Essay on Liberation*, 1969.
38 Paul Lawson, 'The tribal fire brands' (*New Christian*, 7 August 1969), p. 5.
39 *New York Tribune*, 17–18 May 1969.
40 John Wilcock, Editor of *Other Scenes* claims that 'it's impossible to under-estimate how important pot was as a unifying banner and rallying post' (*Bitman*, 3, 1971), p. 11.

41 Roger Lovin, cited in *Penthouse*, 4.5 (1969), p. 16.
42 Richard Neville, *Playpower* (1970), p. 120.
43 There is a detailed account in Neville, ibid., pp. 120–62. For a recent study see Roger Lewis, *Outlaws of America: The Underground Press and its Context*, 1972.
44 Roger Lewis, op. cit., p. 82.
45 See Jeremy d'Agapeyeff, *Release: a progress report*, 1972, and his article, 'Release: the routinisation of charisma, or three years of self-help' (*Drugs and Society*, 9.1, 1972), pp. 8–11.
46 Richard Neville in *Evening Standard*, 6 April 1972.
47 On the Manchester scene see *Mole Express* and *Manchester Free Press*. The *Guardian* claimed on 13 June 1972: 'There are more than forty radical groups in the city dedicated in one way or another to setting up what is loosely described as an "alternative society"'.
48 See the journal *Community Action*, 9 Pattison Road, London, N.W.2.
49 The ELF Manifesto was printed in *Peace News*, 23 June 1972.
50 *Ink* (25 February 1972), p. 5.
51 *Frendz*, 17 March 1972.
52 'A GLF answer to the psychiatrist' (*Red Rat*, Summer 1972), p. 6.
53 Liberation News Service, 'Women and the Underground Press' (*The Spectator*, 29 July 1969), p. 15.
54 Cited in Roger Lewis, op. cit., p. 35.
55 Germaine Greer, *The Female Eunuch* (1970), p. 44.
56 Ibid., p. 45.
57 See Juliet Mitchell, 'Women are exploited' (*Forum*, 3.4, 1970), pp. 4–8. For a general view of Women's Lib writing see the anthology *The Body Politic* (Women's Liberation Workshop, 3 Shavers Place, London, S.W.1., 1972).
58 Stokeley Carmichael and Charles V. Hamilton, *Black Power*, 1967.
59 Stokeley Carmichael in *The Dialectics of Liberation*, p. 172.
60 Roger Lewis, op. cit., p. 59.
61 See C. Eric Lincoln, *The Black Muslims in America*, 1961.
62 For a more detailed account see Joseph C. Hough, Jr., *Black Power and White Protestants*, 1968.
63 Obi Egbuna, *Destroy this Temple* (1971), p. 17.
64 See his *The Wretched of the Earth*, 1967, and *Black Skin White Masks*, 1967.
65 Martin Luther King, *Chaos or Community?* (1969 edn), p. 58.
66 Frantz Fanon, *The Wretched of the Earth* (1967), p. 251.
67 Ibid., pp. 252, 254, 255.
68 Agriculture and Hand-Industries Mutual Support Association.
69 On this phase see Kenneth Leech, *Keep The Faith Baby* (1973), pp. 63–72.

70 See Clem Gorman, *Making Communes*, 1972.

71 David Black, 'Wholes within wholes' (*Peace News*, 23 January 1972).

72 Cf. Kenneth Keniston, 'A second look at the uncommitted' (*Social Policy*, July–August 1971), p. 12.

73 See Andrew Rigby, 'Live the future now' (*Peace News*, 28 January 1972).

74 N. I. Whitney, *Experiments in Community*. Pendle Hill Pamphlets.

75 See Andrew Rigby, 'Problems of communes. 1.—Authority and sexual freedom' (*Peace News*, 27 October 1972).

76 *Newsweek* (18 August 1969), p. 89.

77 David E. Smith and Alan J. Rose, 'Health problems in urban and rural "crash pad" communes' (*Clinical Pediatrics*, 9.9, 1970), pp. 534–7.

78 Dr David Smith, Medical Director of the Haight-Ashbury Free Clinic, at a seminar at St Anne's House, Soho, London, on 17 September 1970.

79 See Dan L. Garrett, Jr., 'Synanon: the Communiversity' (*The Humanist*, U.S.A., September–October 1965), pp. 185-9.

80 Jill Maguire in *Peace News*, 2 February 1973. See also her earlier article, 'For ourselves alone or for social change?' (ibid., 28 January 1973).

81 *Community Music*, Newsletter No. 1. January–February 1972.

82 See Peter B. Smith, 'The varieties of group experience' (*New Society*, 25 March 1971), pp. 483–5.

83 See *The Case for Radical Alternatives to Prison* and *Alternatives to Holloway*. RAP.

84 'Blueprint for Survival' (*The Ecologist*, 2.1, January 1972).

85 John Maddox, *The Times*, 3 February 1972.

86 John Wilcock, Editor of *Other Scenes*, interviewed in *Bitman*, 3 (1971), p. 11.

87 Richard Mabey, *Food For Free*, 1972. See also Audrey Wynne Hatfield, 'How To Enjoy Your Weeds' (*Mother Earth News*, P.O. Box 38, Madison, Ohio 44057).

88 *Seed*, 8a All Saints Road, London, W.11.

89 Michael Allaby, *The Eco-Activists*, 1971.

90 Dave Cunliffe in *Peace News*, 25 August 1972.

91 From Rodale Press, Berkhampstead, Herts.

92 *King Mob 6: Work. Notes from the Underground.*

93 *Sub 70*, 6 Cambridge Gardens, London, W.10, No. 4.

94 Henry Anderson, 'The case against the drug culture' (*Peace News*, 17 March 1967).

95 Ibid.

96 Editorial, 'Humanism with a difference', ibid.

97 See *Berkeley Barb*, 5-11 February 1971, and an abridged version in *Rolling Stone*, 4 March 1971. The *Daily Telegraph* on 29 January 1971 reported Leary's arrest by the Black Panthers in Algiers.

98 *Berkeley Barb*, op. cit.

99   Dave Widgery in *International Socialism* 51 (April–June 1972), p. 4.

100 Alasdair MacIntyre, *Marcuse* (1970), p. 89.

CHAPTER 7

1   'The New Rebel Cry: "Jesus is Coming!"' (*Time*, 21 June 1971), pp. 32–43.

2   Ibid., pp. 32, 39.

3   Edward E. Plowman, *The Jesus Movement* (1971), p. 9.

4   Clay Ford, *Jesus and the Street People* (1972), p. 25.

5   Roy Wallis, 'Dilemma of a moral crusade' (*New Society*, 13 July 1972), pp. 69–72.

6   See *Buzz*, Festival for Jesus Edition (1972): 'Jesus is no Superstar. He is the Son of God. Accept No Substitute'.

7   *The Jesus People Speak Out!* compiled by Ruben Ortega, 1972.

8   Ibid., p. 72.

9   Ibid., p. 75.

10   Larry Norman, 'Upon This Rock' LP. Key Records, 10 Seaforth Avenue, New Malden, Surrey.

11   See Michael Harper, 'New harmony for dissident crash-pad group' (*Renewal*, 40, August–September 1972), pp. 29–30.

12   See Roger C. Palms, *The Jesus Kids* (1972), p. 68.

13   Ford, op. cit., p. 101.

14   Ibid., p. 90.

15   Palms, op. cit., p. 41.

16   *The Street People*, Selections from *Right On!* (1972), p. 18.

17   *Tomorrow's World* (Graduate School of Theology, Ambassador College, Pasadena, California, June 1971), pp. 18–31.

18   Dennis Barker, 'Black sheep in the flock' (*The Guardian*, 2 November 1972).

19   *Evening News*, London, 7 September 1971.

20   *Truth*, 3.7.

21   Letter dated 3 June 1972 from the Children of God, 1 Sherman Road, Bromley, Kent. This address is now occupied by another group, The Jesus Family.

22   Plowman, op. cit., p. 62.

23   Micheal Jacob, *Pop Goes Jesus* (1972), p. 24.

24   Cited in *Renewal* 36 (December 1971–January 1972), p. 4. The writer of the article did not accept the criticism.

25   Francis Schaeffer, *The New Super-Spirituality* (1973), pp. 28–30.

26   *The Times*, Parliamentary Report, 2 February 1973.

27   Alan W. Jones, 'The Jesus freaks—what think ye of Christ?' (*New Fire*, Winter 1971), p. 12.

28   Editorial in *Renewal* 36, p. 39.

29 Cited in Jacob, op. cit., p. 41.

30 Ibid., p. 16.

31 Cited ibid., p. 30.

32 For example, in *Renewal*, 36, p. 3.

33 David Wilkerson, *The Cross and the Switchblade* (New York, 1964 edn), p. 157.

34 Ibid., p. 167.

35 'Life or Death' (*Teen Challenge* 1), p. 2.

36 Ibid., pp. 9–10.

37 David Wilkerson, *What Every Teenager Should Know About Drugs* (New York), p. 36.

38 'Life or Death', p. 19.

39 Elizabeth Braund, 'The Cross, the switchblade—and us' (*The Evangelical Magazine*, November—December 1965), p. 16.

40 David Wilkerson, *The Jesus Person Pocket Promise Book*, 1972.

41 David Wilkerson, *Purple Violet Squish* (1969), p. 18.

42 Ibid., pp. 26, 28.

43 Ibid., pp. 51, 52.

44 Ibid., p. 61.

45 Ibid., p. 113.

46 David Wilkerson, *Get Your Hands Off My Throat* (1972), p. 8.

47 Ibid., pp. 27–38.

48 Ibid., p. 63.

49 Ibid., p. 65.

50 Ibid., p. 68.

51 *Newscope*, Life for the World, Blockley, Moreton in Marsh, Glos., February 1973.

52 Walter J. Hollenweger, *The Pentecostals* (1972), p. xix.

53 Ruben Ortega, op. cit.

54 Cited in Michael Harper, *As at The Beginning* (1965), p. 67.

55 On Catholic Pentecostalism see Donald L. Gelpi, s.j., *Pentecostalism: a Theological Viewpoint*, 1972, and Edward D. O'Connor, *The Pentecostal Movement in the Catholic Church*, 1971.

56 Hollenweger, op. cit., p. 17.

57 Cited in *The Times*, 5 March 1973.

58 See Larry Christensen, *Speaking in tongues: a gift for the Body of Christ* (Fountain Trust, 1965). The author was a Lutheran pastor in Los Angeles.

59 Ibid., p. 17.

60 Michael Harper, *Power for the Body of Christ*, 1966 edn.

61 See, for example, Felicitas Goodman, 'Speaking in tongues' (*New Society*, 7 December 1972), pp. 565–6.

62 The *New English Bible* adds the gloss 'ecstatic' in 1 Cor. 12.10.

63 Michael Harper, letter in *New Society* (14 December 1972), p. 651.

64 Simon Tugwell, O.P., 'The gift of tongues in the New Testament' (*Expository Times*, 84.5, 1972), pp. 137–40. For a valuable study of the phenomenon see John P. Kildahl, *The Psychology of Speaking in Tongues*, 1972.

65 See, for example, F. D. Bruner, *A Theology of the Holy Spirit*, 1971, described by Michael Harper (*Renewal*, 35), p. 16, as 'a massive attempt to destroy the heart of Pentecostalism'.

66 Op. cit., pp. 168–9.

67 Ibid., pp. 178, 194.

68 Ibid., pp. 282–3, 298.

69 James G. Dunn, *Baptism in the Holy Spirit*, 1970.

70 A. M. Stibbs and J. I. Packer, *The Spirit Within You* (1967), pp. 32–3.

71 Kurt Koch, *The Devil's Alphabet*, pp. 108–11.

72 On West Indian Pentecostalism see Clifford S. Hill, 'Pentecostalist growth—result of racialism?' (*Race Today*, June 1971), pp. 187–90, and Michael J. C. Calley, *God's People: West Indian Pentecostal Sects in England*, 1965.

73 Roy Wallis, op. cit., p. 72.

74 Nationwide Festival of Light leaflet, June 1971.

75 Micheal Jacob, *Pop Goes Jesus* (1972), p. 11.

76 Cited in ibid., p. 11.

77 Ibid.

78 See Colonel Orde Dobbie, *Church Times*, 3 November 1972, as an example of such writing.

79 These quotations are from a leaflet *Evil Triumphs When Good Men Do Nothing*, Nationwide Festival of Light, 1972.

80 Nationwide Festival of Light, 1972 Programme.

81 Examples of this can be found in virtually anything which emanates from the Festival. See, for example, Steve Stevens' letter on the harmfulness of pornography in *The Guardian*, 2 December 1972, which merely quotes four individuals; or the *Living Jesus-style Manual* (1972), pp. 37–41.

82 *Renewal*, 36 (December 1971–January 1972), p. 38.

83 Canterbury Festival for Jesus 1972, leaflet.

84 *Living Jesus-Style Manual* (1972), p. 37.

85 Reprinted in *The Catonsville Roadrunner*, cited hereafter as *Roadrunner* (31 January 1972), p. 4.

86 *Christian Science Monitor*, 19 July 1969.

87 Ibid.

88 *Viewpoints from California: Experimental Youth Ministries*, 1969.

89 Ibid.

90 *Win With Love: A Directory of the Liberated Church in America*, 1969 edn.
91 John Pairman Brown, *Planet On Strike*, 1969, and *The Liberated Zone*, 1970.
92 Cited in John Pairman Brown and Richard L. York, *The Covenant of Peace: A Liberation Prayer Book by the Free Church of Berkeley* (1971), pp. 58–9.
93 *Viewpoints from California: Experimental Youth Ministries*, 1969.
94 *The Liberated Zone*, p. 179.
95 *The Covenant of Peace*, p. 12.
96 Dale W. Brown, 'The new theological radical' (*Christian Century*, 13 November 1968). See also John J. Vincent, 'Beginning with Jesus (*New Christian*, 10 July 1968).
97 For more details of the Catholic Worker movement see *Radical Christian Thought: Easy Essays by Peter Maurin*, 1971, and Dorothy Day, *Meditations*. Catholic Worker Farm, West Hamlin, WV 25571, 1971.
98 'Catholic Worker Positions' (*Catholic Worker*, May 1972).
99 David Hart, ' "Away with palaces" say the Christian Radicals' (*Church Times*, 23 August 1968).
100 David Hart, 'On bogus authority' (*Peace News*, 6 September 1968), p. 3.
101 *New Christian* (16 October 1969), p. 15.
102 *Pop Goes Jesus*, p. 78.
103 *Jesus and the Street People*, p. 27.
104 *Roadrunner* 41 (January 1973), p. 12.
105 Cf. Robin Percival in *Roadrunner*, 36 (June 1972), p. 11.
106 *Roadrunner* 1 (April 1969), p. 2.
107 *Roadrunner* 4 (August 1969), p. 8.
108 Harvey Cox, *The Feast of Fools* (1969), pp. 156–7.
109 Cited in *Roadrunner* 3 (June 1969), p. 6.

CHAPTER 8

1 Paulinus Milner, o.p. 'The new spiritual quest' (*The Franciscan*, June 1970), pp. 133–4.
2 John Pairman Brown, *The Liberated Zone* (1970), p. 113.
3 See Stanley G. Evans, *The Social Hope of the Christian Church* (1965), pp. 156–65.
4 Trevor Beeson, *The Church of England in Crisis* 1973, p. 176.
5 Valerie Pitt in *Prism* (November 1959), p. 10.
6 J. L. and B. Hammond, *The Town Labourer 1760-1832*, 1971.
7 C. Booth, *Life and Labour of the People in London*, 3rd Series, VII (1902), p. 399. For other references see K. S. Inglis, *Churches and the Working Classes in Victorian England*, 1963; R. F. Wearmouth, *Methodism and the*

Working Class Movements in England 1800–1850, 1937; and Neil L. Smelser, *Social Change in the Industrial Revolution*, 1959.

8 Leslie Paul, *The Development and Payment of the Clergy* (1964), pp. 28off.

9 Ibid., p. 23.

10 R. S. Moore, 'Religion and immigration in the urban twilight zone'. Paper to the British Association, Annual Conference, Sociology Section, 7 September 1965. See also John Rex and Robert Moore, *Race, Community and Conflict*, 1967.

11 Alasdair MacIntyre, 'Marxists and Christians' (*Twentieth Century*, 170.1011, 1961), p. 33.

12 Richard Buck, 'Elliptical Spirituality'. Talk given at King's College, London, in Lent 1971, MS.

13 William Hamilton, *The New Essence of Christianity* (1961), p. 55.

14 Bede Griffiths, *Christian Ashram*, 1966.

15 Rudolf Otto, *Mysticism East and West*, 1960 edn.

16 R. C. Zaehner, *At Sundry Times*, 1958, *The Convergent Spirit*, 1963, etc.

17 Klaus Klostermaier, *Hindu and Christian in Vrindaban*, 1969.

18 Kenneth Cragg, *The Dome and the Rock*, 1964, and *Christianity in World Perspective*, 1968.

19 John V. Taylor, *The Primal Vision*, 1963.

20 J.-M. Dechanet, *Christian Yoga*, 1964.

21 H. M. Enomiya-Lassalle, s.j., *Zen-Way to Enlightenment*, 1967.

22 Dom Aelred Graham, *Zen Catholicism*, 1963.

23 Secretarius pro Non-Christianis, *Guidelines for a Dialogue between Muslims and Christians*, 1969.

24 Thomas Merton, *Mystics and Zen Masters*, 1967 edn.

25 Graham, op. cit. pp. 154, 39.

26 Enomiya-Lassalle, op. cit., p. 84.

27 Merton, op. cit., p. 242.

28 F. B. Dalby, s.s.j.e., in *New Fire*, 9 (Winter 1971), p. 15.

29 See also 'Le Zen et nous Chrétiens' (*La Vie Spirituelle*, 592, September–October 1972).

30 See on this dialogue Klaus Klostermaier, 'Hindu-Christian Dialogue' (*Journal of Ecumenical Studies*, 5.1, Winter 1968), pp. 21–34.

31 Griffiths, op. cit., p. 183.

32 Abhishiktananda, *Prayer*, 1969.

33 Thomas Merton, *Seeds of Contemplation*, 1949.

34 Thomas Merton, *Bread in the Wilderness*, 1961 edn.

35 Thomas Merton, *Contemplative Prayer*, 1969.

36 Ibid., p. 11.

37 Teilhard de Chardin, *Le Milieu Divin*, 1960, *Hymn of the Universe*, 1966, *Prayer of the Universe*, 1972, etc.

38   Anthony Bloom, *Living Prayer*, 1966, *Meditations on a Theme*, 1971, *God and Man*, 1971.

39   Monica Furlong, *Contemplating Now*, 1971.

40   Dominic M. Hoffman, O.P., *The Life Within*, 1966.

41   J. Neville Ward, *The Use of Praying*, 1967.

42   Paul Hinnebusch, O.P., *Prayer, the Search for Authenticity*, 1969.

43   Hans Urs Van Balthasar, *Prayer*, 1961.

44   René Voillaume, *The Need for Contemplation*, 1971.

45   See Mother Mary Clare, *Christian Maturity Through Prayer, Learning to Pray, The Apostolate of Prayer and Silence and Prayer*, and Gilbert Shaw, *Christian Prayer: A Way of Progress, Creation and Re-creation* and *A Pilgrim's Book of Prayers*, all obtainable from SLG Press, Convent of the Incarnation, Fairacres, Oxford.

46   Martin Israel, *An Approach to Spirituality*, 1971, *An Approach to Mysticism*, 1968, *The Power of the Spirit in Everyday Living* and *Healing and the Spirit*, all obtainable from the Churches' Fellowship for Psychic and Spiritual Studies, 5–6 Denison House, 296 Vauxhall Bridge Road, London, S.W.1.

47   On the Jesus prayer see Anthony Bloom, *Living Prayer* (1966), pp. 84–8, and A Monk of the Eastern Church, *The Prayer of Jesus*, 1967. On Orthodox liturgical life see Timothy Ware, *The Orthodox Church*, 1967. On Orthodox spirituality in general see A. J. Philippou, ed., *The Orthodox Ethos*, 1964, Nicholas Arseniev, *Russian Piety*, 1964, Vladimir Lossky, *The Mystical Theology of the Eastern Church*, 1957, and *The Vision of God*, 1963, Archimandrite Sofrony, *The Undistorted Image*, 1958, A Monk of the Eastern Church, *Orthodox Spirituality*, 1945.

48   C. G. Jung, *Psychology and Alchemy*, Collected Works, Volume 12, 1953, *Psychology and Religion: West and East*, Collected Works, Volume 11, 1958, etc.

49   Victor White, *God and the Unconscious*, 1952.

50   Michael Fordham, *The Objective Psyche*, 1958.

51   Frank Lake, *Clinical Theology*, 1966.

52   Frank Lake, *Clinical Pastoral Care in Schizoid Personality Reactions* (1970), p. 22.

53   Christopher Bryant, S.S.J.E., *Depth Psychology and Religious Belief*, 1972, and *Prayer and Psychology*.

54   *Lunch*, 18 (March 1973), p. 9.

55   R. A. Lambourne, 'Objections to a national pastoral organisation' (*Contact*, 35, June 1971), p. 27.

56   Simon Tugwell, O.P., *Did You Receive the Spirit?* (1972), p. 29.

57   Ibid., p. 63.

58   Kilian McDonnell, O.S.B., 'The experiential and the social' (*One in Christ*, 9.1, 1973), p. 52.

59 See Howard Elinson, 'The implications of Pentecostal religion for intellectualism, politics and race relations' (*American Journal of Sociology*, 70, 1965), p. 408.

60 Donald Gee, 'Remote or realistic?' (*Pentecost*, 68, June–August 1964), p. 17.

61 Michael Harper, 'Charismatic renewal—a new ecumenism?' (*One in Christ*, 9.1. 1973), p. 63.

62 *Letter from Taizé*, May 1970.

63 See James Klugmann, ed., *Dialogue of Christianity and Marxism* (1968), etc.

64 Roger Lloyd, *The Ferment in the Church* (1964), p. 7. See also John A. T. Robinson, *A New Reformation?*, 1965.

65 R. D. Laing in *The Role of Religion in Mental Health* (1967), p. 57.

66 Frank Lake, *Clinical Theology* (1966), p. xxvi.

67 R. D. Laing, *The Politics of Experience and the Bird of Paradise* (1971 edn), p. 114.

68 Ulrich Simon, *A Theology of Auschwitz* (1967), p. 124.

69 Thomas Merton, *Contemplative Prayer* (1969), pp. 25, 28.

70 Martin Thornton, *The Rock and the River* (1965), p. 141.

71 Martin Thornton, *English Spirituality* (1963), p. xiii.

72 Dom Aelred Graham, 'A new star in the East for the institutional church' (*The Times*, 23 December 1972),

73 Hélène Dicken, *Full Face to God* (1971), p. 55.

74 Foreword to ibid., p. ix.

75 Aelred Squire, *Asking the Fathers*, 1973.

76 Matthew Arnold, stanzas from 'The Grand Chartreuse', lines 85-7.

77 Eric James, ed., *Spirituality for Today* (1968), p. 7.

78 See Louis Bouyer, *The Spirituality of the New Testament and the Fathers*, 1960; Hans von Campenhausen, *The Fathers of the Greek Church*, 1963, and *The Fathers of the Latin Church*, 1964.

79 See A. Hamman, O.F.M., ed., *Early Christian Prayers*, 1961, and Robert L. Simpson, *The Interpretation of Prayer in the Early Church*, 1965.

80 See Jean Daniélou and Herbert Musurillo, eds., *From Glory to Glory: Texts from Gregory of Nyssa*, 1962.

81 Denys Rutledge, *Cosmic Theology*, 1964, is a good account of Pseudo-Dionysius. The Shrine of Wisdom (Fintry Brook, near Godalming) publish *The Divine Names* and *Mystical Theology*, both by Pseudo-Dionysius.

82 See Jean Leclercq, Francis Vandenbroucke, and Louis Bouyer, *The Spirituality of the Middle Ages*, 1968.

83 See Cuthbert Butler, *Benedictine Monasticism*, 1924, and Hubert van Zeller, *The Benedictine Idea*, 1959.

84 M. Basil Pennington, ed., *The Cistercian Spirit*, 1970, Louis Bouyer, *The Cistercian Heritage*, 1958, Étienne Gilson, *The Mystical Theology of St*

Bernard, 1940, and A. Hallier, o.c.s.o., *The Monastic Theology of Aelred of Rievaulx*, 1969.

85   See *Richard of Saint-Victor, Selected Writings on Contemplation*, tr. Clare Kirchberger, 1967; *Hugh of Saint-Victor, Selected Spiritual Writings*, tr. A Religious of C.S.M.V., 1962.

86   All these are available in Penguin Classics.

87   See Ray C. Petry, ed., *Late Medieval Mysticism*, SCM Library of Christian Classics, Volume 13, 1967.

88   See Martin Thornton, *English Spirituality*, 1963, and James Walsh, *Pre-Reformation English Spirituality*, undated.

89   See E. Alison Peers, *Complete Works of St John of the Cross*, 1964 edn, and *Studies in the Spanish Mystics*, 3 vols., 1951.

90   E. W. Trueman Dicken, *The Crucible of Love* (1963), p. 168. This is an extremely valuable account of Carmelite spirituality, as is Edith Stein, *The Science of the Cross*, 1960.

91   See Michael Fordham's essays 'Analytical psychology and religious experience' and 'The dark night of the soul' in his *The Objective Psyche* (1958), pp. 113–48; and Oswald Sumner, *St John of the Cross and Modern Psychology*, Guild of Pastoral Psychology Pamphlet 57, 1948.

92   Hubert van Zeller, *Famine of the Spirit* (1950), p. 21.

93   Evagrius, *Treatise on Prayer*, 60.

94   St Gregory Nazianzen, *Oratio*, 32, p. 12.

95   St John Climacus, *Scala Paradisi*, grade 30.

96   Vladimir Lossky, *The Mystical Theology of the Eastern Church* (1957), p. 39.

97   See further on the relation of theology and spirituality in Orthodox thought A. M. Allchin, ed., *Orthodoxy and the Death of God*, 1971.

98   I. T. Ramsey, *Models and Mystery* (1964), p. 61.

99   Alan Watts, *The Joyous Cosmology* (1962), p. 17; R. C. Zaehner, *Drugs, Mysticism and Make-Believe* (1972), p. 133.

100 Michael Itkin to the US Senate 89th Congress (24–26 May 1966), pp. 158–62 (hearings on LSD).

101 Allan Y. Cohen in Richard E. Horman and Allan M. Fox, eds., *Drug Awareness* (1970), p. 449.

102 *The Ascent of Mount Carmel*. Book 2, ch. 11, para. 3 (Peers, 1964 edn of *Complete Works*), p. 97.

103 Déchanet, op. cit., *passim*.

104 Abhishiktananda, op. cit., pp. 50ff.

105 So Abhishiktananda writes of Yoga: 'Nobody should ever engage in it without the help of a sure guide—the *guru*—that is, somebody who himself has trodden the path, has been granted at least a glimpse of the goal, and is prudent enough to lead others,' op. cit., p. 47.

106 Graham, op. cit., p. 141.

107 Cf. D. E. Nineham, *St Mark* (Penguin Commentaries, 1971), p. 44: '... St Mark's understanding of the ministry of Christ is very largely in terms of this fight between God and the evil powers'. See also A. Fridrichsen, 'The conflict of Jesus with the unclean spirits' (*Theology*, 22, 1931), p. 122; J. S. Stewart, 'On a neglected emphasis in New Testament theology' (*Scottish Journal of Theology*, 4, 1951), p. 300.

108 See W. O. E. Oesterley, 'Angelology and demonology in early Judaism' in T. W. Manson, ed., *A Companion to the Bible*, 1939; E. Langton, *Good and Evil Spirits*, 1942, and *Essentials of Demonology*, 1949.

109 See Trevor Ling, *The Significance of Satan*, 1961.

110 C. D. Morrison, *The Powers that Be*, 1960, and Albert H. van den Heuvel, *These Rebellious Powers*, 1966. Cf. John Pairman Brown, *The Liberated Zone*, (1970), p. 99: ' "Satan" and "Beelzebul" are names for warped institutions'.

111 Michael Harper, *Spiritual Warfare*, 1970.

112 Merrill F. Unger, *Biblical Demonology*, 1952.

113 Kurt Koch, *Between Christ and Satan*, 1965, *Occult Bondage and Deliverance*, 1970 edn, *Christian Counselling and Occultism*, 1972 edn, *Demonology Past and Present*, 1972, and *The Devil's Alphabet*. All Koch's works can be obtained in Britain from Hughes and Coleman, Spar Road, Norwich.

114 See R. K. McAll, 'Demonosis or the Possession Syndrome' (*International Journal of Social Psychiatry*, 1971), pp. 150–8. P. M. Yap, 'The possession syndrome' (*Journal of Mental Sciences*, 106, 1960), p. 442.

115 Jean Lhermitte, *Diabolical Possession, True or False?*, 1963.

116 McAll, op. cit., p. 155.

117 Alfred Lechler, 'The distinction between disease and the demonic' in Koch, *Occult Bondage and Deliverance*, pp. 153–90.

118 A. D. Duncan, *The Christ, Psychotherapy and Magic* (1969), p. 137. For more details on Freemasonry see Walton Hannah, *Darkness Visible*, 1952.

119 Charles W. Lowry, *Communism and Christ* (1954), p. 54.

120 Alasdair MacIntyre, *Marxism—an Interpretation* (1953), p. 54.

121 Conrad Noel, *The Battle of the Flags* (1922), pp. 44–5, 47. On Noel see Reg Groves, *Conrad Noel and the Thaxted Movement*, 1967.

122 P. E. T. Widdrington, 'The return of the Kingdom of God' in *The Return of Christendom* (1922), p. 108.

123 Kenneth Leech, 'What has happened to Christian social theology?' (*Theology*, 68, 537, 1965), pp. 134–9.

124 Jurgen Moltmann, *Theology of Hope*, 1967, and *Hope and Planning*, 1971; Johannes B. Metz, *Theology of the World*, 1969.

125 Brian Wicker, *First the Political Kingdom*, 1967, Slant Manifesto, *Catholics and the Left*, 1966, etc.

126 Harvey Cox, *God's Revolution and Man's Responsibility* (1969), p. 10.

127 Jurgen Moltmann, *Theology of Hope* (1967), p. 329.

Index

Index 245